Studies of Familial Communication and Psychopathology

*In memory of
Roger Andersson*

Rolv Mikkel Blakar

Studies of Familial Communication and Psychopathology

A social-developmental approach
to deviant behavior

Universitetsforlaget
Oslo — Bergen — Tromsø

© UNIVERSITETSFORLAGET 1980
ISBN 82-00-01999-3

Distribution offices:
NORWAY
Universitetsforlaget
Postboks 2977 Tøyen
Oslo 6

UNITED KINGDOM
Global Book Resources Ltd.
37, Queen Street
Henley on Thames
Oxon RG9 1AJ

UNITED STATES and CANADA
Columbia University Press
136 South Broadway
Irvington-on-Hudson
New York 10533

Published with a grant from
The Norwegian Research Council
for Science and the Humanities

Cover design: Per Syversen

Printed in Norway by
Nye Intertrykk as, Lommedalen

PREFACE

The present volume represents a first coherent presentation in English of the research on familial communication and psychopathology that has been conducted at the Institute of Psychology, University of Oslo as from 1971-72. Looking back over these years I feel on behalf of the project(s) indebted to many persons and institutions without whose support and assistance our efforts would most likely have been futile. Special thanks are being expressed in connection to the concrete studies represented in Part II and in the reports from the various projects. Nevertheless, I want to use the opportunity offered by this preface to express my gratitude:

First and foremost, there are all those who, for longer or shorter periods of time, have been associated with and have substantially contributed to the integrated project. Throughout these years the following have prepared their dissertations in connection with the umbrella project, the so-called 'Communication Project':

Helge Sølvberg, Svein Alve, Maureen Hultberg, Rita Bast Pettersen, Svein Mossige Jacobsen (now Svein Mossige), Rolf Wikran, Tor Lagerløv, Steinar Stokstad, Astrid Fætten (now Astrid Lavik), Mette Østvold, Øyvind Reer, Ove Moberget, Kirsti Rotbæk, Bjørn Rund, Berit Haarstad, Tom Sverre Kristiansen, Øistein Øisjøfoss, Øystein Teigre, Claes-Göran Brisendal, Birgitta Glennsjø, Knut Rønbeck, Ole Gerhard Paulsen, Marit Dahle, Roger Andersson, Birgit Pilblad, Anita Endresen, Ingebjørg Strøno, Tove Pedersen, Per Erik Guttelvik, Anders Knutsen, Olav Vassend, Inge Svenheim and Asle Hoffart. At present, Rolf Blisten, Anna Valdimarsdottir, Lise Antonsen, Stein Valstad, Einar Aspen and Freddy Olsen are pursuing the project by preparing their dissertations.

It is to acknowledge the fruitfulness of the friendly and cooperative milieu that has been established, that the present book is dedicated to Roger Andersson, who died a few months after he had finished his excellent dissertation, just at the beginning of a promising life of research work.

Throughout the years a lot of people not directly associated with the project have in various manners contributed substantially to the project. If I tried to list them all, I would for sure forget many. However, Ragnar Rommetveit, Hilde Eileen Nafstad, Olav Skårdal, Astri Heen Wold, Finn Tschudi, Arne Holte, Asbjørn Faleide, Harald

Engvik and Thorleif Lund have contributed so much to the project over so many years that they have to be explicitly mentioned in this context.

I also want to thank all the patients, and in particular their parents/families, who have participated in our studies. For obvious reasons they have to remain anonymous.

Without the kind and generous cooperation by hospitals and health institutions the projects presented in this volume could not have been realized. In connection to the studies covered by the present volume, the support and assistance of the following institutions (presented in alphabetic order) should be acknowledged:

Dikemark Hospital, Lovisenberg Hospital, Oslo Bispedømmeråds Familievernkontor, Presteseter Hospital, Rikshospitalet (Allergiavdelingen ved Barneklinikken, and, Barnecardiologisk avdeling), Ullevål Hospital (Allergologisk poliklinikk ved Barneavdelingen), Universitets Psykiatriske klinikk, and Voksentoppen institutt for barn med astma og allergi.

Thanks are due to Ragnhild Brune and Åse Paulsen-Linnekogel for having typewritten the manuscripts.

Finally, our project have been financially supported by the Norwegian Research Council for Social Sciences and the Humanities.

Oslo, November 1979   Rolv Mikkel Blakar

CONTENTS

INTRODUCTION

Two distinct but mutually supportive reasons for preparing the present volume should
be explicitly mentioned. First and foremost, the present project offers solutions to
some of the conceptual and methodological problems said to hinder progress in the
field of family-oriented research. Second, having been involved in family/communi-
cation-oriented research on deviant behavior and psychopathology for some years,
we feel that a more comprehensive presentation (in English) of our studies is warranted.

With regard to the (lack of) progress of all the efforts invested in this particular
field of research, the optimism characterizing the 1950s and 1960s was in the early
1970s replaced by more critical attitudes, in that a series of reviews appeared in which
it was demonstrated that the yield of all this research was questionable indeed (cf. Haley,
1972, Riskin & Faunce, 1972). Consequently, throughout the 1970s various analyses
have been conducted to identify the conceptual and methodological hurdles hindering
progress (e.g., Haley, 1972, Riskin & Faunce, 1972, Jacob, 1975, Moberget & Reer,
1975, Blakar, 1974a, 1976a, Rønbeck, 1977). Recently reassessments of the field and
attempts to surmount the conceptual and methodological problems encountered in family
interaction research, have appeared (e.g., Doane, 1978a, Blakar, 1978a, in press b, in
press c). Not surprisingly, vigorous arguments over the art of family research have then
been elicited (cf. Jacob & Grounds, 1978, Doane, 1978b, Blakar, in press a, in press
d, Hoffart, 1978, 1979). Therefore, it is toward a field currently under massive de-
bate that we present an alternative approach, which in our contention, surmounts at
least some of the conceptual and methodological hurdles that have hindered progress
in the field.

Ever since 1972 there has existed in Oslo a research milieu devoted to family-
oriented research on deviant behavior and psychopathology. Over the years a series
of empirical reports and theoretical-methodological papers have appeared, the majority
in Norwegian, but some in English too. The research of this group has been 'cumulative'
in the sense that the later studies have in various ways pursued the earlier ones, and
also in that direct replications have been conducted. (Various critics have pointed out
that replicative studies are notedly lacking in this field of research.) Moreover, the
various autonomous studies have been conducted within an integral conceptual frame-

work. The framework has continually been refined in the light of empirical studies, however. Against this background a more comprehensive and integral presentation should be warranted.

To achieve these ends we have applied a combined strategy in that we have first prepared an integral presentation of the general approach, together with a review of the various studies that have been conducted, and then compiled a representative selection of the original reports presenting the various studies.

In Part I the conceptual and methodological framework is outlined, and an explora- tory study is presented. Then care is taken to carry out an exhaustive analysis of conceptual-methodological weaknesses and shortcomings in our own study. Finally, on the basis of this thorough analysis a research program developed to surmount these conceptual-methodological shortcomings is hammered out.

Part III contains a review presentation and discussion of what has been done (until October 1979) in order to implement the research program presented in Part I. Part III is organized in perfect accordance with Part I, in that the various studies are dis- cussed under headings corresponding to the conceptual-methodological issues syste- matically addressed in Part I.

In Part II a selection of five reports from representative studies conducted within this research program is presented. The five papers compiled in Part II thus repre- sent autonomous papers that can be read on their own. To avoid boring repetitions, however, the theoretical-methodological sections common to all the empirical studies are presented only once, that is in connection with the general presentation in Part I. Inasmuch as five autonomous reports are compiled, repetetions of various kinds and some overlap have nevertheless been unavoidable. Consequently, Part I has to be read first to give the general theoretical as well as the more specific methodological back- ground informations needed in order to understand the various studies presented in Part II. Having read Part I, however, the reader can choose to read the studies in Part II of most direct interest, and it is not necessary to read the chapters in Part II in any particular sequence.

Finally, in Part III the various studies presented in Part II are discussed in the light of the general research program presented in Part I. It should be mentioned at this point that Part III is highly intelligible on the background of Part I alone, without the more detailed reports from the specific studies presented in Part II being read.

Depending on the degree of interest and time available, the reader is thus in a way invited to choose between two books: the first book consisting of Parts I and III gives a presentation of our general approach and briefly reviews and discusses what has yet been done to implement this research program. The second book, consisting of all three parts, in addition offers the reader an opportunity to have some of the concrete studies presented in considerable detail.

PART I

Historical background, theoretical framework and an alternative research program

During the last two decades studies of communication and interaction in the schizo-phrenic's family have been given high priority. A number of phenomena considered typical of communication in such families have been described, e.g., double-bind (Bateson et al., 1956), pseudo-mutuality (Wynne et al., 1958), and, marital schism and marital skew (Lidz et al., 1957). It is not always clear whether these (and other) phenomena are to be understood as a cause of or as a product of schizophrenia in a family member (cf. Mishler & Waxler, 1965). However, the double-bind situation is readily offered as one of a series of preconditions or requirements for the develop-ment of schizophrenia (cf. Bateson, 1960, Bateson et al., 1963).

Although the family communication and systems perspective can be said to have evolved gradually, it may even be argued that the family perspective was implicit in some of Freud's writings (cf. Ackerman et al., 1961; Blakar et al., 1980) - it was not before the late 1940s /early 1950s that this perspective was explicitly adopted as an alternative paradigm in the study of psychopathology. Haley, himself one of the pioneers in this field, described in retrospect (1959, p. 358) the change of perspective that took place in the study of schizophrenia in the following way:

> A transition would seem to have taken place in the study of schizophrenia; from the early idea that the difficulty in these families was caused by the schizophrenic member, to the idea that they contained a pathogenic mother, to the discovery that the father was inadequate, to the current emphasis upon all three family members involved in a pathological system of interaction. (My italics.)

This radical shift in perspective was not produced by any compelling findings nor promoted by any new observations. On the contrary, this change in perspective re-flected the general trend to adopt a social perspective and the willingness to re-inter-pret earlier observations from a social perspective. This is clearly seen from Ruesch & Bateson's (1951) arguments in support of their programmatically stated position to conceive of psychopathology 'in terms of disturbances of communication':

> Psychopathology is defined in terms of disturbances of communication. This statement may come as a surprise, but if the reader cares to open a textbook on psychiatry and to read about the manic-depressive or the schizophrenic psychosis, for example, he is likely to find terms such as 'illusions', 'de-lusions', 'hallucinations', 'flight of ideas', 'disassociation', 'mental retarda-tion', 'elation', 'withdrawal', and many others, which refer specifically to dis-turbances of communication; they imply either that perception is distorted or that expression - that is, transmission - is unintelligible. (Ruesch, 1951, p. 79-80. My italics.)

No new observations, no new empirical findings are offered. What is offered, however, is an alternative perspective. (Cf. Kuhn's (1970) general descriptions of 'the structure of scientific revolutions' in terms of shifts of paradigms.) Two reasons for this change of perspective at this particular time can easily be identified. In addi-tion to the general trend to adopt a social perspective, the widespread frustration with regard to the lack of efficiency of traditional, individually oriented therapy, definitely represented a motivational impetus for a (any) shift.

As would be expected, this shift of theoretical perspective posed a series of conceptual and methodological problems in this field. Again Haley (1971, p. 274) has described the situation in retrospect:

> Once the hypothesis was posed that schizophrenia was a product of a certain kind of relationship, a problem became apparent. There was no language for describing relationships, no theoretical models, and no means of testing the relationship between two people. Previous research had tested a person. (My italics.)

One might have expected that in adopting a communication perspective, the field would have turned to the various traditional social disciplines - in particular to social psychology - to resolve the problems related to the adoption of a social perspective. Surprisingly enough, this did not happen. And, as Riskin & Faunce (1972) observed in their extensive and systematic overview of the field: 'Interdisciplinary isolation is striking' (p. 369).[1]

After the breakthrough of the social perspective in the early 1950s, the field can be said to have developed over three (or four) more or less distinct phases. That the adoption of the social perspective really represented a 'breakthrough', is reflected for example in the fact that Weakland (1974, p. 269) in 'a self-reflexive hindsight' characterized the launching of the double-bind theory as representing almost a 'scientific earth-quake'.

The first phase, from the beginning to the mid or late 1950s, was characterized by the launching of 'the great theories'. A variety of theoretical models and conceptual frameworks, aiming at an understanding of psychopathology (in particular schizophrenia) in terms of the communication patterns of the family, were introduced. Amongst the variety of models and theories outlined, the highly different theories of Bateson et al. (1956); Lidz et al. (1957); Wynne et al. (1958) have gained a somewhat special status. Due in part to the authoritative review of various theories and models of the field by Mishler & Waxler (1965), the theoretical positions of these three research groups have been canonized.

The next phase, partly overlapping the first one and passing away gradually in the early 1970s, was characterized by an intense empirical research activity, where literally hundreds of studies were conducted for (or against) the various theories launched in the first phase. For reviews, see for example Riskin & Faunce (1972); Jacobsen & Pettersen (1974); Blakar (1978a, 1978b). Taken together, the above-mentioned two phases may be termed the 'optimistic period' of family and communication research on psychopathology. The optimism was testified to, for example, by all the readers and textbooks appearing within this young field.

In the 1970s, this optimism has been replaced by a more pessimistic and critical attitude. A series of reviews and analytical papers identifying methodological and conceptual weaknesses hindering the progress of all this empirical work, have appeared (Haley, 1972; Riskin & Faunce, 1972; Jacob, 1975; Blakar, 1974a, 1975a, Blakar & Nafstad, 1980a; Rønbeck, 1977). Recently, attempts to proceed beyond this criticism and to approach the identified problems of the field by more general and coherent theoretical models and frameworks, developed for example within general social psychology, have been observed (Doane, 1978a; Blakar, 1978a, in press a, Blakar & Nafstad, 1980b).

The lack of progress has been ascribed either to a lack of adequate methods (Haley, 1972) or to a lack of 'intermediate concepts' connecting observable data to the superordinate concepts used when theorizing about families with deviant members (Riskin & Faunce, 1972).

First, when reviewing the empirical research of the field, Haley (1972, p. 35) was forced to conclude that: 'The evidence for a difference between the normal family and a family containing a patient member is no more than indicative'. (My italics.)   At the present stage, what is of particular interest is Haley's explanation of why all this empirical research has not yielded conclusive, but only indicative, evidence. From the above conclusion, Haley (1972, p. 35) starts analyzing the underlying problems in this field.

He concludes by ascribing the lack of progress directly to a lack of adequate methods:

> ... if we judge the exploratory research done to date by severe methodological criteria, one can only conclude that the evidence for a difference between the normal family and a family containing a patient member is no more than indicative. This does not mean that schizophrenia is not produced by a type of family, nor does it mean that a family with a schizophrenic is grossly different from the average family. It means that sufficient reliable evidence of a difference has yet to be provided. The methodology for providing that evidence is still being devised. (My italics.)

Secondly, in their comprehensive critical overview of the field, Riskin & Faunce (1972) identified various conceptual and methodological shortcomings. The major problem, according to their analysis, seems to be a lack of 'intermediate concepts' connecting observable phenomena to the superordinate concepts used in theorizing about the pattern of communication in families containing deviant members. They point out that family research involves abstract, theoretical concepts (such as double-bind, pseudo-mutuality, and marital schism and marital skew), while, at the same time, a number of relatively simple phenomena (for example, 'Who speaks to whom?'), which can easily be measured, are in operation. The connection between these abstract concepts and the readily operationalizable phenomena is, however, lacking. Moreover, the following quotation is telling with regard to their criticism of the conceptual unclarity in the field in general:

Many terms in today's research are often used in a formula-like ritualistic or ambiguous manner, and this tends to interfere with, or substitute for, clear thinking. For example, the word 'systems' at times does seriously represent a point of view that guides one's thinking and research strategy. At other times it seems to be used as a cliche, almost as a badge of high status, in a way similar to the use of the concept 'dynamics' in psychoanalytic case presentations. 'Process' is another 'in' term which is at times used by researchers who are actually dealing with outcome scores. An instance of ambiguous usage is 'communication', which sometimes seems to be synonymous with 'behavior' and at other times appears to refer specifically to verbal messages. And 'interaction' is used in exceedingly variable ways. One wonders, if these expressions were stricken from the vocabulary, would hard thinking be encouraged, or would other terms immediately fill the vacuum?' (1972, p. 371). (My italics.)

In addition, the research in this field has been seriously criticized for more specifically technical reasons, for example, that the experimenter has often not been 'blind', that clinical rather than statistical assessments have been used, etc. (cf. Jacob, 1975; Riskin & Faunce, 1972).

We agree with both Haley's (1972) and Riskin & Faunce's (1972) observations. However, we hesitate to characterize either of these factors as the cause of the lack of progress in the field. To be sure, if one wants to study the communication patterns of families with and without psychopathological members, it will of course be critical that one has (a) adequate methods for investigating the process of communication, and (b) intermediate concepts connecting the observations made to the superordinate concepts used in theorizing. However, in our contention the lack of adequate methods and intermediate concepts are 'symptoms' only. These identified factors are linked to a more fundamental deficiency, namely, that the concept of communication used in family-oriented research is vague and left undefined (see Blakar, 1975c, in press b, Sølvberg & Blakar, 1975; Blakar & Nafstad, 1980a).

An explicated and clarified concept of X (in casu, communication) should logically represent a prerequisite for developing methods for studying X. Or, how could one even hope to construct adequate methods for studying a process so vaguely defined as is the concept of communication in this field according to Riskin & Faunce's description in the above quotation. A theory of communication, for example elaborated in terms of preconditions for (successful) communication, would represent guidelines and give ideas in method development with respect to variables to be manipulated and conditions to be controlled (see below). Thus, to surmount the obvious problems and shortcomings with respect to adequate methods in the study of family communication, one has to start by defining communication and explicate the concept of communication.

Moreover, with regard to the lack of intermediate concepts, the lack of an adequate theory of communication in general, is even more striking. A major objective for a theory of communication would be to specify exactly the connections between the observable, overt behavior and the superordinate concepts of that particular theory.

In conclusion, instead of throwing oneself into time-consuming empirical research on communication patterns in various categories of families (cf. the optimistic period described above), much more work should have been or would have to be invested in clarifying the conceptual framework of communication theory. Or in general, if the adoption of a communication perspective in any specific field is going to be productive and beneficial, and not only represent a popular programmatic position, the communication theory of that particular field has to be worked out in quite some detail. On this point there are no short-cuts. The communication perspective is not a magic wand that can be exploited by everyone everywhere. On the contrary, the adoption of a communication perspective presupposes a thorough understanding of the multiple social realities involved. As a minimum, the adoption of a communication perspective, for example in the field of family interactions, presupposes an adequate definition and (at least an outline of) a theory of communication. Ignorance of these problems, that is, to adopt a communication perspective without bothering about exploring the corresponding communication theory, is bound to result in conditions of absurdity where one mystery (e.g., psychopathology) is being explained by means of another mystery (e.g., familial communication, or more accurately, deviant familial communication).

More specifially, our criticism with regard to the concept of communication as employed in current research can be summarized as follows: (1) To the extent that attempts have been made toward presenting definitions of 'communication', they are much too general and extensive, almost all-inclusive. (2) In most studies in the field the operationalizations of 'communication' represent trivial over-simplifications, which fail to grasp essential aspects of communication. The almost paradoxical co-occurrence of (1) and (2) only adds to our criticism.

With regard to the too extensive definitions (usually the 'definitions' are left implicit), they can be classified as of two types: first and foremost, communication is often conceived of as almost synonymous with behavior (see also the above quotation by Riskin & Faunce). Watzlawick et al. (1967) in Pragmatics of Human Communication provided a classic and in many respects 'authoritative' example when they claimed that: '... all behavior, not only speech, is communication - even the communicational clues in an impersonal context - affects behavior' (p. 22). Secondly, communication is often vaguely characterized as 'the flow of information'. This type of a definition is usually only reflected indirectly in the scoring of categories such as 'information exchange' (Ferreira & Winter, 1968a, b), 'information giving' (Goldstein et al., 1968), 'informing' (McPherson, 1970), etc. The underlying concept of communication, however, appears to be as all-embracing as the definition put forward by Athanassiades (1974, p. 195): 'Verbal and non-verbal communication, i.e., the flow of information, impressions, and understandings from one individual to others'. (My italics.)

A little sarcastically, one might ask why a concept of communication is needed at all, and in particular, why it is such an essential concept, when all behavior is communication? In such a case, it seems, one would rather need a more specified concept of behavior. Similarly, one could pose analogous questions to those who conceive of communication as 'the flow of information'.

Ideally, definitions should prove useful in revealing and specifying the subject matter. Vague and extensive definitions of the above type only serve to disguise and veil fundamental distinctions. That this is actually so, should be realized only by briefly juxtaposing the above definitions of communication with the following quotation by Rommetveit (1968, p. 41): 'The communicative medium is related to the message it conveys only via an intentional act of encoding'. Without taking a definite stand on Rommetveit's general theoretical position, it will be realized immediately that a number of crucial issues, which are neglected in the above definitions, are exposed. To be of any use, a definition of communication must make explicit issues such as: Does it make sense to speak about 'not-intended (non-intended) communication'? Are there any fundamental differences between 'receiving messages' and 'getting information'? (For a more detailed exposition of the crucial issues that definitions of communication should explicitly incorporate, see Blakar, 1978a, in press c.)

Our second point of criticism was that the operationalizations of communication in most studies involve trivial over-simplifications. Variables of the type: Who speaks? Who speaks to whom? How long (much) does each of the participants speak? Number of interruptions? Who interrupts? Who is interrupted? How long and/or how complex sentences are used? etc. We do not say that these aspects of communication are of no interest. However, the interpretation of each one of these observations depends on one's theory of communication (which may involve vague definitions or none at all). For example, an interruption may reflect a power struggle, but it may just as well reflect perfect mutual understanding between the participants ('I have already understood/anticipated what you are going to say'). Nothing much, therefore, can be learned by an atheoretical counting of interruptions. Correspondingly, incomplete sentences may reflect lack of verbal or communicative competence, but it may also reflect perfect mutual understanding (ellipsis) where elaborated sentences would not be needed, and could even create an impression of alienation. These examples should illustrate, first, that the operationalizations of communication frequently involve over-simplifications, and, secondly, that a more explicit and elaborate theory of communication is needed, so that the observations may be interpreted adequately.

In defining communication, the main problem (see above) is to capture the essential aspects of this common and universal human activity, while at the same time distinguishing 'communication' from processes and activities bearing basic resemblances to communication. The most essential characteristic of communication is that something is being made known to somebody. It follows from this that an act of communication is social and directional (from a sender to a receiver). A crucial characteristic distinguishing communication from the general flow of information is that the sender has an intention to make something known to the (particular) receiver. (The intentionality in acts of communication is reflected, for example, in the equifinality of different means.) When communication is defined as a (sender's) intentional act to make something (the message) known to others (the receiver), then the behavioral as well as the informational aspects of the definitions discussed above become integrated, at the same time as we manage to distinguish communication from behavior and information processing in general. Two comments may be warranted in connection with the launching of a definition of this kind. First, the fact that a particular 'act of communication' is not classified as communication, i.e., is excluded by the definition, does not of course imply that it is of no interest to our analysis of human interaction and behavior. It implies only that is has to be grasped and handled by means of other concepts. Second, acts of communication are embedded in and have to be analyzed within wider behavioral contexts of social interaction. Hence, whereas the above definition supports us with a more refined analytical tool, it does not exclude any relevant aspects, for example, non-intentional or unconscious behavior from our total integral analysis. We are forced, however, to develop or refine our conceptual framework in order to grasp all the various aspects and nuances of human interaction in terms of adequate notions. To exploit a vague and extensive concept of communication only conceals distinctions that may prove fundamental to our understanding.

A comprehensive exposition of a conceptual framework developed along these lines is given by Rommetveit, 1972a, 1974, 1978, Rommetveit & Blakar, 1979; Blakar, 1973b, 1978a. From the above definition methods for studying, and concepts for analyzing, processes of communication can be derived (cf. Blakar, 1972a, 1973a). In this perspective, a whole series of intriguing enquiries and corresponding strategies whereby research may gain insight into the riddles of human communication readily offer themselves. We will return to this below.

By the above analysis the challenges to social psychology in general and communication theorists in particular should have been made explicit: that is to transform communication theory from a programmatic, but vague and diffuse perspective into a specific and refined tool of analysis in the study of human behavior. To enable us to conduct studies, for example, of schizophrenia that could possibly add to our understanding of schizophrenia, as a minimum the following issues have to be seriously addressed, and not be ignored any longer.

First, there is the major problem with regard to an adequate definition of communi-

cation. In most communication-oriented studies no definition is explicitly offered
at all, or the definition offered is too general and extensive (see below).

Second, a conceptual framework by which the process of communication can be adequately grasped and conceived has to be developed. The ultimate aim on this point
naturally is to develop an elaborated and refined theory of human communication and
corresponding models which would enable us to analyze acts of communication in their
total social, developmental and dynamic complexities.

At this point it should be stressed that we do not criticize the lack of progress and
success of communication-oriented research in the various fields per se, as the development of an adequate theory of human communication represents an extremely complex task. At present there is no fully elaborated theory of communication available.
Our criticism, therefore, refers to the predominant tendency to pretend that problems
are being solved by means of vague and too extensive definitions. Furthermore, there
is a strong tendency to employ the existing concepts as if they were unproblematic and
everyone would know and agree about what, for example, 'communication' and 'normal'
family communication' is or implies.

Third, methods explicitly anchored in communication theory have to be designed.
Only by means of methods developed from the perspective of communication and grounded
in theory of communication, can we ever hope to enlarge our knowledge about human
communication in general and enable us to conduct sensible studies of particular phenomena (for example, schizophrenia) from an explicit communication perspective.

Fourth, the empirical knowledge about human communication in general under varying social and situational conditions has to be considerably enlarged. At present, our
knowledge about, for example, what is the variation of 'normal familial communication
patterns' across different socio-cultural backgrounds is much too restricted to allow
any safe conclusions with regard to what is (is not) deviant (familial) communication
patterns.

Logically, the latter two enterprises presuppose a certain degree of progress with
regard to the first two. However, here a word of warning is needed: if communication-
oriented empirical work (for example, in connection to development and maintenance
of schizophrenia) were to be postponed until a refined and fully satisfying theory of
human communication in general is developed, we are afraid that one would never get
involved in empirical work, and that communication-oriented studies of schizophrenia,
or of any other phenomenon, would never be conducted. Moreover, there is a dialectical
relation between empirical studies and theoretical clarifications, so that empirical
studies in connection with, for example, familial communication may promote the development of general communication theory. What we have been criticizing above is
the predominant tendency to carry out a lot of communication-oriented empirical

studies almost at the expense of conceptual and methodological clarifications (cf. the above analysis of communication-oriented research on schizophrenia).

Consequently, the following sections will be devoted to an outline of an alternative approach to human communication, where we have tried to take the above challenges explicitly into consideration. We will start by addressing problems in connection with the definition of communication. Then we will continue to comment upon various models underlying the study of communication within the social sciences, and point out what we consider as minimal requirements for a model to be fruitful in the analysis of acts of communication. Finally, we will briefly outline a conceptual framework for the study of communication, and give an exposition of what we consider to be fundamental enquiries which may direct and guide communication-oriented research.

Communication - a fundamental perspective on man

Communication constitutes a basic precondition for all social intercourse. No social system, organization or society can be established and maintained - or changed - without communication. Only through the participation in communicative activities does man become a truly social being. This can easily be demonstrated in various ways.

In the first place, if we, utilizing all our imaginative potentials, try to conceive of man as completely lacking communicative abilities, we immediately realize the absurdity of this autistic being - unable to participate and unqualified for membership in any social organization. Secondly, if we try to define concepts such as 'social fellowship', 'social system', or 'society', we discover that one decisive factor is whether members or participants have developed or have at their disposal a communication system. And in deciding whether a person is a member of a particular society, social system or group, a fundamental criterion is whether or not the person in focus knows the relevant communicative system that enables him to engage in communicative activities with other members.

The implications of these observations are far-reaching and profound: in order to gain insight into and understand ourselves and our fellow man (qua individuals) as well as the society surrounding us (qua social system) it is absolutely necessary to adopt a communication perspective and develop a communication theory.

Historical theories are basic to our understanding of society because society is not static, but develops and changes over time; economic theories are essential for understanding society because society comprises economic relations. This seems to be generally accepted. Similarly, the communication perspective and theories of communication are necessary in order to understand society, because society is constituted through communication and interaction.

Historical, economic, communicational and other relevant perspectives supplement each other. They are not mutually exclusive or of a competitive nature. The historian understands history precisely by attempting to reconstrcut and understand communication and interaction systems that existed in the past in different societies. The object of historical change in a society is, among other things, its communication systems. And the development of a written language, the art of printing as well as television, all illustrate how changes in communicative systems may promote revolutionary social changes. Society cannot, of course, be understood from the point of view of communication alone, but neglect of this perspective will necessarily result in an inadequate understanding.

On a par with the historical perspective, the communication perspective is a general one. A historical perspective can facilitate our understanding of an individual's life situation as well as the situation of a family, a local community, a town or city, an organization, a corporation, a nation or culture, etc. In a similar manner we may conceive of an individual as a member of various communication systems and as a participant in various communcation acts. We may analyze a family in terms of the patterns of communication existing within the family as well as between the family and the environment. A society can be described by means of the communication systems it has developed. A particularly relevant criterion for evaluating the degree of democratic development within a given society is whether and to what extent members have equal access to and control over communication facilities (cf. Blakar, 1973b, 1979a). Moreover, the relations between super-powers cannot be completely understood without a communication perspective. The inclusion of China (in addition to the Soviet Union and the USA) as a super-power has necessarily made this communication pattern much more complex than earlier.

Under these circumstances it is really surprising to observe that the communication perspective has not been more frequently exploited within the various disciplines, and that theories of communication have not been elaborated and refined to a further extent than proves to be the case (see below). It is difficult to identify the reason(s) for this relative neglect, apart from the fact that communication represents a very complex phenomenon, but so do most social phenomena and processes. Within the discipline of psychology, for example, much more effort has traditionally been invested in understanding the related phenomena of language, language processing, and thinking than communication proper. This relative lack of studies - empirical as well as theoretical - on communication is the more surprising as it is our contention that an adequate understanding of language and language processing presupposes the adoption of a communication perspective.

Toward a model of communication

Irrespective of which topic is studied, it is rare in communication-oriented research (see above) that the underlying model of communication is made explicit and presented. This state of affairs is unfortunate indeed, since there is every reason to presume that, owing to the very nature of social realities and social processes, most communication-oriented research is restricted by the model that is adopted. Although it represents an exaggeration, it can be argued that as social scientists we conduct research on our model(s) rather than on the social realities and processes directly. To a large extent the underlying model determines the type of questions that will be asked, and even more decisive, which questions are unlikely to be posed. Hence it is of the utmost importance to examine critically the model(s) underlying communication-oriented research, and continually to refine and elaborate one's model(s).

Since the various models are rarely made explicit, it becomes difficult to evaluate them. Two predominant models in the study of language and communication - for convenience they may be termed the model of individual psychology and the model of sociology respectively - will be briefly presented, because in different and supplementary ways they illustrate our general arguments with regards to how critical the choice of model(s) is.

First, in the dominant model of individual psychology (Fig. 1), the individual is represented as a complex O-variable located between input (stimulus) and output (response) variables. Depending on each psychologist's theoretical interests, the model of 'O' is equipped with complex mechanisms for language processing; associative processing and associative networks; short and long term memories; information-processing procedures; encoding and decoding processes; etc. Prototype designs for studying language and communication according to this model are, for example, varied word association techniques and verbal memory experiments.

This model is very well suited to investigating the individual as a language user in various respects. But this model is totally inadequate with regard to the social and situational aspects of communication, and even hinders critical questions to be posed.

Fig. 1 The model of individual psychology. For explanations see text.

An example will illustrate: word association tests have traditionally been extensively employed in the study of schizophrenia and distorted thinking. Imagine a young male schizophrenic in the setting of a free word association test responding to critical stimulus words such as 'mother', 'sex', and 'love'. The above model is excellent for assessing his 'distorted thinking' in terms of frequency of idiosyncratic associations, response time, etc. This model is totally inadequate, however, with regard to questions of the following type: How would the above client respond if the stimulus words were presented by an elderly, gray-haired male psychiatrist versus by a young, sexy nurse? Actually, this model is not open to enquiries of the latter type. An implicit presupposition of the model seems to be that the individual's processing of language (within his or her head) is unaffected by such social and situational variations. (For a more systematic analysis of the potentials and restrictions of various types of word association techniques, see Blakar, 1972b, 1978a.)

On the other extreme we have the sociological model (Fig. 2), within which the individual actors are represented as positions or locations within the communication network only. This model is particularly well suited for studies of who is in direct (versus only indirect) contact with whom; who has a central versus a peripheral position in the communication network; who is in control (power) of the information; which channels are used for transferring what kind of information; etc. However, this model is totally inadequate with regard to enquiring into the processing of each individual communicant. Questions concerning encoding and decoding of messages, not to say how the received message is preserved by the receiver, are left outside this sociological model.

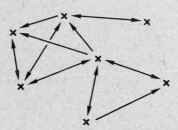

Fig. 2 The model of sociology. For explanations see text.

Although the limitations of the above models are obvious, we have a strong impression that in various more or less refined versions the above models prevail within psychological and sociological research on language and communication respectively. On this background and in connection with our communication-oriented project on psychopathology, we have invested much effort in the explication of an integral model that encompasses the social and situational aspects of the act of communication as well as the individual communicant's processing (for example, the encoding and decoding of messages). In Fig. 3 are outlined what we consider to be the absolute <u>minimal requirements</u> of what is to constitute a tenable model of communication (cf. Blakar, 1970, 1974b). Since model and conceptual framework are so interrelated, the structure and function of the model will be further amplified through the presentation of key concepts in the next section.

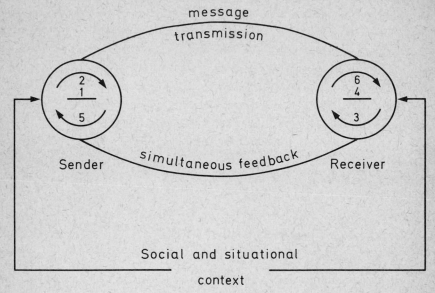

Fig. 3   The minimal requirements of a model of communication. 1: 'Production' of message(s); 2: Encoding of message(s); 3: Decoding of message(s); 4: Processing and memory of received message(s); 5: Sender's anticipation of receiver's decoding; 6: Receiver's listening on the premisses of the sender. 5 and 6 are particularly crucial in the monitoring of the process of communication, revealing how the sender has to speak on the premisses of the listener and the listener has to listen on the premisses of the speaker. For further explanations see text.

Outline and explication of a conceptual framework

A reservation should be stated explicitly at this point: It follows from what has been maintained above (p. 20) that at present we (this seems to be the case for the field of communication-oriented research in general) do not have a fully developed and refined conceptual framework to offer. To underline that at present we are in the process of explicating the conceptual framework, the presentation of the conceptual framework will be done in connection with a presentation of the research we are conducting in order to pursue these issues (see also Parts II and III).

    What has so far been guiding and integrating our enquiries and theory construction within the field of human communication is the following basic question: What are the prerequisites for (successful) communication, i.e., under what conditions will somebody succeed (to a reasonable degree) in making something known to somebody else? To (clinically oriented) psychologists the counterpart of this enquiry may be even more intriguing: Which of the preconditions have not been satisfied when communicacation fails? An important aim of research, with obvious theoretical as well as practical implications, is, hence, an identification and systematic description of the various prerequisites for (successful) communication. Such a research program needs to emcompass individual and situational as well as social variables (Blakar, 1974c, 1977).

Consequently, a theory of communication should involve a specification of the individual, social and situational preconditions for (successful) communication, and a description of the interplay between these preconditions.

In an effort to identify and describe some of these prerequisites for communication, we developed a particular experimental method (Blakar, 1972a, 1973a). The method was directly derived from our general conceptual framework, and it was further inspired by various studies of communication breakdowns, especially those typical for children (for example, Piagetian studies on egocentrism), and also by analyses of everyday misunderstandings and how they occur (for example, Ichheiser, 1970, Garfinkel, 1972).

The general idea of the method was very simple, but in practice it proved very difficult to realize. This was to try to create a communication situation in which one of the preconditions for (successful) communication was not satisfied. If one were able to create such a situation, one would be able to study, at least: (1), the impact of that particular variable on communication, (2) the potential 'missing' requirements or preconditions to which the subjects would attribute the resultant communication difficulties, and (3) what the subjects acutally do in order to try to 'improve' their communication when it goes astray.

It can be hypothesized that the most basic precondition for successful communication, in order that it may take place at all, is that the participants have established 'a shared social reality', a common 'here-and-now' within which exchange of messages can take place (Rommetveit, 1972a, 1972b, 1974; Blakar, 1970, 1975b; Blakar & Rommetveit, 1975). An ideal experimental situation would thus be one where two (or more) participants communicate with each other under the belief that they are 'in the same situation' (i.e., have a common definition of the situation's 'here' and 'now'), but where they are in fact in different situations. In other words, we tried to create a situation where each participant speaks and understands what is said on the basis of his own particular interpretation of the situation and falsely believes that the other (others) speaks and understands on the basis of that same interpretation as well (as in everyday quarrels and misunderstandings).

The problems that we encountered in developing an experimental situation that 'worked', i.e., a situation where the subjects would communicate for a reasonable period of time without suspecting anything awry, will not be dealt with here (see Blakar, 1972a, 1973a). The final design, however, was simple and seemed quite natural. Two persons, A and B, are each given a map of a relatively complicated network of roads and streets in a town centre. On A's map two routes are marked with arrows, one short and straightforward (the practice route), and another longer and more complicated (the experimental route). On B's map no route is marked. A's task is then to explain to B the two routes, first the simple one, then the longer and more complicated one. B will then, with the help of A's explanations, try to find the way through town to the predetermined destination. B may ask questions, for example, ask A to repeat the explanations, or to explain in other ways, and so on. The experimental manipulation is simply that the two maps are not identical. An extra street is added on B's map/a street is lacking on A's map. So, no matter how adequately A explains, no matter how carefully B carries out A's instructions, B is bound to go wrong. The difference between the two maps affects only the complicated route, however; the practice route is straightforward for both.

The practice route was included for three reasons: (1) to get the subjects used to the situation, (2) to strengthen their confidence in the maps, and (3) to obtain a sample of their communication in the same kind of situation, but unaffected by our experimental manipulation (a 'before-after' design). The two participants sit at opposite ends of a table, with two low screens shielding their maps from each other. The screens are low enough for them to see each other and allow natural eye-contact (Moscovici, 1967; Argyle, 1969). Everything said is tape-recorded, and for certain analyses the tape is subsequently transcribed. For more detailed presentations of the method and its theoretical background, see Blakar, 1972a, 1973a.

In the above presentation we have been strictly descriptive. The following excerpt of a thorough analysis of this particular cooperation situation (Blakar & Pedersen, 1980a, p.35) clearly demonstrates how core social variables such as control and self-confidence are involved:

> ... the subjects participate two-and-two in a rather common type of interaction situation. One subject is going to explain something to the other, and the latter is going to carry out the task according to the explanations and directives given by the first. The communication situation is structured so that one subject is given some information which the other one needs. In other words: The two subjects are ascribed to the roles of an explainer and a follower. Furthermore, the standardized interaction situation consists of two apparently similar, but in reality highly different communication tasks, in that whereas the first one is simple and straightforward the other one is more complicated and a communication conflict is induced.

While the roles as explainer and follower involve different types and degrees of control, the subjects' reactions to situational variants - simple versus conflict communication situation - may reflect their self-confidence and self-esteem. In order to resolve the communication conflict induced in the more complicated situation, the subject has to demonstrate confidence in himself/herself (as well as in the other). (For a detailed analysis of the patterns of control in the two communication situations, see Blakar & Pedersen, 1978, 1980a.)

A study in which students served as subjects convinced us that the experimental manipulation was successful (Blakar, 1972a, 1973a). Blakar (in press a, p. 18) summarized the most interesting findings from this first exploratory study as follows:

1. It took an average of 18 minutes from the start on the experimental route before any doubt concerning the credibility of the maps was expressed. During this time the subjects communicated under the false assumption that they were sharing the same situation (the same 'here').

2. Moreover, the situation proved successful in demonstrating how the subjects 'diagnosed' their communication difficulties, and what kinds of 'tools' they had at their disposal in order to remedy and improve their communication. The experimental situation seemed to make great demands on the subjects' powers of flexibility and ability to modify their communication patterns, and also on their capacity to decenter and see things from the other's perspective.

The latter involves actually a tentative specification of prerequisites for (successful) communication, which was exactly our aim for developing this standardized communication conflict situation. Therefore, let us take, for example, 'capacity to decenter and see things from the other's perspective' as an illustrative example in a further exposition of our conceptual framework.

The ability and/or willingness to decenter (at least to some extent) and take the perspective of the other(s), is a basic prerequisite for successful communication, and extreme egocentrism may strongly hinder communication. In particular, when problems are encountered in the communication process, a minimum of decentration is required in order to re-establish shared premisses for further communication.

Decentration in communication is characterized by the fact that the sender anticipates the receiver's decoding, takes the receiver's perspective into account, and encodes on the receiver's premisses. Similarly, decentration on behalf of the receiver is reflected in the receiver's listening and decoding on the premisses of the sender. The following statement, in which the sender in the above communication conflict situation tries to describe a point on the map, is an example:

'... then you come to a crossing, there you are in the upper left-hand corner of a rectangle which is to your right under the crossing ...'

Egocentrism, on the contrary, is characterized by the fact that the participants do not take each other's perspective, and do not speak and listen, respectively, on each other's premisses. In a situation resembling the one just mentioned in the above example, an egocentric statement would be: '... and then you go down here and across there, and then you come to a crossing ...'

Our use of the concept of egocentrism is inspired by Piaget's (1926) analysis of children's language, but the concept's more social flavour is influenced by Mead's (1934) 'the generalized other'. Closely related to these concepts is Rommetveit's (1968) notion that 'encoding involves antecipated decoding'. Only by the communicants taking the perspective of the other(s) into account, so that they (sender and receiver) may establish commonality, is communication rendered possible.

In addition to the actual lack of sharing of perspectives, there is another important aspect of egocentric communication, i.e., that this lack is constantly covered up in that the communicants act as if their communication were not egocentric. 'Egocentrism ... is characterized by an underlying postulate that the other always sees and keeps the same thing in mind as oneself, i.e., by an unreflected presupposed convergence of memory and attention between speaker and listener' (Rommetveit, 1972a, p. 48-49). (My translation.)

The concept of egocentrism/decentration may thus be applied to characterize both the persons involved (he/she is egocentric) and the communication process itself (the communication is egocentric)(cf. Blakar, 1974c, 1977).

That these two levels do not necessarily coincide may be seen from the following example. If a person (sender) is egocentric in his way of speaking, this can be compensated for by a particularly decentered receiver, so that the communication may nevertheless flow tolerably well. This is for example often the case in child-adult interactions.

Before we continue to amplify our conceptual framework by specifying a few more preconditions for (successful) communication, some general theoretical-methodological issues should be explicitly commented upon.

First, the relationship between the various prerequisites on the one hand and the process of communication on the other, is of a logical type. For example, it can be concluded on the basis of logical analysis of the concepts involved that a greater capacity to decenter and take the perspective of the other will make communication run more smoothly, and that extreme egocentrism will hinder communication.[2] Nevertheless, when undertaking systematic identification and specification of the various preconditions and analysis of the subtle interplay between them, illustrative empirical material of the kind envisaged in the communication conflict situation above is almost indispensable (cf. Blakar, 1978d). Moreover, when it is reported (Sølvberg & Blakar, 1975, Mossige Pettersen & Blakar, 1976, 1979, Blakar, Paulsen & Sølvberg, 1978) that the pattern of communication in families containing schizophrenic members is characterized by more (extreme) egocentrism than that in comparable control families, this represents empirical findings that could not be derived by logical analysis of the concepts involved (Blakar, 1978d).

Second, the concept of egocentrism-decentration illustrates the openness in models of communication with regard to aspects of social processes as well as of individual capacities that we claimed (see p. 26).

Third, the above analysis of egocentrism-decentration in communication highlights in various ways the problems connected with the study of human communication (i. e., the communicant's establishing and maintenance of intersubjectivity) from the perspective of an outside observer. In assessing an utterance as being egocentric/decentered, the wider context and the communication process as such has to be taken into account. Only on the basis of what the participants at a certain point of time have established as a shared social reality (cf. Rommetveit, 1974, Blakar & Rommetveit, 1975), can anything uttered be assessed as egocentric/decentered. Hence, the observer has to follow the communication process carefully over time in order to 'know' at each point of time what the participants may tacitly take for granted. However, the outside observer to the communication process has no immediate access to the participants' experiences. A particularly salient fallacy for such an outside observer is to judge as egocentric a sequence of communication which actually is characterized by ellipsis (Rommetveit, 1974, Strøno, 1978) and thus in a way reflects almost perfect commonality on behalf of the participants. Consequently, analyses of the process of communication ideally enforce some sort of oscillation between the 'from-within perspective' of the communicants and the 'from-outside perspective' of the observer (Blakar, 1978a, in press c).

Finally, the above analysis should have given clues as to why we have termed our approach social-developmental. In an earlier section (p. 23-25) we refuted the models of individual psychology and sociology respectively, and a model integrating individual, social and situational preconditions for communication was envisaged. A social-individual model open to situational variation thus seems optimal. The most obvious and only general perspective in order to conceive of the individual communicant is definitely the developmental perspective.[3]

On the basis of the above general theoretical-methodological considerations, we will now briefly exemplify a few more of the prerequisites for communication. In so doing, we will exploit the above standardized communication conflict situation, and refer to some of the studies conducted with this particular method. This for two reasons: first, this will constitute a somewhat standardized observational framework, which, it is hoped, will help one to see the subtle and extensive interplay between the various preconditions. Second, because of the experimental manipulation, we are granted systematic situational variation (the simple situation versus the conflict situation).

The directional and the social character of acts of communication was underlined in the above explication of the concept of communication (p. 19). Another essential aspect of human communication is the <u>contractual</u> aspect (Rommetveit, 1972a, 1972 b, 1974, Blakar, 1972a, 1975b). In various respects the process of communication and the premisses for intersubjectivity are fundamentally negotiable. The communicants continually face critical moments of choice at which their underlying premisses have to be coordinated in order to render communication possible. For example, in the above situation the critical concepts of 'right' and 'left' can meaningfully be exploited from the perspective of the participants as seated at the table as well as from the perspective of the driver. In order to make the routes common (i.e., communicate), they have to endorse contracts monitoring their communication with regard to this particular aspect. The communicants' ability to endorse contracts monitoring the process of communication thus constitutes an essential prerequisite for communication. In the present standardized communication conflict situation it has been shown that the communicants endorse contracts concerning topic, perspective, categorization, orientation, roles, strategy as well as meta contracts (Blakar, 1972a, 1973a), and schemes for analyzing the process of communication in terms of contracts have been developed (Moberget & Reer, 1975). A finding worth reporting here is that on the basis of the quality of the contracts endorsed in the simple and straightforward situation, relatively good predictions concerning the communicants' degree of success and failure with regard to unravelling the induced conflict could be made (Moberget & Reer, 1975).

Communication conflicts, misunderstandings, and situations involving lack of mutual understanding are inevitable in any human intercourse. When communication runs into more or less serious trouble, it is essential in order to re-establish commonality that the difficulties are adequately <u>attributed</u> (Heider, 1958). The induced communication conflict offers an almost optimal opportunity to study patterns of attribution during the process of communication. Schemes for assessing patterns of attribution have been developed (Hultberg, Alve & Blakar, 1978, see ch.2 in Part II, Haarstad, 1976), and Brisendal (1976) enquired more systematically into the communicants' creativity with regard to producing hypotheses concerning 'the cause' underlying the communication conflict the subjects found themselves involved in.

Exploiting the prediction procedure mentioned above, Teigre (1976) analyzed the influence of another basic precondition for communication, i.e., the communicants' <u>confidence</u> in oneself and in one another. To a certain extent it was possible to predict a married couple's degree of success or failure with regard to unravelling the induced conflict on the basis of the patterns of confidence assessed in the simple and straightforward situation.

In the above section we have outlined singular concepts (for example, contract, attribution of communication difficulties, conficence, egocentrism vs. decentration). Obviously, these concepts are <u>interconnected</u>; they are all derived from the same conceptual framework (Blakar, 1978a). The existence of such interrelations may be illustrated thus: the egocentrism of one of the communicants may result in his tacitly taking for granted (as free information) something that could not possibly be known by the others. This may result in communication difficulties, either directly or indirectly. In order to re-establish commonality, the communication difficulty experienced has to be identified (attribution of communication difficulties). As a consequence of the (adequate or inadequate) attribution of communication difficulties, the underlying contracts are frequently modified or new contracts are endorsed to prevent further tangles of the same kind (Blakar, 1978a).

Naturally, the above brief exposition can give nothing but vague ideas about the conceptual framework in terms of preconditions for communication. Hopefully, the studies presented in Parts II and III will apmlify our approach.

Toward a more fruitful communication-oriented research on schizophrenia

A reasonable test of the social-developmental alternative we have advocated above would thus be to see whether this conceptual framework enables us to promote a sensible understanding of schizophrenia from the perspective of communication. In this context it should be kept in mind that the lack of progress in spite of all the effort invested in communication-oriented research on schizophrenia was attributed, in particular, to a lack of adequate methods (for example by Haley, 1972), whereas we, on the contrary, argued that the lack of methods was only a symptom reflecting the lack of an explicit communication theory (see p. 16). The above-presented communication conflict situation (Blakar, 1972a, 1973a) offers a method grounded in the above-presented conceptual framework. Of the first observations made in connection with the use of this method, the following in particular led to the idea that the method could possibly be used to illuminate communication deficiencies in families with schizophrenic members:

> Moreover, the situation proved successful in demonstrating how the subjects 'diagnosed' their communication difficulties, and what kinds of 'tools' they had at their disposal in order to remedy and improve their communication. The experimental situation seemed to make great demands on the subjects' powers of flexibility and ability to modify their communication patterns, and also on their capacity to decenter and see things from the other's perspective. (Blakar, in press a, p. 18.)

These observations coincide well with core aspects of earlier research, as summarized by Haley (1972, p. 35):

> If we accept the findings of the research reported here and assuming it is sound, evidence is accumulating to support the idea that a family with a patient member is different from an 'average' family. As individuals, the family members do not appear different according to the usual character and personality criteria. Similarly, evidence is slight that family structure, when conceived in terms of role assignment or dominance, is different in normal and abnormal families.

On process measurements there is some indication of difference: Abnormal families appear to have more conflict, to have different coalition patterns, and to
show more inflexibility in repeating patterns and behavior. The most sound
findings would seem to be in the outcome area: When faced with a task on which
they must cooperate, abnormal family members seem to communicate their preferences less successfully, require more activity and take longer to get the task
done. (My italics.)

The present standardized communication conflict situation was designed precisely
for the purpose of making possible more detailed analyses and descriptions in 'the
outcome area'. In this situation communication difficulties are bound to emerge. Concepts such as attribution (how and to which cause the induced communication difficulties are attributed), the ability to decenter and take the perspective of the other,
the capacity to endorse, maintain and modify interactional contracts, and so on, become consequently of central significance in the analysis. Our method thus enabled
us to draw upon theorists within general social and developmental psychology such
as Heider (1958), Mead (1934), Piaget (1926), Rommetveit (1972a, 1974), and others
in the description of deviant patterns of communication in abnormal families.

In the first exploratory study (Sølvberg & Blakar, 1975) we chose, both for theoretical and practical reasons, to concentrate on the parent dyad. Obviously, this is the
core dyad in the milieu into which the child is born and within which he later matures
into a healthy or pathological person. Moreover, we did not want to include the patient
himself in this very first study in which the method and conceptual framework itself
was to be tried out.

Since the communication task given to each couple was in principle unsolvable, we
had to decide beforehand the criteria for terminating the experiment:

1. The task would be considered finished successfully as soon as the error was correctly localized and identified.

2. The task would also be considered resolved when the route was correctly recon-
   structed to the location of the error and when one or both of the subjects insisted
   that the maps were not identical and, hence, that it was pointless to go on. In this
   context, it must be mentioned that the experimenter was instructed to neglect all
   suggestions that something might be wrong and give the impression, for as long
   as possible, that everything was as it should be (Blakar, 1973a, p. 418).

3. If no solution according to criteria one or two was reached within 40 minutes, the
   communication task would be brought to an end. The subjects would then be shown
   the discrepancy between the maps and told that the task was actually unsolvable.
   The 40-minute limit was based on findings of earlier experiments (Blakar, 1973a)
   and pre-tests.

4. Finally, it was decided that if the task should upset the couple too much, the experimenter would stop it and reveal the true nature of the experiment.[4]

In connection with this latter criterion, a few more general comments on the ethical dilemmas intrinsic to clinical research may be warranted. Ethical considerations have to be central in research involving human beings in general and in clinically oriented research in particular. Even though ethical considerations are of necessity essential in all research involving human subjects (cf. the APA ethical standards for research), such problems are seldom dealt with explicitly in written presentations of the research. It seems, so to speak, to be an implicit contract underlying the scientific culture that serious ethical considerations are being respected. Without questioning that this really is the state of affairs in the art of clinical research in general, it is our contention that the problems and dilemmas of an ethical nature intrinsic to this kind of research ought to constitute an integral part of the presentation of the designs and the studies.

The fundamental ethical dilemma confronting everybody undertaking clinical research (be it within the framework of medicine, psychiatry or psychology) is that from a certain perspective this type of research is by its very nature unethical. The argument then goes as follows. People who are suffering (i.e., the patients and their families) are invited and/or more or less forced to participate as subjects (i.e., to spend some of their very often highly restricted resources and time) in research which it is very unlikely that they themselves will ever benefit from. It is hoped, though no guarantee can ever be given in research, that future patients will benefit from the research. The ethical justification of clinical research in general lies in this hope. The ethical dilemma intrinsic to clinical research is then: How to justify (in terms of potential future clinically relevant knowledge) putting any extra burdens (in terms of participating as subjects in research) on severely suffering individuals and families? This ethical dilemma has to be faced and considered at every stage of any clinical research project: Does this situation/instrument/test/interview impose a greater strain than is necessary? How many patients and/or families do we really have to bother by including in the study? Is the chance to obtain any potentially useful knowledge high enough to justify having this category of people participate in this study when taking their total life situation into account? etc. Naturally, these ethical dilemmas and considerations are well-known to everybody familiar with clinical research. Therefore, we have to state briefly our more specific reasons for commenting explicitly upon these problems in this context.

First and foremost, a fascinating experimental method, which has proved very creative in clinically oriented research, is being presented. We want to ascertain, therefore, that anybody who might be attracted to pursue this work realizes beforehand that an exploitation of this particular method (as of any other instrument in clinical research) presupposes a systematic and thorough examination of the total experimenter-subject interactions, particularly with specific reference to the ethical dilemmas mentioned above. Second, as criterion 4 above suggests, this particular communication situation involves misunderstandings and communication conflicts. Consequently, as is the case with most instruments applied in clinical research (be it tests, clinical interviews, standardized communication situations, or whatever), the participation definitely represents a certain strain on behalf of the participants. Third, in connection with our research in general and the use of this method in particular, we have taken care to develop procedures and strategies for the experimenter to be prepared for all eventualities (cf. Moberget & Reer, 1975, Endresen, 1977, Blakar, 1978a). The experimenter has to go through a standardized training procedure. In particular, the experimenter has to be trained to manage phases of communication conflict and to cope with the crucial de-briefing period just after the termination of the experimental session (see Part II). Anybody who wants to exploit the present method should pay attention to these aspects, in particular to the essential training of the experimenter. A final reason for explicitly commenting upon these ethical issues is that in the earliest phases of the clinical research to be reported in the present volume, we once or twice had our application to obtain subjects rejected because the method involving an induced communication conflict was said to be 'unethical'. (As clinical researchers associated with the University, we have to get access to the subjects via various clinical institutions and hospitals.) Although based on a lack of knowledge regarding the real nature of this communication situation and what actually takes place during the interaction, this argument naturally forced us to make explicit the ethical considerations underlying our research on a par with the theoretical and methodological considerations. It should be unnecessary to mention, but if we had found the situation to be harmful for the participants, we would of course immediately have terminated the exploitation of this particular method. (Or, if we as stubborn, short-sighted scientists had continued to use a harmful method, the responsible clinical institutions would not have allowed us to have any more subjects.) In this connection it should be mentioned that in the very first exploratory studies we were extra cautious, in that the clinician in selecting subjects excluded families that were judged to be emotionally very unstable, and that therefore perhaps would not stand the potential strain of the situation. (This involved in reality that we counteracted our hypotheses with regard to finding different communication patterns.) However, as we have been forced on the basis of rather massive experiences with the method (see Part II and Part III) to conclude that the situation does not do any harm, we have in later studies been more keen on establishing more representative samples of the various categories of subjects (families). With specific reference to the fundamental ethical dilemma intrinsic to clinical research (see above), the present study will now be discussed in greater detail to corroborate the aspects that will be of special relevance in the ethical considerations with regard to this particular method.

First and foremost, there is the possibility that clinical research unintentionally may add to and enhance the problems of people who are already suffering severely. In the following two respects in particular one has to be on guard against such unwanted effects. First, the participants themselves may interpret the study in ways that create or enhance their feelings of guilt, or even worse, the study as presented and framed by the researcher may add to their feelings of guilt. Second, the participation may elicit or promote processes that may prove to be negative and harmful to the individuals and families. A classic example in the literature of the first type is the launching of the notion 'schizophrenogenic mother', which no doubt created an enormous amount of extra guilt feelings in a whole generation of unlucky and vulnerable mothers. In designing clinical research, the parents' and other family members' sensitivity with regard to their own responsibility and guilt has to be taken into account. Moreover, it has to be acknowledged that the subjects experience the situation and the purpose of the study on their own premisses, not on the premisses of the experimenter. It is particularly essential to be aware of these aspects in the pre- and post-experimental interaction with the subjects, to ensure, as far as possible, that they do not interpret the study in ways that, for example, enhance their feelings of guilt. Contrary to what is the case with many instruments and tests exploited in clinical research and practice, the experimental manipulation with the maps, the resultant communicative difficulties, and the striking different patterns of communicative behavior revealed in the two apparently similar situations, make it easier to give a generally understandable explanation of the aim of the study.

Second, there is the possibility that the participation in a clinical research project may initiate or promote processes (be it for good or for bad) in the families or family members. For example, by this particular method the subjects are exposed to a situation in which problems of communication are bound to emerge. In this context, three comments seem warranted. First and foremost, in assessing the potential strain of this situation, it should be acknowledged that the induced communication conflict resembles the type of conflicts and misunderstandings that are inevitable to everybody in everyday life. We are all frequently exposed to misunderstandings or conflicts with regard to premisses and information of this kind. The difference being that in this context the differences with regard to premisses are intentionally arranged by the experimenter. (See the comments on the experimenter as an authority below.) It may be difficult, if not impossible, to prove that exposure to, for example, meaningless inkblots and communication situations of the above kind is not in some subtle way harmful. However, the potential strain of such exposures in the context of clinical research has to be realistically compared to the kind of situations and conflicts that people encounter in their everyday lives. Second, the experimental manipulation is very helpful in defining (or, more adequately, in re-defining) the total social interaction situation. The revelation of the experimental manipulation (at the termination of the experimental session) furnishes the participants with an understanding of what it was that caused the difficulties of communication they encountered. In various ways this is reflected in the subjects' spontaneous comments and behavior in this phase; relaxed laughter, active support to each other: 'Heh, it's no wonder we did not get across since the bridge was gone', etc. This constitutes a real advantage of this particular method as compared with most comparable methods. For example, in the widely used Family Rorschach setting, family members are invited to disagree and argue over issues (meaningless inkblots) which in principle cannot be settled. Finally, the revelation of the manipulation not only supplies the participants with a certain understanding of what it was that caused their communication difficulties, it also offers those who during the interaction process might have become annoyed with each other an excellent opportunity to square things up: 'It was neither your fault nor mine'. Again this represents a clear advantage when compared to, for example, married couples in a situation where they have become annoyed with each other over the interpretation of a series of meaningless inkblots. The experimenter is trained actively to exploit the possibilites that the manipulation offers in the de-briefing period (cf. the training procedure for the experimenter to be).

Let us now turn to the other pole of the fundamental ethical dilemma intrinsic to clinical research, i.e., the fact that the participating subjects and families themselves are not likely to benefit from it. If the conditions could be arranged so that the participating patients and/or their families themselves could benefit, this would naturally highly reduce the force of this fundamental ethical dilemma. Consequently, this is a possibility that should be explicitly considered as an integral aspect in the planning of clinical research, the more so as the participation of people with minimal resources is required. With regard to the use of this particular method, this can be realized in the following two ways, either separately or in combination. First, the post-experimental interaction, with the communication difficulties the subjects have just been through still present, can very easily be transformed into a family therapeutic session. The closeness in time between the interaction conflicts constituting the material and the therapeutic session may optimalize the outcome. Often the participating family members themselves invite or promote such a transformation. In cooperation with the actual patients' therapist this can easily be organized to the benefit of the patients and their families. The categories 'subject' versus 'client' have to be explicitly clarified in the cooperation between the experimenter and the therapist (see below). Second, systematic feedback to the therapist from the experimenter on the basis of thorough analyses of the communication in this situation, which has proved to highlight various aspects of a family's pattern of communication, may prove useful in the therapeutic process. The degree to which these possibilities have been exploited in our studies has varied from study to study. In a few studies it has been optimalized, in that the experimenter has been identical with the clinical psychologist responsible for the patient's therapy. This eliminates the problem with regard to the categories 'subject' versus 'client' (see above). In conclusion, potential users of this method should be aware of these possibilities of 'giving something back' to the participating families.

We cannot leave these ethical considerations without explicitly commenting upon the relationship between the experimenter and the participating subjects in clinical research in general and in this experimental situation in particular. This the more so, as the results obtained have to be interpreted with specific reference to the frame constituted by this relationship. Essential to this relationship is the subjects' definition of the experimenter as an authority. Consequently, the subjects' obedience to authority is definitely a factor to be taken into account when interpreting results and findings from clinical research. For example, the fact that grown-up people interact for quite some time exchanging information concerning totally meaningless inkblots (in the Family Rorschach setting and in the Rorschach test) is not at all understandable without specific reference to the subjects' obedience to the experimenter's authority. The present cooperation situation as such, however, is not meaningless. On the contrary, it appears immediately to make sense to the subjects, in that it resembles interaction situations they know very well from their everyday lives. However, the fact that the subjects continue for 40 minutes under circumstances of rather severe communication difficulties is only understandable with specific reference to the experimenter's authority vis-à-vis the subjects. That the behavior of the subjects is really dependent on subtle experimenter-subjects' interactions is also clearly testified to in Dahles (1977) study (cf. Part III). Totally to eliminate in clinical research this element of obedience to authority may be impossible. The total life situation of patients and their families makes it reasonable that any person or activity that may be associated with the health system is ascribed authority and status. Therefore, this element has explicitly to be considered in designing studies, in choosing methods, in analyzing the resultant data, etc.

The fact that the experimenter deceives the subjects in the context of a clinical research project may deserve a few comments in this context. With specific reference to the relationship between the experimenter and the subjects, it is essential that the experimenter never explicitly asserts that the maps are identical. The experimenter is thus not lying to the subjects. On the other hand, everything is being done (see the above description of the experimental design) to make the participants <u>assume</u> that the maps are identical. One might fear that this deception could be damaging to the relationship between the psychologist (the experimenter) and the subjects (the patients and their families) in general. Massive experiences from a whole series of studies involving varying diagnostic categories (see Part II and Part III), however, have forced us to conclude that this is not the case. The subjects readily realize and accept the rationale behind the experimental manipulation (i.e., to establish systematically varying conditions of communication). The experimental manipulation proves again (see above) helpful in discussing and explaining the various aspects of the study to the participants. A comparison with the most frequently exploited instrument in clinical research in general on this issue is telling. It is not unlikely that most subjects would find it easier to accept and understand on their own premises the exposure to these two different communication situations (the simple versus the one inducing the communication conflict), than to understand that they have to exchange information and hold opinions concerning entirely meaningless inkblots.

In conclusion, ethical dilemmas are intrinsic to clinical research involving suffering patients and their families. In the planning and designing of clinical studies, ethical considerations should therefore constitute an integral part on a par with the usual theoretical and metodological considerations. The choice and use of methods should be grounded in ethical considerations of the above nature. With the above ethical dilemmas and considerations in mind, we will now return to the practical problems in connection with our very first exploratory study in which this particular method was exploited in a clinical context.

In order to simplify comparisons between the various couples, the distribution of the two different maps among the spouses had to be standardized. To counteract culturally determined male dominance, we gave the map with the routes drawn in to the wives so that the husbands had to follow the directives and explanations of their wives.

A very important issue in this exploratory study was to establish two comparable groups, one consisting of parents <u>with</u> schizophrenic offspring (Group S) and one matched control group <u>without</u> (Group N). During this exploratory research we chose to limit ourselves to small but strictly controlled and matched groups.

We concentrated on establishing Group S first. We decided to accept the definition of schizophrenia generally held in Norwegian psychiatry, i.e., according to Kraepelin. Our point of departure was that <u>the reference person</u> in Group S had been diagnosed as being a schizophrenic at a psychiatric institution. The use of the diagnostic category entailed that all reference persons would be over 15 years of age. We put the upper age limit at 30, and within this range we sought the youngest possible reference persons to ensure that they had not been separated from their families for too long.

Establishing Group S was a long and laborious process (Sølvberg, 1973, Sølvberg & Blakar, 1975). Once Group S was established, much effort was put into assembling a matching Group N. Variables such as age, number of years of marriage, education, employment, social group, annual income, domicile, living conditions, number of children and their sex and age, were all matched satisfyingly (for details of the matching see Sølvberg, 1973, p. 62-67). Group N represented a 'normal group' in the sense that it included ordinary couples without problems that had brought them or their children into contact with treatment or penal institutions. Nothing else is implied by 'normality' in this study.

The fact that in the earlier phases of our research in this field, traditional, individual diagnostic categories ('schizophrenia', 'borderline', 'anorexia nervosa', etc.) have been used as a point of departure in selecting families, should not be interpreted in the sense that we conceive of this strategy as the ideal one. However, at the time when this research was initiated (1972), there did not (at least not to our knowledge) exist any valid family-based nosology. Therefore, to get started at all we had to use index persons in terms of individual nosology. For a general discussion of all the problems encountered in the development of a family-based nosology as opposed to categorizing families in terms of individual nosology, see Blakar & Nafstad (1980a). At this point the 'cumulative' effects of our integral studies (see Introduction, p. 9) are clearly reflected, in that we are presently involved in efforts to develop family-based categorization systems on the basis of the thorough empirical investigations of different patterns of familial communication carried out in the studies presented in this volume (see Part III, and Blakar & Nafstad, 1980a).

Since the primary purpose of this exploratory study was methodological, our hypotheses bearing upon the differences between Group S and Group N couples were not very refined. The following rather general hypotheses may in fact be considered tentative conclusions based upon reviews of the literature:

1. Couples from Group S will communicate less efficiently than those from Group N if the cooperation situation is vague and complicated, requiring critical evaluation and change in patterns of communication. In other words, the Group S will have more problems and will require more time in solving the experimental route where the communication conflict is induced.

2. Couples from Group S will manage just as well as couples from Group N if the cooperation situation is plain and simple, in the sense that no readjustment is required from their usual pattern of communication or cooperation. In other words, no difference in time spent on the simple task (the practice route) is expected.

3. Qualitative differences in the communication between Group S and Group N couples

will be revealed, and such differences are expected regardless of whether the communication situation is simple or complex. In addition, it is expected that such qualitative differences observed in communication in the simple and straightforward situation will shed some light on why Group S communication fails when the communication situation is more demanding.

All couples became involved in the task. The experimenter had no particular problems getting them to grasp the instructions and start on the practice route, although some of the couples put some pressure on the experimenter to structure the situation more explicitly.

Let us start by examining some quantitative measures related to efficiency in solving the communication task. None of the couples seemed to experience serious problems with the practice route. The actual time spent, however, ranging from 2 min 2 sec to 9 min 56 sec, indicates that the task and communication situation were not equally easy for all of them. If we compare the two experimental groups, we find that Group S used 4 min 50 sec on an average (ranging from 2 min 5 sec to 9 min 56 sec) while Group N used 4 min 57 sec on an average (ranging from 2 min 2 sec to 8 min 52 sec). Actually, this is very close to the student dyads, with a mean of 4 min 27 sec on the simple situation (Blakar, 1973a). Until then, all the student dyads we had run had solved the induced communication conflict according to criteria one or two above, and within the 40 minutes limit. However, only six of the ten parent couples managed to solve the communication conflict according to criteria one or two. Four of the ten couples went on for more than 40 minutes, and were consequently stopped and shown the discrepancy between the maps. In dealing with the conflict situation, therefore, the ten couples formed two sub-groups: six solvers and four non-solvers, and the crucial question is how the Group S and the Group N couples were distributed over these sub-groups. While all five Group N couples solved the induced communication conflict, only one of the Group S couples managed to do so. All the four non-solvers were thus Group S couples. [5]

As regards the simple situation, where no conflict was induced and hence no critical evaluation and readjustment of communication strategy was required, Group S parents performed as well as Group N parents, and actually similarly to the younger and more highly educated students dyads. However, when a discrepancy with respect to premises was induced, most Group S parents failed.

The primary aim of the Sølvberg & Blakar study was methodological, and the data presented already suggest that our method is worth the investment of more effort in further elaboration and refinement. Further qualitative analysis, however, was performed at this stage of the research. Three types of analysis were conducted in order to further identify differences and similarities in patterns of communication between the two groups of couples:

(1) The tapes were blind-scored by a communication-oriented student trained in clinical psychology.

(2) A detailed analysis (on utterance level) of the organization of the communication process was carried out.

(3) The emotional climate was assessed on a set of five-point scales.

For two reasons we present these analyses here. First, the findings reached by means of these preliminary and not very sophisticated analyses were in fact revealing with respect to qualitative differences in patterns of communication. Secondly, this detailed presentation is intended to represent very convincing support for our argument (p. 46) that this field of research is in severe need of theoretically founded methods for analyzing patterns of communication. On the basis of this exploratory study, we started, within the framework of social-developmental psychology (see p. 155-161 and p. 28-30), to develop systematic procedures for describing the communication process in terms of degree of egocentrism/decentration, patterns of attributions of communication difficulties, proposed and endorsed contracts, etc.

(1) Clinical Analysis of Communication: In order to get (a) some sort of a clinical 'validation' of the differences revealed by the mere time measures, and (b) a more global and qualitative description of the communication patterns, a student trained in clinical psychology was given the ten recordings and the following instruction:

These tapes record what took place when ten parent couples were presented with a standardized cooperation task. Five couples are parents of a person diagnosed as schizophrenic. The other five couples have offspring with no obvious form of psychopathology. You may listen to each of the ten tapes as many times as you want, and then give a short description of each couple and what takes place between them. Then tell which of the recordings you believe to be of the schizophrenic's parents and which are not.

On the basis of her clinical evaluation, she correctly identified four couples who she felt certain belonged to Group S. In the communication of the other six she found no particular characteristics which, according to her clinical knowledge, would lead her to classify them as belonging to Group S. When forced to guess at the last Group S couple, she was incorrect, but she stressed that she was in severe doubt. For what this finding may be worth, it suggests that potential pathological characteristcs of communication are highlighted in this situation to such an extent that they can be identified fairly easily by a clinical psychologist. In comparison, the extensive notes on how each couple appeared to the experimenter outside the experimental setting revealed no systematic differences between Group S and Group N couples. They all appeared to him (also trained in clinical psychology) to be normal, well-adjusted, middle-age couples (cf. Sølvberg, 1973).

A closer examination of the scorer's descriptions of the communication pattern shows that the Group S couples (as compared to the Group N couples) were characterized by (a) more rigidity (in explanation strategy, in role distribution, etc.); (b) less ability and/or willingness to listen to, and take into account, what the other said; (c) a more unprecise and diffuse language (unprecise definitions, concepts, etc.); and (d) more 'pleasing' and/or pseudo-agreement in situations in which the erroneous maps had made them lose each other.

(2) Utterance Analysis of Communication: The categorization system that was developed and applied in order to analyze the organization (on utterance level) of the communication represented a preliminary attempt to bridge the gap between the communication-oriented studies of schizophrenia and general theory of language and communication. Our categorization system as applied in this study was immature and very laborious, and the more promising aspects of it have been further developed and refined in follow-up studies (see below). Hence we will not present it in detail here, but will outline it only to the extent that may be indicated by some of the most interesting of the preliminary findings.

Every single utterance - as well as every sequence of two and two utterances - was classified with respect to some formal and some content aspects. For practical as well as theoretical reasons, the practice route was chosen. For practical considerations, the couples spent much less time on the practice route, and such an analysis is extremely time-consuming. Theoretically, if any qualitative differences were found on the practice route, where the two types of couples had been equally efficient and where they had not been influenced by our experimental manipulation, these qualitative differences could, it was hoped, shed some light on why the Group S couples failed when the communication conflict was induced.

Our detailed analysis of the utterances on the practice route revealed various differences between the two groups, of which only the three most significant will be presented briefly and commented upon:
(a) Every utterance was classified as being either active (in the sense that it was initiated by the person himself) or reactive (in the sense that it represented a reaction to something the other had said or done). When we examined the distribution of active utterances within each couple, we noted that the Group S wives tended to have a larger proportion than the Group N wives. Four of the five Group S wives had more active utterances than their respective husbands, whereas three of the five Group N husbands had more than their respective wives. This tendency toward 'marital skew' in the schizophrenic family (cf. Lidz, 1963), however, becomes much clearer if all 'questions' and 'comments' are excluded from the active utterances, so that one is left with 'directives' only ('go there and there', 'do so and so', etc.). In all five Group S couples, the wife gave many more

such active directives (on the average, almost twice as many as the husbands), where-as in the Group N couples the distribution between the spouses was much more equal (in three couples the husband gave more, and in two the wife gave more such active directives).

(b) The active utterances, furthermore, were classified into 'directives', 'questions', and 'comments'. Comments again were classified as being either task-relevant (comments that could be of help in solving the task) and task-irrelevant (comments that were judged to be entirely irrelevant from the point of view of solving the communication task). First, at group level the Group N couples had many more comments (almost twice as many) as the Group S couples, but there was some overlap. However, if the distribution of task-relevant and task-irrelevant comments within each couple is inspected, it is found that a much larger proportion of the comments in the Group S couples were task-irrelevant (a mean of 57 per cent of the comments were irrelevant) as compared to the Group N couples (in mean 19 per cent of the comments were irrelevant). And, with respect to the total number of relevant comments, there were on the average three times as many in the Group N as in the Group S couples.

This finding is of particular theoretical interest in that relevant comments may reflect a capacity and willingness on behalf of the spouses to decenter (e.g., one describes to the other how the map looks where he or she is) and thereby reestablish a shared here-and-now within which meaningful communication can take place (cf. the theoretical framework briefly outlined above).

(c) Furthermore, for every active utterance elicited by either member of the couple, the reaction of the other was classified as being adequate (confirmation, disconfirmation, relevant answer of question, etc.) or inadequate (in particular, ignoring and no response). In Group S a larger proportion (an average of 36 per cent) of the active utterances were ignored by the other as compared to Group N (an average of 21 per cent). In addition there was almost no overlap between the two groups, with the exception of one Group S couple, whose extremely few active utterances were ignored. This couple was obviously characterized by pseudo-mutuality, as described by Wynne and collaborators (1958).

(3) The Emotional Climate: The emotional climate was assessed on five-point scales (from 'very much' to 'very little') of the following type: 'To what extent is the interaction characterized by warmth (openness, confidence, helplessness, intimacy, mutual respect, etc.)?' All ten couples were scored by two students of psychology. This scoring procedure did not reveal any differences between the two groups. Analysis of variance (2 groups x 2 raters) did not show more significant differences than would be expected by chance (cf. Bakan, 1967). The reasons for this may be many - apart from the obvious one that there may really be no such differences. (An obvious counter-argument

against this latter hypothesis was the fact that in the above analysis a student of clinical psychology easily picked out four of the five Group S couples.) Of the other possible reasons: Our two student raters were not well enough trained to detect more subtle differences, and on a lot of variables the interscorer reliability was too low. (However, separate analyses for each of the two raters did not give any more significant group differences.) Furthermore, on many of the variables all 10 couples scored either very high or very low, so that no differences could possibly be demonstrated. With regard to the standardized communication conflict situation as such, it is promising that all ten couples scored high on 'To what extent is their interaction characterized by involvement?' Regarding this particular analysis, the evidence thus seems to be inconclusive.

Emergence of new questions

Our results were in line with earlier findings and conclusions (cf. e.g., Haley's 1972 summary), while many intriguing new questions also emerged from the above analyses. Instead of presenting the preliminary findings in greater detail, some of the questions and some of the observations upon which these questions were based, will be outlined:

1. Do Group S couples have a more egocentric and less decentrated communication? In other words, are Group S spouses less able and/or willing to take the perspective and speak on the premisses of the other? For instance, utterances such as '... and then you go up there', '... and from here you take a right' when 'here' and 'there' respectively could obviously not be known to the other - were frequently observed in the Group S couples.

2. Are Group S couples less able and/or willing to endorse (and adhere to) contracts that regulate and monitor the various aspects of their communication (e.g., role distribution, perspective, strategy of explanation)? Few contractual proposals were found (regarding, for example, categorization, explanation strategy). Furthermore, many cases were observed in which implicitly or explicitly endorsed contracts were broken or ignored.

3. Do Group S couples show less ability and/or willingness to attribute (adequately or inadequately) their communication difficulties to any potential causes? The Group S couples could apparently return to the starting point again and again without any (overt, explicit) attempt to attribute their communication difficulties to anything.

These were some of the most significant questions that emerged from our first exploratory study. All these questions are formulated within a conceptual framework dissimilar to that usually employed in the study of schizophrenia. The formulations are inspired by the theoretical work of people such as Heider, Mead, Piaget, Rommetveit,

etc. (see above). More systematic research has to be carried out in order to settle
these questions (see Parts II and III). But the mere posing of these questions may represent a contribution in the direction of describing (and hence in part explaining)
schizophrenia within the framework of general social-developmental theory.

At this stage a tenable conclusion seems to be that a standardized communication
conflict situation that is really sensitive with respect to the participants' abilities/
inabilities to unravel underlying conflicts has been established. From the perspective
of social psychology in general and communication theory in particular, this will come
as no surprise. In the present method so fundamental preconditions for (successful)
communication are systematically manipulated that if there is any reality in the idea
that families containing schizophrenic members demonstrate deviant communication
patterns, this should indeed be revealed under these conditions of communication.
Moreover, the conceptual framework explicated in the present experimental design
allows for specifications of situational conditions under which the differences will be
salient (cf. the hypotheses).

On the background of the above study, it seems reasonable to conclude that the severe lack of adequate methods in this field could be surmounted if the general theories
of the social sciences (for example communication theory) were drawn upon (cf. p.16)

The fact that it has proved possible to develop a theoretically grounded method that
proves sensitive with regard to differences in patterns of communication is important.
However, with respect to understanding the development and maintenance of schizophrenia in terms of family communication patterns, this constitutes only a first, albeit
critical, step. One next step is the development of methods that enable systematic analyses to be made of qualitative characteristics pertaining to the communication of families
and parental couples. But at this point the field faces the serious problems described
by Riskin & Faunce (1972), in that there are no concepts connecting the observations
made to the superordinate concepts used in theorizing. And, in our contention, in
particular when it comes to qualitative analyses of communication in families with
and without psychopathological members, most researchers seem to have given up
or forgotten all about general communication theory. Overwhelmed by the richness
and variation of the material, they have resorted to mere clinical-casuistic descriptions, freely employing everyday language and 'private' terms. (For a critical review of this conceptual and terminological chaos, see Riskin & Faunce, 1972, Blakar
1976a, in press b.)

But again, if one goes, for example, to social-developmental psychology, a whole
set of relevant and theoretically grounded concepts offer themselves. To illustrate,
a few examples will be given. A basic precondition for successful communication is

the participants' ability to take the perspective of the other (Mead, 1934), and egocentrism (lack of decentration) (Piaget, 1926) may strongly hinder communication. Related to this is Rommetveit's (1968) notion that 'encoding involves anticipatory decoding'.
Another essential prerequisite for successful communication is that the participants
have to endorse contracts (contracts concerning categorization, topic, perspective etc.)
by which the act of communication is being monitored (Rommetveit, 1972a, 1974, Blakar, 1972a). And when communication runs into more or less serious trouble, it is
essential, in order to re-establish successful communication, that the difficulties are
adequately attributed (Heider, 1958) by the participants. Even the slightest knowledge
about communication in relation to psychopathology and deviant behavior should enable
one to see that these concepts from social-developmental psychology may be of direct
relevance in the analyses of communication patterns in the families. In the studies presented in Parts II and III, various of the above-mentioned concepts will be developed
further and exploited in analyses of patterns of communication in various categories
of families.

Theoretical-methodological constraints of the Sølvberg & Blakar study

Retrospectively, this first exploratory study may be conceived of as a lucky shot.
However, this should not be understood to mean that the project and the findings represented mere chance. The method was derived so directly from general psychological
theory of language and communication, and the experimental manipulation interferes
with such fundamental preconditions for communication (Blakar, 1975b) that if it is
the case that the family/immediate environment of the schizophrenic demonstrates abnormal patterns of communication, then it would certainly become apparent in this
particular situation. As an incentive for future research, however, it was our good
fortune that the method proved to be even more sensitive in revealing such abnormali-
ties in communication patterns than we could have dared to hope beforehand.

This first exploratory study should hence be conceived of more as a point of departure for further research than as providing answers to or final clarification of the
issues focused above. We will therefore identify the theoretical-methodological shortcomings, and then describe control and follow-up studies which would appear to be
logically and methodologically necessary and/or desirable in order to render conclusions possible.

A satisfactory solution to the problem complex of schizophrenia would necessarily
involve integration of knowledge obtained within different disciplines from studying the
subject matter from differing perspectives (psychology, genetics, pharmacology, anthro-
pology, etc.) (cf. Blakar & Nafstad, 1980a). In the following analysis, however, we will

restrict ourselves to desirable and/or necessary continuations of the present project conceptualized within the present framework of communication theory. An integration with other disciplines and perspectives belongs to the future.

Furthermore, our theoretical and methodological considerations were at this stage also determined by the fact that we did not want to make any changes regarding the communication conflict situation itself. Given the promising results achieved in the first exploratory study, this seemed to represent a reasonable choice (cf. Sølvberg & Blakar, 1975, Blakar, 1974a).

In analyzing theoretical-methodological shortcomings in connection with the exploratory Sølvberg & Blakar (1975) study, we identified six different issues or aspects on which further work had to be conducted in order to render conclusions possible (cf. Blakar, 1975a, 1978f). The classification is primarily of a formal-logical character. In practice, work and research along any one of these six lines will be mutually supportive, and follow-up studies should therefore be planned and designed to address two or more of these theoretical-methodological shortcomings.

It should be emphasized that whereas some of the controls (for example No. 2) are really needed in order to render any conclusions possible, other of the follow-up studies can be conceived of more as an attempt to outline a general research program. Moreover, it should be mentioned that the order of presentation does not reflect a hierarchy of importance.

(1) Replications and expansions of the samples: First and foremost, the two samples have to be enlarged. Even though the matching between Groups S and N with regard to relevant background variables was almost perfect, groups of 5 and 5 couples seemed too small. But merely to increase the sample size without improving the conceptual framework (pt. 6 below), and developing more adequate methods of analysis (pt. 5 below), would be nonsensical.

(2) Different demand characteristics: A vital requirement, in fact a sine qua non for studies designed to obtain conclusive evidence with respect to differences and similarities in the behavior of different categories of subjects (families), is that their behavior is observed under identical or comparable conditions. In particular when it comes to social behavior (for example communication), it is very difficult indeed to establish identical or comparable conditions (social situations) for different categories of social actors. Social behavior is a product of subtle person(s)-situation interactions (Bowers, 1973, Bem & Allen, 1974, Stokstad, Lagerløv & Blakar, 1979, Rommetveit, 1979a). And the meaning of a situation may vary from person to person, and from time to time for the same person. And the subjects do not act upon the situation as defined by the experimenter. They act upon the situation as defined and experienced by themselves. Hence the experimenter has to take great care to control how the various

categories of subjects (families) experience and define the actual situation. Only in terms of their (the subjects') definition of the situation, is it possible to reach an adequate understanding of their (social) behavior (Blakar, 1978a, in press a).

At first glance, the treatment of the participating couples in the Sølvberg & Blakar study may seem to be identical. However, a closer examination of the two different categories of couples reveals that highly different expectations may be held toward the study as such. The Group S couples, recruited via a psychiatric institution, knew that they participated because they were the parents of a schizophrenic person. The Group N couples, on the other hand, participated in a general study of the social sciences on cooperation, and no reason was given for selecting exactly them as subjects. There is every reason to assume that the different expectations entail different definitions of the standardized communication situation. Even though Sølvberg & Blakar took great care to use a standardized procedure and have all the couples interact in the same two communication situations, there is every reason to ask whether their results were indeed tautological, in that they have merely revealed that people behave and communicate differently in different situations.

The social situation encountered by the Group S couples may be described as follows. As they are participating because they are the parents of a schizophrenic offspring, they may feel accused or guilty (cf. Haley, 1972). However, they are neither told what the accusations are, nor what they are assumed to do (how to behave) to be found 'not guilty'. This is a social situation at great variance from the one that the 'innocent' control couples encountered.[6] In conclusion, this analysis of the meaning for different categories of families of the 'standardized' situation reveals that the Sølvberg & Blakar study - on a par with the great majority of studies in the field, is left inconclusive.[7]

Since the subjects will always define the situation(s) on the basis of their different expectations, and the resultant social situation will be a product of person(s)-situation interactions, this methodological source of error is almost impossible to eliminate totally. Four different strategies seem tenable in order to handle this problem of different situational demand characteristics:

First, the subjects (families) can be studied and observed without their being aware of it. By this procedure they are not participating as subjects in a study, and by definition, they will hold no particular expectations toward the 'experimental' situation. The obvious problem with this strategy is to have the various families communicate in the 'same' situation or under comparable conditions. Second, the expectations of the subjects can be systematically manipulated. An obvious objection to this strategy (this objection is of relevance to the first strategy too) in connection with families containing psychopathological members is the ethical one. Moreover, by this strategy the experimenter himself may be deceived, in that the false or misleading expectations induced may in subtle ways interact with the (always) underlying expectation that in reality we are participating because our family contains a schizophrenic member. Third, a systematic network of groups of different categories of control families other than and in addition to Group N families can be established. In our contention, theoretically and methodologically (as well as ethically, since one can 'play with open cards') this is the most sound strategy. We will therefore return to this strategy in some detail to demonstrate how it was possible to corroborate the Sølvberg & Blakar findings. Fourth, for practical as well as ethical reasons it will often be the case in clinical psychology, that none of the above strategies is applicable. In such situations, findings and observations should be interpreted with great care, while explicitly trying to take into account the varying situational demand characteristics. The fifth strategy, although by far the one most frequently adhered to, cannot be reommended at all. This strategy is to ignore the very issue of varying demand characteristics, and compare the behavior of Group N and Group S families as if they have been exposed to the same social situation. Considering that, within social psychology, Orne gave a coherent analysis of varying situational demand characteristics as long ago as 1962, we have here found another piece of strong support for Riskin & Faunce's (1972) claim with respect to the interdisciplinary isolation of the field.

These notorious ignorances of the multiplicity and the pluralism (cf. Rommetveit, 1979b, 1979c) of social realities may in part be explained by the almost exclusive preoccupation with one diagnostic category (schizophrenia) only. In the same way as 'hysteria' once was the star syndrome of psycho-analysis, the substantial part of the family- and communication-oriented studies of psychopathology has been carried out in relation to schizophrenia. The three main research groups in the field - organized around Bateson, Lidz and Wynne respectively - seemed to make the condition of schizophrenia the main focus of interest (cf. Mishler & Waxler, 1965). However, there is nothing in the communication approach or perspective itself which restricts it to schizophrenia exclusively. On the contrary, the earlier programmatic positions formulated underlined the general scope of the communication perspective.

In retrospect, the communication theorists' preoccupation with merely one diagnostic category (schizophrenia) may represent part of the explanation of the present state of affairs. First of all, this preoccupation with one particular type of psychopathology has resulted in a too restricted empirical basis for the theories of communication and psychopathology. (Not to mention that all the other types of psychopathology have not been subjected to or blessed with the potential benefits of being redefined in terms of communication.) Grolnick's (1972) paper, in which he examines 'A family perspective of psychosomatic factors in illness', can be seen as illustrating this point. Second, the description and understanding of the condition of schizophrenia itself has been hindered by a lack of relevant control groups (Haley, 1972, Riskin & Faunce, 1972, Blakar, 1975a). Because as Bannister (1968, p. 182-183) argues:

Schizophrenics are a subgroup of the class of 'psychiatrically ill', and any research designed to cast light on the nature of schizophrenia as a specific category must include non-schizophrenic control groups as well as normals. Otherwise any findings relate to the superordinate distinction between people under psychiatric care and people outside it and cannot carry implications for the subordinate class of schizophrenics.

More urgent than enlarging the samples (pt. 1), therefore, is the need to 'test' the parents of children with diagnoses other than schizophrenia in this particular communication conflict situation. In selecting alternative diagnostic categories as additional control groups, it will be decisive how sweeping this particular source of methodological error is assumed to be: (a) If it is assumed that our findings do not pertain exclusively to the familial communication of the schizophrenic, but are characteristic of the communication pattern in the family of all (seriously) ill patients, then it would follow that one should start by studying the communication of parents to patients with an (serious) illness where there is little or no theoretical reason to assume that there should be any connection between the familial communication patterns and the pathological development of the offspring. Illnesses such as congenital heart disease and cancer should then constitute appropriate controls. (b) If on the other hand it is assumed that the findings do not pertain to the familial communication of all who are seriously ill, but only of those with some kind of psychopathology, then obviously other forms of psychopathology than schizophrenia would be relevant as control groups.

(3) Parent-child interaction: Even though the present design does not address the issue of causality directly (cf. Blakar, 1974a, Blakar & Nafstad, 1980a), it would be very interesting to investigate the communication between the parents and the child (schizophrenic versus control) in this particular communication conflict situation. In order to obtain a more exhaustive understanding of the connection between the development and maintenance of schizophrenia and the familial communication, it will be essential to see whether (and how) the peculiarities of the parental communication pattern which we have exposed affect their interaction with the child. As in the study of parental communication, this design involving the parent-child constellation will necessary require control groups in addition to Group N families (cf. pt. 2 above).

(4) General variables in communication: In our critical analysis of this field of research (see above, and Blakar, 1974a, in press a) we pointed out that many of the theoretical and methodological weaknesses could be explained by the lack of contact with general theory. The fact that the present method was explicitly derived from general communication theory (Blakar, 1972a, 1973a) constituted an obvious improvement, but nevertheless there is an obligation to examine our findings concerning schizophrenia (deviant behavior and psychopatology) further in terms of general theory, and to relate our findings to general social, personality and developmental variables.

(a) Anthropological and sociological studies have testified to how people from different cultural and social (class) backgounds employ differing patterns of communication and language use (cf. Hall, 1959, Labov et al., 1968, Bernstein, 1971). Moreover, it is known that the occurrence and distribution of various forms of psychopathology vary in different cultures and classes. In other words, communication characteristics that prove to be specific to and 'normal' in certain subcultures (e.g., a social class) could easily be interpreted as deviant characteristics in the familial communication of the schizophrenic. Hence it is desirable to obtain knowledge about how general social variables such as socio-economic status, urban as opposed to rural background, etc., are reflected in the pattern of communication in this communication conflict situation.

(b) In spite of the fact that the concept of personality for many reasons is both problematic and controversial (cf. Bem & Allen, 1974, Mischel, 1968, 1973), there is nevertheless no doubt that the kind of variables that have traditionally been conceived of as 'personality traits' will be reflected in different ways in patterns of communication. General variables such as anxiety, aggression, degree of conficence (in oneself and others), rigidity as opposed to flexibility, etc. will obviously affect the communication process. To assess the implications of the (deviant) communication patterns found in the family of the schizophrenic, it will thus be of vital importance to know how the communication patterns of rigid (or other relevant variables) persons deviate from the communication patterns of more flexible persons within the so-called normal range. In addition to indicating whether the communication pattern of rigid (or flexible) persons have common characteristics with the pattern found in the familial environment of the schizophrenic, this type of study would, it is hoped, entail a conceptual clarification in the field with respect to variable labels (e.g., aggression) which have been used both as individual and as social variables (cf. Blakar, 1974c, 1977).

(c) Many of the concepts we have employed in describing the familial communication patterns of the schizophrenic obviously involve developmental aspects and are based on developmental theory. For example, the communication of the Group S couples was characterized as egocentric (lacking the capacity to decenter and take the other's perspective) (Sølvberg & Blakar, 1975). In the literature (Piaget, 1926, Glucksberg et al., 1966, Øvreeide, 1970, Nafstad & Gaarder, 1979, Strøno, 1978) it is demonstrated how capacity to decenter develops from the child's nearly total egocentrism to the adult's (periodical?) decentration. Analogous to (a) and (b) above, knowledge about the communication patterns in conflict situations demonstrated by children at various stages of development, i.e., with differing capacity regarding decentration, could illuminate the 'deviations' found in the communication pattern in the family of the schizophrenic.

(5) Methods of analysis: Our explanatory study revealed that we, like others in this

field of research, are practically without systematic methods for analyzing and describing the qualitative aspects of the communication exposed in the communication conflict situation. A blind scorer, basing his predictions on clinical judgment only, correctly identified four of the five Group S couples by listening to the tape recordings from the communication conflict situation (Sølvberg & Blakar, 1975). This indicated that our conceptual apparatus is not yet sufficiently explicit and detailed (see pt. 6 below). Although we do have some relevant concepts (such as egocentrism), we lack corresponding, adequate methods (with the exception of descriptive case reports) by means of which systematic scoring (of e.g. egocentrism/decentration in the communication process) could be conducted.

(6) Conceptual framework: The outcome of this exploratory study constituted a great challenge toward further development of our theoretical framework and conceptual apparatus, to enable us to capture and understand the various patterns of communication which were so vividly exposed in the present communication conflict situation. Actually, it was the need for further explication and clarification of communication theory which originally led us to the development of this communication conflict situation (Blakar, 1972a, 1973a). Problems in connection with theory construction in this field have thus been focused on within the project (Blakar, 1978a, in press c).

A few comments have to be made concerning the above list. First and foremost, in this connection, we have discussed the various potential studies either as follow-ups or just as controls in connection with the study of the complex problem of schizophrenia and familial communication. This is of course too narrow a perspective to take toward the various potential studies mentioned under points (2), (3), and (4), not to mention points (5) and (6). Work in connection with points (5) and (6) will be important to the study of communication in general, while studies pertaining to points (2), (3), and (4) represent substantial contributions in themselves, quite independently of the study of schizophrenia.

Secondly, in the above analysis we have concentrated on purely methodological issues. Nevertheless, there is every reason to emphasize that the examples we have chosen as illustrations of the various approaches may prove to be substantially interesting in their own right. This latter point is illustrated when the various examples given above are compared with the descriptions the blind scorer gave of the communication patterns demonstrated by the Group S couples:

> A closer examination of the scorer's description of the communication pattern shows that the Group S couples (as compared to the Group N couples) were characterized by (a) more rigidity (in explanation strategy, in role distribution, etc.) (b) less ability and/or willingness to listen to, and take into account what the other said, (c) a more unprecise and diffuse language (unprecise definitions, concepts, etc.), and (d) more 'pleasing' and/or pseudo-agreement in situations in which the erroneous maps had made them lose each other. (Sølvberg & Blakar, 1975, p. 527-8.)

PART II

A Presentation of Studies Conducted within the Research Program Outlined in Part I

SCHIZOPHRENIA AND COMMUNICATION EFFICIENCY: A MODIFIED REPLICATION TAKING ECOLOGICAL VARIATION INTO CONSIDERATION

R.M. Blakar, O.G. Paulsen and H.A. Sølvberg[8]

In their highly readable review of communication-oriented research on psychopathology, Riskin & Faunce (1972) identify a series of weaknesses characterizing the communication-oriented research on psychopatology. One particularly striking characteristic is the almost total lack of replications of one's own and others' studies.
Naturally, replicative studies are not as prestigious as original and innovative ones,
but without systematic, critical, controlled replications it is difficult to see how
systematic progress can ever be made. The need for replicative studies in this
field is convincingly illustrated by Ringuette & Kennedy's (1966) totally negative
findings in their highly controlled 'replication' of Weakland & Fry's (1962) sen-
sational and frequently cited study of double-binds in the letters of mothers of
schizophrenics (for a critical discussion see Schuham, 1967, Blakar, 1975a, 1975c).

Another weakness of communication-oriented research on psychopathology is the
lack of ecological variation and the relatively high social homogeneity found in the
samples of most studies. Variation of social and ecological background variables
should be included for the following reasons, at least. First and foremost, there is
no reason a priori to conceive of the pattern of communication of 'normal' control
families as being constant over social and ecological variation. On the contrary,
evidence indicating systematic style and language use according to social background
is being accumulated (Bernstein, 1971, Dahle, 1977). Secondly, epidemiological
studies have testified to very uneven distributions of various kinds of psychopathology (e.g. schizophrenia) in different types of societal environments (Sorokin &
Zimmermann, 1929, Ødegaard, 1945, Brooke, 1959, Folkard & Mandelbrote, 1962).
This knowledge seems often not to be taken seriously in communication-oriented
studies. And finally, if the two factors are combined, a potential interaction
effect may result, in that what proves to be pathological or deviant communication
may vary according to different social backgrounds.

Starting from a general theory on language and communication (as developed by
Rommetveit, 1968, 1972a, b, Blakar, 1970), Blakar (1973a) designed a method
directed toward identification of some prerequisites for communication. And
Sølvberg & Blakar (1975) demonstrated that the method was sensitive with respect

to differences in the communication of parental couples with and without schizophrenic offspring.

On the basis of the above discussion,the aim of the present study was: (1) To conduct a replication of Sølvberg & Blakar's study to see whether their findings were reproducible. (2) To take potential ecological variation in patterns of communication seriously, in that we would see whether Sølvberg & Blakar's findings made in a typical urban city population would be reproduced in a typical rural population. The latter approach apparently contradicts a strict replication, but when the original study and the replication are taken together, the ecological variation will put us in a favourable position to determine the generalizability of our findings.

Method

In the present study Blakar's standardized communication conflict situation as described on p. 27-28 was employed. Theoretical background as well as rationale for the clinical application of this method is given on p. 23-27 and on p. 32-33. In the present replication the experimental procedure used in the original study was followed in every detail. Even the experimenter was the same (cf. Sølvberg & Blakar, 1975).

Samples

As in the original study we chose to restrict ourselves to small, but heavily controlled and strictly matched, groups. In selecting parental couples with schizophrenic offspring (Group S), exactly the same set of criteria as in the Sølvberg & Blakar study was followed, the only difference being that whereas the subjects in the original study lived in a city (Oslo), the subjects in the present replication lived in a typical rural region of Norway. Having established Group S, much effort was put into establishing a matching control group (Group N). Variables such as age, number of years of marriage, education, employment, social group, annual income, domicile, living conditions, number of children and their sex and age, were all satisfyingly matched. (For further details on the matching, see Paulsen, 1977.) Group N therefore represented a 'normal group' in the sense that it comprised comparable, ordinary couples without problems that had brought them or their children into contact with treatment or penal institutions. Nothing else is implied by 'normality' in this case.

Hypotheses

The hypotheses to be tested in the present replication are the very same as were put forward in the original study. These hypotheses may actually be regarded as tentative conclusions based on extensive reviews of the literature on communication and schizophrenia. The hypotheses were:

1. Couples from Group S will communicate less efficiently than those from Group N if the cooperation situation is vague and complicated, requiring a critical evaluation and change in patterns of communication. In other words, the Group S couples will have more problems and use a longer time in solving the experimental route where the error is induced.

2. Couples from Group S will manage equally as well as couples from Group N if the cooperation situation is plain and simple in the sense that no adjustment is required from their usual pattern of communication or cooperation. In other words, no difference in time spent on the practice route will be expected.

3. Qualitative differences in the communication between Group S and Group N will be revealed, and such differences are expected whether the communication situation is simple or difficult. It is expected, moreover, that such qualitative differences observed in communication on the simple practice route will shed some light on why Group S communication fails when the situation is more demanding.

Since the ecological variable (rural-urban) was primarily included for methodical reasons, little effort was put into elaborating hypotheses regarding this variable. An earlier study (Fætten & Østvold, 1975) applying the present method in mapping the communication patterns of married couples, in which the wife was given/was not given the diagnosis 'hysteria', may give some clues. In this study the participating couples were recruited from a typical rural district. Fætten & Østvold (1975) revealed interesting qualitative differences in patterns of communication; the most striking differences were the 'hysteric' wives' active behavior in order to avoid the responsibility for the communication process given them as 'explainers', and their almost desperate search for help from the husband and the experimenter to structure the situation. The most relevant finding in connection with the present study, however, was that with respect to efficiency in the present 'city-like' communication task, the rural control couples managed less well than the urban control couples in Sølvberg & Blakar's study. It thus seems reasonable that the present communication situation and task favour people with an urban as compared with a rural background.

Results

In order to get a broader basis for a more general discussion the results from the original study will be presented and commented on, together with the results from the present replication.

All the couples became involved in the task. And the experimenter had no particular problems in getting them to grasp the instructions and start on the practice route, although some of the couples put some pressure on the experimenter to structure the situation more.

Let us start by examining the quantitative measures bearing upon efficiency in solving the communication tasks. In Table 1 the time used by each of the 20 couples on the simple and straightforward practice route, is presented. The variation in time used, ranging from 1 min 49 sec to one couple who did not manage even the simple practice route within 40 min, indicates that the situation and type of task as such was not equally simple for all. An analysis of variance (in this analysis the time of the non-solver is given as 40 min), however, shows that there are no significant differences in communication efficiency in the simple situation between the four experimental sub-groups; nor were any significant main effects (schizophrenic - 'normality'; urban - rural) or any interaction effect, found. If only mean time used is examined, no difference with respect to the 'schizophrenic-normality' variable is found. This holds whether we examine the urban and the rural samples separately or combined. With respect to the ecological variable there seems to be a tendency, though not a significant one, for the urban couples to use shorter time. This holds whether we examine the 'normal' and the schizophrenic samples separately or combined.

In conclusion, there is considerable variation in how efficiently the different couples manage this type of a communication situation as such, but this variation is not systematically correlated with the ecological variable rural-urban or to whether or not the couple are the parents of a schizophrenic child. This conclusion is warranted on the basis of the analysis of variance, but may be corroborated by pointing to the total overlap between the experimental sub-groups; the couple with the most efficient, as well as the one with the most inefficient, communication belong to the same sub-group, namely the rural Group S.

With the above findings and conclusions in mind, it becomes particularly interesting to see how the different groups of couples manage the communication conflict induced on the experimental route. In the original Sølvberg & Blakar study a distinction was made only between solvers (couples who resolved the induced conflict according to the above criteria) and non-solvers (couples who did not manage, and hence were shown the erroneous maps when more than 40 min had elapsed). Further

Table 1. *Time used in the simple and straightforward communication situation (the practice route)*

Ecological background	Diagnostic category		Mean
	Schizophrenic	Normal	
Rural	7 min 57 sec	7 min 48 sec	
	—*	19 min 17 sec	
	30 min 25 sec 11 min 27 sec	4 min 38 sec 8 min 36 sec	9 min 52 sec
	5 min 37 sec	7 min 16 sec	
	1 min 49 sec	4 min 02 sec	
Urban	6 min 47 sec	2 min 02 sec	
	9 min 56 sec	8 min 52 sec	
	2 min 09 sec 4 min 50 sec	4 min 05 sec 4 min 57 sec	4 min 54 sec
	3 min 11 sec	4 min 55 sec	
	2 min 05 sec	4 min 52 sec	
Mean	7 min 46 sec	6 min 47 sec	7 min 15 sec

* This rural S couple did not manage the practice route within 40 min. The mean times calculated in the table are based on the 19 couples who managed the route.

use of the present standardized experimental cooperation situation (Alve & Hultberg, 1974, Endresen, 1977, Hultberg et al., 1978, Wikran et al., 1978), however, has revealed two problems concerning this rather rough classification. First, it may happen that the experimenter accepts (according to criterion 2 above) the task as being solved, or is pressed or misled by the couple to reveal the erroneous maps to them in cases where careful examinations of the tape-recordings (particularly the subject's spontaneous comments afterwards) could throw serious doubts on whether the couple had gained insight into the error and thus really had solved the communication conflict, or not. Hence an uncertainty category resulted.

Of the 19 couples who were started on the experimental route (the one couple who

Table 2. *Distribution of solvers/non-solvers over the four experimental sub-groups*

Ecological background	Diagnostic category	Solvers	Uncertain	Non-solvers	Total
Urban	Normal	5	0	0	5
	Schizophrenic	1	0	4 (2 with, 2 without)	5
Rural	Normal	2	0	3 (2 with, 1 without)	5
	Schizophrenic	0	1	3* (1 with, 2 without)	4*
Total	Normal	7	0	3	10
	Schizophrenic	1	1	7	9
Total		8	1	10	19*

* The one couple who did not manage the simple practice route was not started on the more complicated experimental route.

did not manage the simple practice route was naturally not started on the more complicated one), eight couples managed to solve the induced communication conflict according to the predetermined criteria. On the basis of a vague and diffuse doubt concerning the maps and the experimental situation, one couple emotionally pressed the experimenter to admit the error before they themselves had identified and localized the induced error. Hence one case of uncertainty resulted. The remaining 10 (11 when the couple who did not even manage the simple practice route are included) were non-solvers.

Secondly, among the non-solvers it seems reasonable to distinguish between those couples who at least once explicitly question the credibility of the maps (but without their doubt leading to an acceptable solution) and those who throughout the communication process never explicitly questioned the credibility of the maps. Five of the non-solving couples never explicitly questioned the credibility of the maps, whereas the remaining five did so at least once, but without the expression of their doubt leading to any solution of the communication conflict.

The crucial question then is how the solvers and non-solvers were distributed over the experimental sub-groups (Table 2). That the distribution is far from random is clearly reflected by the variation in the proportion of solvers from all (five solvers in the urban Group N) to none (0 solvers in the rural Group S) in the different experimental sub-groups.

The difference in the distribution of solvers/non-solvers in Group S versus N (one versus seven solvers out of 10) is highly significant (Fisher's P=0.01). The difference between Groups S and N may be corroborated further by a closer examination of those couples who failed most completely to handle this cooperation situation, in that four of the five couples who never explicitly questioned the credibility of the maps, and the one single couple who failed even in the simple situation, belong to Group S.

Even with our relatively small samples, the distribution of solvers/non-solvers is close to significantly different (Fisher's P=0.08) in the urban versus the rural samples (six solvers versus two out of 10 respectively). The same method that is sensitive with respect to differences in communication efficiency in couples with and without a schizophrenic offspring is thus also sensitive with respect to influences of ecological background variables. Hence a much more detailed examination of the data is recommended.

Let us start with the urban sample (original study). Within the urban sub-sample the Group S couples showed significantly (Fisher's P=0.02) less efficient communication; whereas all the five Group N couples managed to solve the induced communication conflict, four of the five Group S couples failed.

If we turn to the rural sample (replication study), we again find that the Group S couples demonstrate an extremely inefficient communication; none of them managed to solve the induced communication conflict. The main difference between the urban and the rural samples is the relative failure of the rural Group N couples to solve the induced communication conflict (only two solvers) as compared with the urban group N couples (all five of whom were solvers).

The theoretically urgent question, then, is whether or not the rural Group S couples demonstrated a more inefficient communication than the matched rural Group N couples. With only two solvers in the total rural sample, the distribution of solvers/ non-solvers over Groups N and S could not possibly become significantly different. However, all the results point in the same direction as in the urban sample. First and foremost, the two rural solvers both belong to the Group N couples. Hence, the distribution of the very few solvers is as unequal as possible, and in the direction predicted. The difference may be corroborated further by pointing to how inefficient the rural Group S couples really were; one Group S couple did not manage even the simple and straightforward communication situation, and another two of the five rural Group S couples never explicitly questioned the credibility of the maps.

Finally, it completes the general picture that there was no difference in communication efficiency - or more adequately, communication inefficiency - between the urban and the rural Group S.

In Sølvberg & Blakar's study as well as in other studies in our project (cf. our general research program part I, and Blakar 1974a, 1978a) the quantitative measures bearing upon communication efficiency (time used and proportion of solvers/non-solvers) have represented only a frame or point of departure for the qualitative analyses. Degree of egocentrism/decentration (Mossige et al., 1976, Kristiansen et al., 1977), patterns of attribution of communication difficulties (Alve & Hultberg, 1974, Hultberg et al., 1978), power and control patterns (Glennsjø, 1977, Blakar & Pedersen, 1978), etc., have been used to describe the styles and patterns of communication (cf. hypothesis 3 above). (For an integrated presentation, see Blakar, 1978a). In connection with the present study, Paulsen (1977) has analyzed the communication of the 20 couples in terms of how they at each point of time during the communication process manage or fail to establish the information they must take as "free information" in order to exchange further information (i.e. 'bound information') (Rommetveit, 1974, Blakar & Rommetveit, 1975). Paulsen found that the Group S couples, irrespective of ecological background, more frequently tacitly took as given or granted something which was not as yet established as common (i.e. 'free') information (Paulsen, 1977). This analysis thus represents a corroboration of our earlier more global findings that families containing a schizophrenic member demonstrate more severe egocentrism in their communication than matched control families (Mossige et al., 1976, Kristiansen et al., 1977).

In order to discuss the more general methodological issues focused upon in the present paper, however, the more 'atheoretical' data on communication efficiency represent the most appropriate point of departure.

Discussion

Before any general conclusions are attempted, we have to remind ourselves of the complexity of the present experimental design, in that we have a 2x2x2 design. From (1) two different ecological backgrounds (rural versus urban) we have (2) couples with and without a schizophrenic offspring who (3) interact in two different cooperation situations (one simple and straightforward and one in which a communication conflict is induced). This design enabled us to specify the conditions under which couples having a schizophrenic child demonstrate inefficient or deviant communication. (For more general discussions of the specific situational influences upon the communication process, cf. Stokstad et al., 1976, Blakar & Pedersen, 1978.)

Two more general conclusions, one methodological and one substantial, seem warranted on the basis of the above results. Firstly, couples having a schizophrenic offspring demonstrate a less efficient communication than matched control couples in vague and complicated situations in which a critical evaluation of, and a change in pattern of, communication is required. However, in plain and simple situations in which no critical evaluation and readjustment of their usual pattern of communication is required, no difference in communication efficiency is found. Hence the generally held view within this field of research regarding the inefficiency of communication of families containing a schizophrenic member has to be qualified and specified with respect to type of interaction situation: if the situation is (relatively) plain and simple, no difference in communication efficiency is revealed. If the situation is (more) complicated and vague, thus requiring a critical re-evaluation and change or readjustment of the pattern of communication, then families containing a schizophrenic member demonstrate a much more inefficient and helpless communication than matched 'normal' control families (cf. Mossige et al., 1976).

Secondly, the differences in communication efficiency found between the urban and the rural 'normal' control couples pose severe methodological problems. If we cut across all kinds of subtle reasoning, it seems to be the case that we - as experimental researchers - have demonstrated a particular experimenter ethnocentrism, in that we have developed an urban-biased method. Conducting research at a university located in a city (Oslo), having university students and urban (middle class) couples as the subjects and main frame of reference in the study of communication, a communication situation or task based on and typical to urban student/middle class communication has been developed. (In connection with the present project it should be noted that we have been aware of and made this cultural/social/ ecological 'sensitivity' of methods and theoretical frameworks a topic of study - cf. Blakar, 1975a, 1978a, Dahle, 1977. However, we have an unpleasant feeling that in general these aspects are almost totally ignored, and that the 'norm' for 'adequate communication' is implicitly given by the communication of 'the normal middle class family living in cities'.) As a consequence the baseline, i.e. the communication efficiency of the 'normal' control couples, varies, depending on background variables. Our method, which proved highly sensitive with respect to communication efficiency in a particular ecological sub-society (urban couples), seemed to lose most of its potentiality in another ecological sub-society (rural couples).

The general methodological lesson to be learned is that every study of psychopathology, whether communication-oriented or not, has to take social/cultural/ ecological variation seriously, so that, for example, a rural family containing a schizophrenic member should be described as 'deviant' on the basis of what is a typical rural style and pattern. In order to pursue this course the theoretical framework(s) and method(s) to be adopted have to be established on the premises of the actual social/cultural/ecological sub-society.

Dahle (1977) has undertaken a more systematic mapping of communication efficiency and patterns of communication in 'normal' couples with differing social backgrounds. In her study she included couples with an urban versus a rural background, and the urban group was further divided into labour and middle class couples. Her findings show that the three groups of couples reveal highly different patterns of communication in the present standardized communication situation. This systematic variation in patterns of communication and communication efficiency in 'normal' couples, depending on ecological/cultural/social background, has to be taken seriously into account when 'deviances' in the communication of families containing schizophrenic members are being assessed.

The general methodological implications of the present study are the more penetrating when it is realized that Norway represents a very homogeneous society. In a global perspective the differences between our urban sample (Oslo, the biggest city in Norway is only a 'small' city with about half a million people) and our rural sample (not at all 'isolated' couples) are 'microscopic' - nevertheless, significantly different patterns of communication occurred. Thus the present study, together with the study of Dahle (1977), should represent an obligation on every researcher and practitioner in the field to make explicit the underlying model or idea about 'normal' or adequate communication from which the communication of families containing psychopathological members deviates.

PATTERNS OF ATTRIBUTION OF COMMUNICATION DIFFICULTIES IN COUPLES WITH A 'BORDERLINE', A 'SCHIZOPHRENIC', OR A 'NORMAL' OFFSPRING

Maureen Hultberg, Svein Alve & Rolv Mikkel Blakar.[9]

Introduction

In the same way as 'hysteria' once was the star syndrome of psychoanalysis, the substantial part of the communication-oriented studies of psychopathology has been carried out in relation to schizophrenia. The three main research groups in the field - organized around Bateson, Lidz and Wynne respectively - seemed to make the condition of schizophrenia the main focus of interest (cf. Mishler & Waxler, 1965). However, there is nothing in the communication approach or perspective itself which restricts it to schizophrenia exclusively. On the contrary, the earlier programmatic positions formulated underlined the general scope of the communication perspective. For example, in Ruesch & Bateson's 1951 book Communication: The Social Matrix of Psychiatry it is programmatically stated that: 'Psychopathology is defined in terms of disturbances of communication'. (p. 79. Our italics).

This redefinition in terms of communication initiated much research, and various theories were developed. (For reviews, see Mishler & Waxler, 1965, Framo, 1972, Riskin & Faunce, 1972, Pettersen & Jacobsen, 1974, Blakar, 1976a, 1978a.) However, the initial optimism has been followed by much more critical attitudes toward the communication-oriented studies, and the way in which they have been carried out. (For critical reviews and/or analyses, cf. Haley, 1972, Riskin & Faunce, 1972, Blakar, 1976a, 1978c.) A particularly illuminating example is represented by the so-called double-bind theory (Bateson et al., 1956), which exerted a great impact and initiated a lot of research (cf. Bateson et al., 1963, Olson 1972), but which has later on been seriously criticized for being almost 'empty' (Schuman, 1967, Olson, 1972, Blakar, 1975c, 1978a).

In retrospect, the communication theorists' preoccupation with merely one diagnostic category (schizophrenia) may represent part of the explanation of the present state of affairs. First of all, this preoccupation with one particular type of psychopathology has resulted in a too restricted empirical basis for the theories of communication and psychopathology. (Not to mention that all the other types of psychopathology have not been subjected to or blessed with the potential benefits of being redefined in terms of communication.) Grolnick's (1972) paper, in which he examines 'A family perspective of psychosomatic factors in illness', can be seen as illustrating this point. Second, the description and understanding of the condition of schizophrenia itself has been hindered by a lack of relevant control groups (Haley, 1972, Riskin & Faunce, 1972, Blakar, 1975a). Because as Bannister (1968, p. 182-183) argues:

> Schizophrenics are a subgroup of the class of 'psychiatrically ill', and any research designed to cast light on the nature of schizophrenia as a specific category must include non-schizophrenic control groups as well as normals. Otherwise any findings relate to the superordinate distinction between people under psychiatric care and people outside it and cannot carry implications for the subordinate class of schizophrenics.

Consequently, an empirical study should not be restricted to only one diagnostic category. (For a further elaboration on these issues, see Part I, p. 48-51.)

The borderline syndrome of personality represents a neglected psychiatric category. Reviewing the literature, we have found none or few studies taking an explicit communication perspective on this syndrome. The reasons may be multiple, but the following two seem evident: first, the borderline diagnosis is often used loosely and in many cases is too badly defined; this results in a mixed group, which has not been very attractive to the more scientifically oriented theorists (cf. Frosch, 1964, Grinker et al., 1968, Crafoord, 1972). Secondly, the lack of adequate methods seems to have presented a serious problem: 'We would wish to relate specific family constellations to specific psychiatric entities - in this case Borderline - but this is not possible with our present concepts and methods applicable to family functions." (Grinker et al., 1968, p. 19).

This ignorance seems to us regrettable. First of all, the borderline syndrome gives a picture of a very complex personality, and would hence present a challenge calling for a critical re-examination of everything said to be 'known' about correlations between the communication pattern of the family and the development of the (pathological) personality (cf. the too restricted empirical basis for theories on this issue).

Secondly, the borderline diagnosis is both different from and related to schizophrenia, and would thus offer a most interesting control in the communication-oriented studies of schizophrenia.

Having reviewed the literature, we found that the most reliable and coherent descriptions of the borderline syndrome were given within the framework of ego-psychology (cf. e.g., Grinker et al., 1968, Knight, 1953, Masterson, 1972). On the basis of descriptions of the structure and organization of personality, it is possible to differentiate between those deficiencies which are typical of the borderline personality and other types of pathological development (Shafer, 1958). Such descriptions of personality within the framework of ego-psychology are not, however, easily 'translatable' to the framework of communication theory.

The purpose of the present paper is hence three-fold:

I. Taking the description of the borderline personality (as used within the framework of modern ego-psychology) as given, we will systematically explore the typical borderline symptoms in order to generate hypotheses about the context within which this type of personality is most likely to have developed. The familial context will be described in terms of the communication pattern within the family.

II. Having generated hypotheses about the communication context of the borderline person's family (I), we will develop methods for empirically testing some of these hypotheses, and an exploratory study will be presented.

III. Finally - taking the methodological arguments discussed above seriously - the borderline category will be introduced as a control in a communication-oriented study of schizophrenia (or, vice versa, schizophrenia will be introduced as a control in the study of borderline).

Thus the present study represents a direct extension of Sølvberg & Blakar's (1975) study on communication in couples with and without a schizophrenic offspring (see Part I).

Consequently, the paper will consist of two sections. Section I is devoted to the theoretical analysis where hypotheses about the communication in the family of the borderline patient are generated on the basis of descriptions of the borderline personality. Section II is devoted to the development of methods for testing (some of) these hypotheses, and a presentation of a first exploratory study carried out along these lines.

The familial context of the borderline patient

There is a lack of consistency and clarity around the use of and content of Borderline as a diagnostic category. The diagnosis has often functioned as a 'sack' in which patients are placed who do not obviously fit other more common diagnostic categories. Perhaps what is most characteristic of the borderline group is its lack of homogeneity regarding symptomatology, and it is difficult to see exactly what this group of patients does have in common. The group has been identified clinically as being more seriously disturbed than psychoneurotics whilst not being manifestly psychotic. The borderline person shows persistent instability and severe maladaptation regarding everyday life (Frosch, 1964, Grinker et al., 1968, Crafoord, 1972).

The group of patients characterized as Borderline is large and, in Norway as in other countries, the diagnosis is used with increasing frequency (Kringlen, 1972).

Patients with this diagnosis are known to be 'bad' cases and have been described as having a bad prognosis and as being difficult to treat (Chessick, 1968). The behavior of persons described as Borderline is said to be 'stable in its instability', uneven in level of functioning, a functioning that can swing from adequate and social acceptability to near psychotic breaks and infantile outbursts.

According to modern theory on the development of the ego, the borderline personality is characterized by its incomplete and unevenly developed ego structures. The borderline ego is neither 'strong' nor 'weak', but is characterized by an uneven profile regarding its ability to function. The person we would describe as having borderline characteristics, is one who lives in constant crisis because he lacks the appropriate and relatively permanent personality structures, that endow new situations with familiarity. The borderline person lacks stability and consistency both in his behavior and in his experience of the world.

The genesis of this type of developmental failure is supposed to be connected with the failure to resolve the original mother-child symbiosis (Masterton, 1972). The person's basic conflict will thus be concerned with the problems of individuation - separation, making independence and continued symbiosis equally threatening. On the one hand the person suffers from acute loneliness, whilst on the other hand intimacy involves the threat of inescapable and complete fusion with another.

In the following section the most typical characteristics of the borderline personality as given in the literature will be described, and in each case a hypothesis will be made about the familial context within which such a personality is likely to have developed. Since the parental couple plays a basic role as the core sub-system in constituting the familial context into which the child is born, particular attention will be paid to the communication of the parental couple.

(a) Inconsistent level of functioning. Perhaps the most typical characteristic of the borderline patient is his unevenness regarding level of functioning. Because he has not developed a well-organized and stable identity, the person will be unpredictable and inconsistent over time. This is in contrast to the neurotic person whose reactions are often rigid and restricted - only too predictable. The schizophrenic on the other hand substitutes reality with his own constructions and reacts on the basis of whatever these may be; within this context his reactions may be very consistent and predictable.

What sort of parental relationship would one expect to be related to this aspect of borderline functioning? We assume that the parents will probably have met the child with opposite and irreconcilable reactions and expectations - typically mirroring a polarization within the relationship. The parental relationship will be characterized by strife and conflict and in many respects unsatisfactory.

(b) The regulation of interpersonal relationships. There is general agreement in the literature that the borderline personality lacks the ability to establish permanent and satisfactory relationships to other people. This does not mean that efforts to achieve contact with others are given up, but rather that the person will alternately seek out others and cling to them only to reject them with hostility in order to maintain sufficient distance. Unlike the schizophrenic the borderline person cannot cut out object relations to minimize anxiety and suffering, but he is instead doomed to oscillate between the fear of intimacy and the fear of being alone. We take the following illustration from Becket's 'Waiting for Godot'. Here we have an example of a type of communication reflecting such basic ambivalence:

Vladimir: You again, come here until I embrace you.

Estragon: Don't touch me.

Vladimir: Do you want me to go away?

Estragon: Don't touch me. Don't question me. Don't speak to me. STAY WITH ME.

Vladimir: Did I ever leave you?

Estragon: You let me go.

Vladimir: Look at me.

What in the familial atmosphere the parents have created would have resulted in this type of contact pattern? First and foremost the parents must have made the child dependent on them. Having an unsatisfactory relationship with each other, the parents may have used the child to satisfy their own frustrated dependency needs and avoid direct communication with each other. We will assume, further, that the parents are actually dependent on maintaining a polarization in their relationship, and that episodes of hostility and frustration will alternate with attempts at reconciliation which will come to nothing. Neither will take responsibility for steering the direction of the relationship. Communication will thus be preoccupied by the relationship aspect (Watzlawick et al., 1967), i.e., conflict about the definition of the relationship. This preoccupation will hinder the parents in other aspects of living, i.e., in rational problem solving. Communication will also be characterized by mutual blaming and accusations, which nevertheless have little consequence for the following interaction.

(c) The ability for realistic and detached self-observation. The borderline person is often characterized by role playing. He can often complain that he is unsure who he really is, and that he only plays up to other people's expectations. Because of this he can feel 'alientated' or a stranger to himself (the 'as if' personality described by Deutzch, 1942). Litzowitz and Newman (1967) claim that the borderline syndrome is typical of modern times. Crafoord (1972) and Grinker (1968) also mention this. They believe that this type of disturbance is connected to a general alienation of modern man - the 'outer directed' man - as portrayed in literature by Camus, Albee, Becket, etc. Being unsure of who he is, the person is compelled to construct a way of being. This, however, he experiences as ungenuine and suffers on account of his own falsity. Uncertainty about his own identity will result in the person having difficulties with proper differentiation between himself and others. This in turn will make genuine empathy difficult and inevitably lead to isolation.

We would assume that the parents have not managed to present themselves as clear,unambiguous figures of identification for the child. They have probably had difficulty in exposing themselves as they really are - as people with a clear-cut profile for better or for worse. We believe that their communication will mirror this difficulty, and will be lacking in clarity and in the ability to make decisions. Taking a clear point of view involves a risk that these parents probably do not feel able to take - a risk of taking responsibility - and of changing. A risk of change involves possible conflict about whose decisions shall weigh most heavily. In general we will expect the parental relationship to be characterized by lack of clarity and lack of decision, and that this has the function of maintaining the polarization in the relationship without threatening their mutual dependence.

(d) Regulation of self-esteem. Low self-esteem is one of the characteristics of the borderline personality (Kernberg, 1967). His inconsistent changeable mode of being will inevitably lead to difficulties in maintaining a permanent occupation and a stable field of interests. It is usually found that borderline patients have difficulties in holding a job or concentrating sufficiently on educational projects which would lead to the experience of mastery. After the earliest years of childhood, self-esteem is maintained by a person experiencing that he 'is something', 'can do something'. Without this inner security which competence can give, the person is constantly dependent on supplies from outside himself (White 1963). Borderline patients often act in a demanding and clinging way in order to ensure their supplies.

We would expect that the parents have not supported the child when they spontaneously have taken the initiative. On account of their own disillusionment and resignation, they have sowed doubt in the child and undermined their child's attempts at mastery. Action and participation are seen as not being worth it, the likeliest result being disappointment. A possible example of such communication we find in Alice in Wonderland. If we think of our developing borderline personality as Alice - the child asking naive questions, believing that its question will be

answered, and if we think of the Cheshire cat as the adult who answers on the basis
of a deep scepticism and sows doubt and confusion in the child, (it doesn't matter
what you do, the world is evil and meaningless. We never get anywhere anyhow and
we only talk past each other in our attempts to leave our isolation), the parents of a
schizophrenic might have ignored or redefined Alice's question (cf. Laing, 1969).
In this case the question is answered at face value, but in such a manner that it becomes meaningless to choose or to take a firm standpoint. The basis for a decision
disappears because the reply to the question increases doubt and indecision, instead
of yielding constructive information that can be used. The premises for further interaction are constantly challenged. We suppose that the parents themselves lack the
necessary confidence to take initiative and instigate change, and that they undermine
each other's attempts in this direction. It will, therefore, be difficult for them to
encourage and support their child in his attempts to take the initiative, try out new
things, and gradually master new skills.

(e) Testing of reality. The ability to test reality adequately is necessary for
normal adult functioning. It develops from the early experience of that which is
'me' as opposed to that which is 'not me', which is the basis of the ability to
discriminate between outer and inner experience. The child must gradually grow
out of his fantasies and imaginative constructions about the world, and gradually
exchange these for more realistic and objective understanding. The fact that we
can have a common interpretation of things that happen is dependent on the ability
to differentiate between perception by the senses and imagination (Piaget 1926,
Becker 1962). The borderline person can have a partial failure in his ability to test
reality, i.e., it is not a question of a generalized disability but specific, personal
variations in the operation of the various ego-functions. Frosch (1964) mentions
that the feeling of having contact with reality can disappear, but the person may be
able to test reality enough to know that the ability is missing. Such insight may, of
course, lead to considerable suffering for the person concerned. This is in
contrast to the psychotic patient who replaces the real world with his fantasy.
Patients with this type of difficulty react strongly with anxiety and confusion when
placed in unstructured or ambiguous situations, and therapeutic intervention will
thus consist of creating a clearly structural situation for the person (Knight 1953,
Chessick 1968).

We assume that the parents' attention has been largely concentrated on the
conflicts in their own relationship, but that these conflicts have not resulted in
direct confrontations. Disagreement is abundant, but there is no real will that
problems shall be solved.

Again an illustration from Samuel Becket.

E: I wonder if we wouldn't have been better off alone, each one for himself. We
   weren't made for the same road.

V: It's not certain.

E: No, nothing is certain.

V: We can still part, if you think it would be better.

E: It's not worth while now.

   (From 'Waiting for Godot', p. 53.)

The relationship is characterized by a constant stream of hostile exchanges which
always lose their impetus and run out in sand. Neither is willing to take responsibility for the hostility, since this could have consequences for the relationship. Our
hypothesis is that a relationship that does not allow the partners to try to solve
conflicts and disagreements will hinder the child's development and its ability to
test reality. Smedslund (1964) is of the view that it is conflict situations and their
resolution which develop intellectual capacities. We assume that the parents will
not make serious attempts to solve the conflicts which occur, because they are in
a state of constant oscillation and polarization, which in fact represents stability
in the relationship.

(f) Regulation of defence system. The borderline personality lacks a firm defensive
system on which he can rely to protect him from the most acute anxiety. The
defensive system he does have is of a primitive 'all or nothing' character. Primitive defence mechanisms such as denial, introjection, and projection, are operative.
The borderline person's life will be characterized by a series of crises in which
he will from time to time be overwhelmed by impulses in their primitive form;
these may take the form of infantile temper tantrums, acute depression, acute
fits of anxiety, paranoia, etc. Minor difficulties and frustrations can lead to
breakdowns of these types - lack of a steady system of defence means that crisis is
always at hand.

Other categories of disturbed individuals avoid anxiety by the establishment of
a rigid defensive system. The neurotic person limits his activity and area of
experience by the establishment of a rigid defence system, and the psychotic individual hides from terrible reality and anxiety by the construction of an alternative
world of hallucination and fantasy. The borderline individual's life may often appear
to be extremely painful, desperate, and hopeless, in that he must live in full
awareness of suffering without adequate defences against it.

What sort of family situation and parental communication would be associated
with the development of an inadequate system of defence? We assume that the
parents have been unpredictable and inconsistent, and that it must have been
difficult for the child to interpret the constantly changing moods that they have

presented. They can have met the child with badly controlled hostility one minute and in the next clung to the child with exaggerated attempts at reconciliation. Faced with this kind of behavior, it would be difficult for the child to develop any steady way of dealing with the parents which would give him security - the attack always coming from an unknown quarter.

Whilst the parents of the schizophrenic will react to their child by ignoring it, redefining its opinions and mystifying, we expect the parents of borderline patients to be unpredictable, suspicious, and inconsistent, and more openly destructive and confusing. To sum up, we assume that the parents of borderline patients are caught up in a conflictual relationship on which they are also dependent. Any attempt to resolve the conflicts will be experienced as a threat to the relationship itself, and will therefore not be seriously tried. We can assume that this polarization has the function of maintaining a balance between closeness and intimacy, on the one hand, and the necessary distance and separation, on the other. The interaction will be destructive and characterized by inconsistency and unpredictability. Initiative will be met with ambiguity and uncertainty. Disagreements will not be solved, but will be left hanging in the air though perhaps recognized. Communication between the parents will be characterized by suspicion and lack of confidence regarding each other and other people. Because their relationship is strained and irreconcilable, a third person (often a child) will often be 'used' in the conflict between them and thus function as a 'scapegoat'. 'Solutions' of this type will, of course, not work, and interaction will thus be characterized by pessimism, confusion, and despair. The underlying premisses for their life in common will constantly be questioned, even though this does not lead anywhere.

The experimental approach

The above exposition of the literature has clearly demonstrated that a systematic examination of communication patterns in the family of borderline patients might represent a substantial contribution. As was demonstrated in the above review, on the basis of the literature, even rather specific hypotheses about the communication in such families could be put forward. However, at the present stage it would seem more reasonable to conduct exploratory, though systematic, studies with the purpose of identifying and describing qualitative characteristics of the communication typical to such families, rather than to test specific hypotheses. (For a presentation of our general program on communication-oriented studies on psychopathology, see Part I, p. 47-53, Part III, and Blakar, 1978a.)

Every communication-oriented study on psychopathology - irrespective of which diagnostic categories one chooses to study - is immediately confronted with two substantial problems. First, there is the vague or even entire lack of relevant communication theory (cf. Part I and Riskin & Faunce, 1972, Blakar, 1976a). Secondly, there is the serious lack of adequate methods (cf. Part I and Grinker et al. 1968, Haley, 1972, Blakar, 1974a).

The choice of, or development of, methods in this field should ideally be based on (a) an explicit theory of communication, and (2) knowledge about families with psychopathological members. Regarding the latter, Haley concludes in his review of the field: 'The most sound findings would seem to be in the outcome area: When faced with a task on which they must cooperate, abnormal family members seem to communicate their preferences less successfully, require more activity and take longer to get the task done.' (Haley, 1972, p. 35. Our italics.)

Our own expectations concerning the communication in the family of the border-line patient (cf. the above review) would also point to the suitability of a cooperation task. And we felt that an experimental situation of the type envisaged by Haley would yield a good point of departure.

In the present study Blakar's standardized communication conflict situation (Blakar, 1972a, 1973a) was employed. A presentation of the method, its theoretical background, and the rationale for clinical application is given in Part I (p. 26-33).

In the present study we have chosen to study the parental communication pattern. This for two reasons: first, we did not intend to have the patient himself present, as eventual differences could then be 'explained' as a function of special consideration made to the patient member. Secondly, the parents create the basic dyad of the family, the child being born into a milieu created by the parents. It is essential to emphasize that a study of this type cannot say anything definite about causality (Blakar, 1974a). On the other hand, there scarcely any longer exist good reasons (i.e., in communication-oriented family research) to think in terms of simple chains of causality; one has surely to regard the family as a complex system (Jackson, 1959, 1965, 1966, 1967, Watzlawick et al. 1967, Mossige, Pettersen & Blakar, 1976). However, in family systems the parents do play a conclusive role in the constitution of the family.

Since the communication task given each couple is in principle unsolvable, we had to decide upon the criteria for terminating the experimental session beforehand. The set of criteria used in the first study exploiting this particular method (Sølvberg & Blakar, 1975) is presented in Part I (see p. 33). Re-analyses (Blakar, 1978a, Endresen, 1977, Moberget & Reer, 1975) of tape-recordings from preceding studies, however, have revealed two problems concerning these criteria. First, the experimenter could, according to criterion (2), accept the task as being resolved in cases where examinations of the tape-recording (particularly the subjects' spontaneous comments afterwards) could throw doubt on whether they had really solved the communication conflict or not. Naturally, this would result in a loss of essential information. Secondly, it happened in some cases that only one of the spouses recognized the discrepancy between the maps, while the other one would show great surprise when the error was afterwards uncovered by a direct comparison of the two maps. This type of resolution, which we will classify as an individual solution, is very different from cases where the two of them are both firmly convinced about the error (a social solution). Again, if the experimenter too readily accepts an individual solution, we would lose the chance to see how the spouse with insight about the deception would convince or fail to convince the other. Actually, this phase could be very revealing as to factors such as power and control. In order not to lose such critical information, we decided that the experimenter should (a) 'press' the couples as much as possible toward criterion (1), and not accept solutions according to criterion (2) (see p. 33). Furthermore, the experimenter would (b) hesitate to accept individual solutions, and see if the couple could reach a joint conclusion.

In order to simplify comparison between various couples, the distribution of the two differing maps to the spouses had to be standardized. In order to counteract culturally determined male-dominance, we gave the map with the routes marked in to the wives, so that the husbands had to follow the directives and explanations of their wives (cf. Sølvberg & Blakar, 1975).

Samples and matching

As was mentioned in the introduction (p. 67), the choice of adequate control groups is an issue of great theoretical and methodological importance in this type of research. Taking Bannister's argument (see p. 67) seriously, we thus chose to use two control groups, one so-called 'normal group' (Group N) and one group consisting of parents having a schizophrenic offspring (Group S). Group N represents a 'normal group' in the sense that they constitute comparable ordinary couples without problems that have brought them or their children into contact with treatment or penal institutions. Nothing else is implied by normality in this case. Concerning schizophrenia, we decided to accept the definition generally held within Norwegian Psychiatry, i.e., according to Kraepelin. Our point of departure was that the reference person in Group S had been diagnosed as being a schizophrenic at a psychiatric institution.

The use of the diagnostic categories - schizophrenia and borderline - entailed that all reference persons would be over 15 years old. We put the upper age-limit at 30 - and within this range sought the youngest possible reference persons to ensure that they had not been separated from their families for too long.

Groups S and N, each consisting of five couples matched on relevant background variables, were established in connection with an earlier study (presented in Part I, p. 32-47).We thus had to establish a matching Group B. Since Group B was our main focus of interest, and since wide within-group-variation would have to be expected, we decided to have twice as many couples in Group B.

In establishing Group B we encountered all the problems connected with the vague use of this diagnostic category (cf. introduction p. 67). Contrary to schizophrenia, borderline is not an officially used diagnostic category in Norwegian psychiatry. Hence, we had to present the list of criteria (cf. the description of the borderline personality in Section I), and have the institution choose patients according to these criteria. [10]

To establish Group B was a long and laborious process. A large number of potential reference persons were dropped, because either the parents were divorced, one or both parents were dead or had mental or somatic ailments, or because the reference person had been brought up by foster parents. A particular problem was that so many of the parental couples were divorced or separated. Others were dropped because the respective therapists considered the mental state of the parents so labile that they would not expose them to the possible strain of this type of research.

The previously established Groups S and N were satisfyingly matched on relevant background variables such as age, number of years of marriage, education, employment, socio-economic status, annual income, domicile, living conditions, number of children and their sex and age. Just to give an idea of the degree of matching: in Group S the average age was 52 (range 48 to 58) as compared to 51 (range 45 to 57) in Group N, and the average length of marriage in Group S was 25 (range 22 to 29) years, as compared to 25 (range 24 to 27).

Efforts were taken to establish a matching Group B. Although this was relatively successfully accomplished, the Group B couples were, on an average, a bit older (54, range 48 to 63). Furthermore, they belonged to a higher socio-economic level, they were better educated and had a higher annual income. (For further details on background variables and the matching, see Alve & Hultberg, 1974, pp. 69-72.)

All the 20 couples lived in the Oslo area. As regards education, income, and living conditions, they represented a heterogeneous sample. All the Groups S and N couples who agreed to participate in the experiment were run through, but one Group B couple had to be replaced, as the husband turned in the doorway and left the experimental scene when he caught sight of the tape-recorder. Apart from this, there were no real problems in administering the task. The experimenter for Group B was trained to react as similarly to the previous experimenter for Groups S and N as possible.

Hypotheses

Even though the present study is highly exploratory, hypotheses concerning the degree
of efficiency as well as concerning qualitative differences, were set forth. As
regards our possibility of testing specific hypotheses, the very nature of the experimental method is essential. The method consists of two apparently similar, but in
reality highly different, communication tasks. Whereas the first one is simple and
straightforward, the second induces a communication conflict.

As mentioned in Section I, there is a huge literature on communication and
schizophrenia, but none or few studies have been conducted on communication in
families with borderline members. Hence our basis for hypotheses is really very
slight. Actually, the most sound basis for making predictions about the efficiency in
the Group B couples, seems to be Section I of the present paper.

First of all, wide within-group variation is to be expected. However, if we are
right, as we have argued in Section I (p. 68-74), that the communication will be characterized by suspiciousness, inconsistencies, polarization, and changes in levels of
functioning, we would predict that at least some Group B couples would run into (or
themselves create) rather serious communication problems even on the simple task.

Regarding potential qualitative differences, hypotheses will be specified in connection with the presentation of the various analyses that will be carried out. But
again, Section I has to be read as our attempt to put forward more general hypotheses
about the quality of the communication in families with borderline members.

Our specific hypotheses with regard to the patterns of communication across the
varying situations of Groups N and S couples were presented in Part I (p. 40).

A scheme for investigating patterns of attribution

We have elsewhere (Blakar, 1974a) argued that methods and concepts to be employed
in communication-oriented studies of psychopathology should be anchored (a) in a
general theory of communication as well as (b) in characteristics of the specific
category of psychopathology on which attention is being focused. And we have claimed
(Blakar, 1974a, 1976a) that the lack of progress in the field (for critical reviews,
see Haley, 1972, Riskin & Faunce, 1972, Jacobsen & Pettersen, 1974) is primarily
caused by lack of a general theory of communication (see also Part I).

In particular, when it comes to qualitative analyses of communication in families
with and without psychopathological members, most researchers seem to have given
up or forgotten all about general communication theory. Overwhelmed by the richness
of and variation in the material, they have resorted to mere clinical casuistic descriptions, freely employing everyday language and ad hoc terms. (For a critical

review of this conceptual and terminological chaos, see Riskin & Faunce, 1972, Blakar, 1978a.)

Riskin & Faunce (1972) point out that 'interdisciplinary isolation' is striking in this field. However, if one turns to social-developmental psychology, a whole set of relevant and theoretically grounded concepts offer themselves. In Part I (p. 46-47) various examples of such concepts were given.

In the present study we chose to describe the communication in terms of the couples' patterns of attribution of communication difficulties. This choice reflects the preferred two-fold anchoring of concepts, in that we felt that if our description of communication in the family of the borderline patient was adequate, particularly critical moments would occur when they have to cooperate and make decisions about attributions of communication difficulties (cf. for example the polarization and the mutual suspiciousness). Furthermore, the method seemed to be particularly revealing or sensitive to this aspect. This is clearly illustrated by the following quotation from the presentation of the very first study where same-sex student dyads were run as subjects. This quotation will also give the reader a further idea about which aspect of communication we are about to analyze:

> The instructions are usually quickly grasped, and the Ss start directly on the simple route, which is easily carried out. If, for one reason or another, they get into trouble, they may even before starting on the more complex route explicitly 'diagnose' their communicational strategies in manners very similar to those observed in most dyads after series of trials on the more complex route. The simple route usually causes no trouble, however, and the Ss go on to the complex route with an apparent confidence in the maps as well as in the strategy they applied. And the specific strategy applied varies from dyad to dyad.
> In the complex route all dyads soon run into trouble. When missing the route or realizing that Y has come wrong, they usually go back to Point E, the starting point. Mean number of returns to the starting point was 10, with a range from 5 to 14.
> In most dyads, little seems to happen during the first two or three trials, even though directives vary with respect to redundancy. Apparently their trouble in this early phase is attributed to the complexity of the map. At this early phase the Ss are also perfectly willing to attribute failures to themselves, and exchanges like the following are not unusual: 'Oh dear, my fault, I was unaware'. 'No, no ... my explanation was not adequate'. But as they continue to miss the route, they are not any longer as ready to attribute the failure to themselves, and they start accusing each other. ('You'd better follow my explanations carefully.' 'You give damned bad explanations'). This change coincides with a striking change in the emotional climate in the dyad: they generally get more and more excited and sometimes rather furious at each other. (Remember that on an average they go on and on for more than a quarter of an hour without expressing any doubt about the maps at all.)
> For one reason or another, the maps are then at some point brought into focus in the dialogue. The possibility of attributing the difficulties to defects in the maps are suggested more-or-less vaguely. From that stage on, more than half the dyads spend a short time either identifying the error or claiming that there is no reason going on since the maps are different. (Blakar 1973a, p. 421-422).

Communication conflicts, misunderstandings, and situations involving lack of understanding are inevitable in any familial or human relationship. And it seems essential how such events are managed - whether (and how) preconditions for successful communication are re-established, or not. Various couples may react differently to communication conflicts they encounter, and some may even themselves create or enhance such conflicts. How parental couples tackle communication conflicts, should hence tell us a lot about the social environment and familial context they foster for their children to grow up in.

By experimentally inducing a communication conflict, we are in a strategic position to investigate and study the pattern of the couples' attributions of their communication difficulties. As was reflected in the above quotation, we not only get information (from their own explicit replies) about whether or not they attribute their communication difficulties, and to what (adequately or inadequately) they attribute them, but also about who is attributing, and the receiver's response, etc. Furthermore, we may analyze their patterns of attributions as they develop over time.

Before the concrete scoring procedure we developed is presented in detail, it has to be underlined that in the present experimental situation - as in every communication conflict - an adequate attribution of the communication difficulty (in our case to the discrepancy on the maps) is a precondition for successful communication. If not, the failure of communication will continue unchecked and uncorrected on the false premises. In Heider's terms '(one) would be at the mercy of seemingly fickle events in the environment'. (Heider, 1958, p. 257).

In order to be a vehicle of successful change in the process of communication, the act of attribution must be adequate in that (a) the nature of the communication difficulty is identified, and (b) a causal explanation has to be offered. Furthermore, (c) the participants have to reach some consensus or agreement as to the nature and cause of the communication difficulty (e.g., on whose premises is the communication conflict to be understood and resolved).

The first step (0) in our analysis was to identify every occurrence of communication difficulty where an explicit attempt at attributing the experienced communicative difficulty is made, and then analyze each such occurrence according to the following four dimensions:

(1) Who offers or makes the attribution.
(2) To what is the communication difficulty attributed.
(3) The quality of the attribution.
(4) The reaction of the other participant(s).

A few comments have to be made in connection with this procedure. First, we are aware of the fact that by restricting the analysis to explicit acts of attribution only, we may lose essential information about the unverbalized, but nevertheless influential, attributions. On the other hand, the methodological problems connected with the identification and scoring of such 'implicit attributions' (e.g., the scorer feels that the wife/husband signalizes to the other that 'it's your fault that we fail in this situation') seemed insurmountable in the present preliminary study. But this choice did not entirely solve the problem, however. In many cases there is no doubt as to the existence of an act of attribution (e.g., utterances such as 'your explanations are damned bad'), but in other cases there may be some doubt as to whether or not an act of attribution is really involved (e.g., a husband repeating his wife's explanation in a voice indicating that he does not have faith in her explanation). But since we are not interested in how many attributions each couple makes, but in a comparison of patterns of interaction at these critical moments of communication between our 20 different couples (or three different groups), the problem is not that we may overlook some instances of attribution, but rather that we may run the risk of not being consistent over the 20 couples. In order to counteract such tendencies, the couples were scored in randomized order. Two trained scorers scored each half of the couples, both getting mixed groups of S-, B- and N-couples. Two couples were scored independently by both, and their agreement was almost perfect. In cases where the scorers were in doubt, they would consult each other, and only cases where both agreed that this was an act of attribution, were included. The identification of acts of attribution was conducted from the tape-recordings, but the scorers could check against written transcripts. The subsequent detailed analysis of each identified act of attribution was conducted on written transcripts, but could be supported (voice, stress, intonation, etc.) by the tape-recordings.

Each event involving an explicit attribution of the communication difficulty was then analyzed according to the following scheme:

(1) Who makes the attribution? It can easily be seen how this variable may tell us something about, for example, the control in the relationship. A statement involving an attribution of communication difficulties is a statement about the communication itself, and hence an aspect of 'meta-communication' is involved. Such events should thus be particularly revealing as to the control and governing aspects of the couple's interaction (cf. Haley, 1963). It has to be kept in mind, however, that the two roles of the situation - as explainer and follower - may be biased in this respect. But the roles are standardized to the extent that the wife is given the map with the routes marked in. Hence comparisons between couples and groups of couples can be made, even though nothing absolute can be said about control relations within each individual couple.

(2) To what do they attribute their communication difficulties? The content of the attribution, i.e., the experienced cause of the difficulty is naturally highly dependent

upon the nature of the specific situation and conflict. Nevertheless, on the basis of the literature (Hall, 1959, Hymes, 1967, Blakar & Rommetveit, 1975, cf. Blakar, 1975c), we feel that at least two dimensions are universal to all communication situations: personal attributions (I, you and/or us) versus situation-oriented attributions. On the basis of analysis of tape-recordings from earlier studies, we found that attributions in the present experimentally induced communication conflict could be categorized as:

Table 3. To what are the communication difficulties in the present situation attributed?

The communicative difficulty is attributed to:	Examples:
(1) Oneself ('my fault'):	'Sorry, my mistake.. I turned right too early there.'
(2) The other ('your fault'):	'Wait a minute, .. I think you missed a road from the left! '
(3) Both ('our fault'):	'We must be misunderstanding each other.'
(4) The difficulty of the task:	'If you want my opinion this is really difficult.'
(5) The maps being different:	'We can't be doing that bad .. there must be something wrong with the maps! '
(6) Something diffuse (or vague):	'That's strange!' 'How mysterious! ' 'Something must be wrong.'

On the basis of what was said in section I, more person attributions (particularly 'your fault') should be expected in Group B. From the literature (Watzlawick et al. 1967, Riskin & Faunce 1972, Haley, 1972) a preoccupation with the person or relation dimension should be expected in the two psychopathology groups. And in Group N we would expect a development over time in that they start from 'vague and diffuse attributions' and work their way to specific attributions about the deceptive situation. In the Groups S and B more rigidity and less development would be expected.

Furthermore, this content aspect can provide essential clues as to why some couples' communication is more inefficient. In a way, this analysis will reveal their own diagnosis of their own communication difficulties.

(3) The quality of the attribution: An essential aspect of every such act of attribution is whether it is constructive, i.e., whether it represents a positive contribution to the resolution of the communication conflict. Constructive attributions are attributions that make potential changes of the communication possible, and they represent attempts at inquiring into what is 'wrong' in our communication. Non-constructive attributions are attributions that either are entirely task-irrelevant, or they are directly destructive, in that the act of attribution does not involve or reflect any serious attempt to identify the cause of the difficulty, but can more likely be conceived of as, for example, an attempt to blame the other. In scoring an act of attribution as constructive versus non-constructive, the whole communication context would have to be taken into consideration. E.g., a diffuse hint that 'there seems to be something wrong' may be scored as constructive in the opening phase, but as non-constructive if it appears toward the end of the communication task. Every attribution was thus scored as either constructive or non-constructive (destructive or irrelevant).

However, we were interested in the couple's interaction in these critical moments during the communication process, and the constructive versus non-constructive category is applied to the one spouse making the attribution only. But it is evident that the quality and potential consequence of an attribution lies just as much in the other spouse's reaction.

(4) The reaction of the other participant(s). Four different types of reactions were identified: 1) The proposed attribution is accepted, 2) rejected (with or without modifications or counter proposals), or 3) neglected. A fourth category had to be added in order to encompass 4) ambiguous responses, that is a response that neither implies a 'yes' nor a 'no', or implies both a 'yes' and a 'no'. In order to clarify these distinctions a series of examples are presented in Table 4.

If these two aspects are combined, we see that the interaction at these critical moments of the communication process may vary from constructive attributions that are accepted/rejected to non-constructive attributions that are neglected/met with ambiguous reactions. It can easily be imagined how this will define the interaction climate. Qualitative differences between the three different groups were to be expected. The N-group would be characterized by constructive attributions where the receiver takes a stand (accepts or rejects). In the other groups more non-constructive (irrelevant and destructive) attributions would be expected. Furthermore, we would expect a tendency to neglect in the S-group, and a tendency toward ambiguous reactions in the B-group.

The four dimensions of analysis presented so far may be applied to every communication situation where a communication conflict has occurred. Our experi-

Table 4: The various types of reactions upon attributions of communicative difficulties

---

1) Taking a stand (accepting or rejecting):

S: 'Now we have messed it up again! '

R: 'Yes, let us start from the beginning.' (acceptance)

R: 'No . ... We must be at the same place! ' (rejection)

2) Not taking a stand/Ambiguous response:

S: 'These maps must be different.'

R: 'Hmm ....' (ambiguous response implying neither a 'yes' nor a 'no')

R: ' .... (Silence 3 sec.) ... Let's go back to point E.: (ambiguous silence, followed by a change of topic).

R: 'Yes, either the maps are different ... or there is something wrong with the explanation.' (the response implies both 'yes' and 'no')

3) Neglect/Ignorance:

S: 'Did you say "right" and "left" correctly now?'

R: 'And then you take the first road to the right, then straight up .. and the second road to the left ..' (The spouse's attribution is neglected)

R: 'As I said .. go straight on! ' (A tangential response: The receiver responds as if the sender had asked: 'Where did you tell me to go?')

mental design, however, allows us to conduct some more particular analyses that may shed some light on the different communication patterns:

(5) Focusing on or ignorance of communication discrepancies. In this particular experimental situation it is known exactly where the discrepancy is located; hence it is possible to analyze how often the various couples continue past the error. (Here it has to be mentioned that the maps are constructed so that the influence of the error will usually not be detected before they have continued a bit past the error. Cf. Blakar 1973a.) Different 'styles' of communication should be reflected in this measure. Take as an example a couple who for one reason or another actively avoid conflicts; this may for example be done via 'pseudo-agreement'. Such a couple would be likely to continue past the error again and again. Take another couple, in which the spouses are mutually suspicious toward each other and try to fight each other. They may grasp every chance to quarrel, including the experimentally induced error, and hence never or seldom continue past the error. In order to study potential change over time, we counted how often each couple continued past the error in the first and the last third of the time spent on the experimental route. In the Group N couples we

would expect a radical decrease, whereas in the Groups S and B couples we would expect more rigid patterns and less development over time. Furthermore, we would expect the S-group couples to ignore the discrepancy and thus frequently continue past the error.

(6) Re-establishing commonality by returning to the starting point. If communication runs into trouble, particularly in a situation such as the present, a natural strategy is to re-establish commonality by returning to the starting point, i.e. to a point known to be shared or common. However, if the communication is to be improved, the return has to be followed by an attribution of the communication difficulty. If not, it is likely that one will merely run into the very same difficulty again and again. Hence, we counted all returns to the starting point, and for each return checked whether an explicit attribution was made. And again, in order to analyze potential development over time, we analyzed how large a proportion of the first and last third of each couple's returns was not followed by an attribution.

(7) Ratio of attributions to returns. One would expect different styles in different couples with respect to how often they will try to attribute communication difficulties. In some couples there may be a tendency to ignore or even avoid conflicts, hence few explicit attributions will be made. Others may focus upon conflicts, cling to them, or even themselves create conflicts, thus many attributions (particularly many destructive attributions that are rejected or met with an ambiguous reaction) could result. The mere ratio between the number of starts from the starting point and the number of attributions could roughly differentiate different styles. In other words, a high ratio of attributions to starts/returns may reflect a tendency to concentrate upon and focus communication difficulties, whereas a low ratio could reflect a tendency to ignore or even avoid communication conflicts. One would expect that there is an optimal level in this respect, but it is impossible beforehand to know what this optimal level is in a particular situation. If we à priori take the ratio of the N group to be 'optimal', a too high ratio would be expected in the B group and a too low ratio in the S group couples.

Presentation and discussion of results

(a) Efficiency of communication

A first crucial observation was the different reactions to the standardized experimental communication situation as such. In contrast to Groups N and S, the Group B couples' attitude toward the very situation was flavored with suspiciousness. Whereas no particular problems were encountered in making the Groups N and S couples grasp the instructions and start on the simple practice route, the experimenter almost had to negotiate with the Group B couples in order to get them to start. All the couples who came to participate in the study, had of course, agreed beforehand, and appointments with respect to time, place, etc. had been made. Nevertheless, some of the Group B couples had 'misinterpreted' the situation in various ways; they showed a more sceptical or negative attitude toward the tape-recording; they questioned the experimenter's integrity in handling such confidential material; etc. The opening or introductory phase of the experimental sessions with the Group B couples thus in various ways put a heavy pressure on the experimenter. In this respect Group B deviates from all the different samples of subjects who have at present participated in this particular communication conflict situation (Blakar, 1973a, Sølvberg, 1973, Jacobsen & Pettersen, 1974, Lagerløv & Stokstad, 1974, Wikran, 1974, Sølvberg & Blakar, 1975, Rotbæk, 1976, Rund, 1976, Haarstad, 1976, Glennsjø, 1977). [11]

It seems natural to start the presentation of the results by examining some quantitative measures bearing upon the couples' efficiency in solving the two different communication tasks. As can be seen from Figure 4, even on the simple and straight-forward practice route the time used varied greatly (from 1 min 42 sec to 33 min 51 sec), thus indicating strong variation with respect to communication efficiency. However, this huge variation is mainly a product of the very large within-group variation in Group B.

Regarding communication efficiency in this plain and simple situation (the practice route), no difference was found between Groups S and N, either in mean time used or in range. Furthermore, in the simple situation Groups N and S demonstrated a communication efficiency almost identical to that of younger and more highly educated student dyads (cf. Blakar, 1973a, Lagerløv & Stokstad, 1974, Stokstad, Lagerløv & Blakar, 1976).

Group B differs from Groups N and S in that their mean time used is much longer (more than twice as long), but first and foremost in that the range is much wider. Actually, the Group B couples varied from the quickest and most efficient in the total sample to couples being so helpless and inefficient in their communication that they would never have managed even this simple task (the practice route) if the experimenter had not assisted them.

Moreover, as can be seen from Table 5, striking differences in the three different categories of couples' abilities to solve the communication conflict induced on the experimental route, were testified to. As groups, the Group N couples managed, whereas the Group S couples failed, thus demonstrating highly different patterns of communication efficiency. Group B falls in-between, in that about half of the couples succeeded and the other half failed. However, a striking qualitative difference between the Group N and the Group B 'solvers' has to be mentioned at this point. Whereas the Group N couples worked themselves toward a more or less

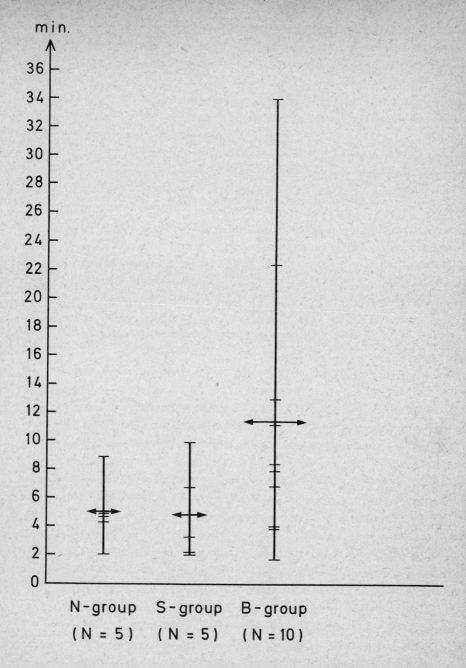

Figure 4: The time used by each of the 20 couples and mean time of each of the
three experimental groups in the simple communication situation.

Table 5: Distribution of solvers/non-solvers in the communication conflict
situation (the experimental route) over Group N, Group B and Group S
couples

Group	Solvers	Non-solvers	Total
Group N	4 *	0	4 * * * *
Group S	1 * *	4	5
Group B	4 * * *	6	10
Total	9	10	19

*   1 individual and 3 social solvers.
* *   1 social solver.
* * *   1 individual and 3 social solvers.
* * * *   With respect to one Group N couple the evidence is inconclusive. According
to Sølvberg & Blakar's criterion 2 the couple was accepted by the experimenter as a
solver, and consequently the session was stopped. However, this couple did not
satisfy more rigorous criteria (see above). Hence we are left inconclusive regarding
this particular couple.

accurate identification and localization of the discrepancy between the maps, and then
turned toward the experimenter for social 'confrontation' and confirmation, the Group
B solvers were much more likely to turn toward the experimenter without having
taken all the trouble to identify the nature of the communication problem. The resolving process amongst the Group N couples was hence more characterized by
cognitive activity, whereas amongst the Group B solvers the process was characterized by the social activity of the couple trying to 'fight' the experimenter and force
him to admit 'something is wrong'.

Even though these quantitative measures on communication efficiency are primarily intended as a point of departure for qualitative analyses of the couples' communication patterns (see Part I and Blakar, 1974a, 1975a), some more general
conclusions may seem warranted at the present stage:

First and foremost, general conclusions regarding differences in communication
efficiency between couples having and not having psychopathological offspring should
never be stated without explicit reference to type(s) of interaction or cooperation
situations (cf. Stokstad, Lagerløv & Blakar, 1976, Blakar, 1978a). From Table 6,
in which the 20 couples are rank-ordered with respect to the time used on the simple
situation (the practice route), and success/failure is indicated by ' + ' or ' - ' res-

Table 6: All the 20 couples rank-ordered with respect to time used in the simple situation (the practice route) and success/failure in the complex one (the experimental route) marked with ' + ' or ' - ' respectively

Group	Practice route	Eperimental route	
B - 2	1'42''	-	
N - 2	2'02''	+	
S - 9	2'05''	-	
S - 6	2'09''	-	
S - 7	3'11''	+	
B - 10	3'51''	-	
B - 8	3'55''	+	
N - 5	4'05''	+	
N - 10	4'52''	+	
N - 8	4'55''	+	
B - 5	6'45''	+	
S - 1	6'47''	-	
B - 6	7'52''	-	
B - 1	8'17''	+	
N - 3	8'52''	? *	
S - 4	9'56''	-	
B - 4	11'09''	+	
B - 3	12'52''	-	
B - 7	22'20''	-	
B - 9	33'51''	-	

* Inconclusive, cf. note to Table 5

pectively, the pattern typical to each group of couples with respect to communication efficiency can be read.

The Group N couples demonstrate an efficient communication in the simple as well as in the conflict communication situation. The communication of the Group S couples was just as efficient as that of the Group N couples in the simple communication situation, but proved to be almost totally inadequate in the communication conflict situation. (For a theoretical discussion of this particular issue, see Sølvberg & Blakar, 1975.) As one might expect, the parental couples with a borderline offspring proved to represent a rather heterogeneous group. Great within-group variance was found in the time used on the simple practice route (cf. Figure 4) as well as in the ability to resolve the induced communication conflict. A closer examination of Table 6 reveals that the 10 Group B couples are divided into three rather distinct sub-groups with respect to the pattern of communication efficiency. The first sub-group BI (4 couples, Nos. 1, 4, 5 and 8) adheres to the pattern most typical of the Group N couples, in that they master the simple communication situation quickly and succeed in resolving the induced communication conflict. The second sub-group BII (3 couples, Nos. 2, 6 and 10) shows the pattern most typical of the Group S couples, in that they master the simple communication situation, but fail in resolving the induced communication conflict. The remaining third sub-group BIII (3 couples, Nos. 3, 7 and 9) differs from both the Group N and the Group S patterns, in that they not only fail to resolve the induced communication conflict, but even the simple and straightforward communication situation (the practice route) seems to represent a severe communication problem to them.

(b) Patterns of attribution of communication difficulties

On the average, 20 such acts of attribution were registered in the couples' communication on the experimental route. The wide range, from 8 to 45 acts of attribution, indicates large variation in style and pattern. But no systematic differences were found between the three experimental groups in terms of mere numbers of such acts. The couples who managed to resolve the induced communication conflict made 15 (8-25), as compared to the non-solvers who made 25 (10-45) explicit attributions, on the average. When the difference in time spent in the situation is taken into account, however, there is no difference between solvers and non-solvers with respect to mere numbers of acts of attributions.

Our first question regarding the quality of the communication was: Who makes the attribution? In total in the whole sample, 58% of the attributions were made by the husbands, thus indicating an expected skewedness in that the informant (the husband) would correct/blame the informer (the wife). However, inspection on individual couple level revealed a large variation, in that the husband's part of the attributions varied from 40 % to 75 %. And in 8 of the 20 couples the wife was responsible for more than 50 % of the attributions.

On group level, there is a more equal distribution between the spouses in Group B (44 % versus 56 %) as compared to those in Group N (37 % versus 63 %) and in Group S (40 % versus 60 %). However, within-group variations are large, and in all the three experimental groups it varies from couples where the wife is responsible for more than 50 % to couples where the husband is responsible for the major part. In conclusion, there is large variation with respect to the distribution of attributions between the spouses, but there seems to be no systematic correlation between this distribution and the group to which the couple belongs. Nor is there any correlation between distribution of attributions and whether or not the couple resolves the induced communication conflict (4 of the 8 'wife-dominated' and 6 of the 12 'husband-dominated' couples failed to resolve the induced communication conflict).

With respect to what the communication difficulties encountered are attributed to, however, different patterns were found in the three experimental groups as well as in the three B-sub-groups (see Table 7.) The table speaks for itself, but

Table 7: The distribution (in percentages) of what the couples attribute their communication difficulties to

Group	N	Me	You	Us	Personal attributions (Me + you + us)	The difficulty of the task	The maps are different	Diffuse attributions	Total
Group N	5	10	36	1	(47)	1	32	19	99%
Group S	5	14	48	15	(77)	7	10	6	100%
Group B	10	21	27	15	(63)	6	18	13	100%
Group BI	4	9	21	17	(47)	9	42	2	100%
Group BII	3	21	16	21	(58)	4	15	22	99%
Group BIII	3	29	44	5	(78)	6	5	10	99%
Solvers	9	9	28	10	(47)	4	38	10	99%
Non-solvers	10	22	36	14	(72)	7	9	13	101%
Total	20	17	34	12	(63)	5	19	13	100%

a few comments may be useful. First and foremost, the much lower proportion of
person-related attributions (me, you, us) in Group N, has to be notified. Again
inspection of the individual couples reveals that there is no overlap between Groups
S and N, but that the Group B couples vary widely. Actually, the couple with the
highest (88%), as well as the one with the lowest (13%), proportion of person- -
related attributions belongs to Group B. Interestingly, sub-Group I (the 4 solving
Group B couples) in this respect almost perfectly fits the Group N pattern. That a
too high proportion of person-related attributions results in inefficient communication is clearly reflected in the fact that whereas none of the 9 solving couples had
more than 70% person-related attributions, 7 of the 10 non-solving couples did
have.

It may be argued that the higher proportion of person-related attributions in
Groups S and B merely reflects the different demand characteristics of the experimental situation (see Part I, p. 48 - 51, and Part II, p. 150). Naturally, this
may represent part of the explanation. However, the following facts cannot be fully
explained by this hypothesis: the four solving Group B couples adhere to the
Group N pattern; the solving Group S couple has a lower proportion of person-related attributions than any other Group S couple; and the only non-solving (the inconclusive one) Group N couple has by far the highest proportion of person-related
attributions of the Group N couples. Secondly, almost all the couples, (with the
exception of two couples) at least once explicitly questioned the credibility of
the maps.

Moreover, the proportion and distribution of the so-called diffuse attributions
is revealing. The relatively high proportion of diffuse attributions in Group N
reflects their particular strategy in unravelling the induced communication difficulty,
in that they started with vague and diffuse attributions and worked their way toward
more specific and adequate attributions. In Groups S and B no such development
over time was found. Vague and diffuse attributions were just as likely to appear
after 40 minutes of communication as in the beginning. As an illustration the
'diffuse' attributions of one Group N and one Group B couple is presented:

All the diffuse attributions made by couple N-10:

After 1 min.   There's something odd here.
After 2 min.   There's something funny.
After 5 min.   There's definitely something wrong here .... it can't be ......
After 6 min.   There is still some mistake here.

All the diffuse attributions made by couple B-6:

After 8 min.   I can't imagine where on earth you are.
After 12 min.   There's definitely something wrong .... I can't quite understand.

After 17 min.   There's something odd here.

After 22 min.   There is something odd.

After 30 min.   I'm not quite sure where you are.

After 33 min.   There must be a catch here.

After 37 min.   There is some sort of mistake here.

After 38 min.   There must be something that's not right.

Sub-group BI is remarkable in that no or few (three of these couples made none and one couple made one) diffuse attributions are made. This finding corroborates the above-mentioned difference in style and strategy of the Group B as compared to the Group N solvers.

Two acts of attribution made by the same spouse (e.g., the wife) to the same cause (e.g., your fault) may nevertheless differ enormously in quality. In Table 8 the distribution of constructive, irrelevant, and destructive attributions as well as the reactions upon attributions, are presented. Three types of reactions are given in the table: reactions taking a stand (accepting or rejecting the proposed attribution), neglect or ignorance, and ambiguous responses (see p. 83).

Table 8: The distribution in percentage of constructive, irrelevant and destructive attributions, and the distribution of the reactions upon the attributions

Group	N	Attribution				Reaction			
		Con- structive	Ir- rele- vant	De- structive	Total	Taking a stand	Ambigu- ous re- sponse	Neg- lection	Total
Group N	5	60	25	16	101%	70	21	10	101%
Group S	5	40	24	36	100%	42	26	32	100%
Group B	10	26	21	53	100%	28	53	19	100%
Group BI	4	59	22	19	100%	34	47	19	100%
Group BII	3	20	22	58	100%	27	52	21	100%
Group BIII	3	12	19	68	99%	23	63	13	99%
Solvers	9	65	22	13	100%	53	32	15	100%
Non-solvers	10	23	24	52	99%	29	44	26	99%

Regarding the quality of the attributions, the three experimental groups differ greatly, in that whereas the Group N couples are characterized by constructive attributions, the Group B couples are characterized by destructive ones. In Group S the attributions are more evenly distributed over the three categories, this being in perfect accordance with the above hypothesis. However, again sub-group BI turns out to adhere to the Group N pattern, and sub-group BII and particularly sub-group BIII demonstrate a very destructive behavior in these critical moments of the communication process (in that respectively 58 % and 68 % of their acts of attribution were classified as destructive). Furthermore, the solvers are characterized by constructive, and the non-solvers by destructive, attributions.

Regarding the other spouse's reactions to the attributions made, the differences are even more revealing. In Group N the other spouse takes a stand, in that the proposed attribution is either accepted or rejected. In the Group S couples there is a surprisingly high proportion (32%) of cases in which the attribution proposed is either ignored or neglected. This means in plain words that every third explicit attempt made by either of the spouses to unravel their communication difficulties is ignored by the other spouse. This fact may be interpreted as reflecting the tendency toward pseudo-mutuality and as-if communication reported in families containing schizophrenic members (Wynne et al., 1957, Sølvberg & Blakar, 1975). Finally, the Group B couples are characterized by ambiguous reactions in which they do not take a stand, or the answer implies both a 'yes' and a 'no'. In more than half of the cases when an explicit attempt is made by either of the spouses to unravel their communication difficulties, the other spouse in Group B gives an ambiguous reaction. Interestingly enough, the Group B solvers (sub-group BI) do not adhere to the Group N pattern at this point, although they are not as extreme as the other Group B couples.

A closer examination on individual couple level corroborates the qualitatively different patterns of attribution identified. For example, only seven of the 20 couples showed a higher proportion than 50 % destructive attributions, but all the six non-solving Group B couples (sub-groups BII and BIII) and none of the Group N couples were amongst them.

In only six of the couples was a stand taken (accepted or rejected) in more than 60 % of the attributions proposed; in the remaining 14 a stand was taken in less than 50 % of the cases. All five Group N couples belonged to these six; the last one was the one Group S couple who resolved the induced communication conflict. In fact, this particular Group S couple almost perfectly fitted the average Group N pattern with respect to the quality of the attributions as well as the reactions to them.

In ten of the 20 couples an ambiguous reaction was made to 40 % or more of the attributions proposed. Nine of the 10 Group B couples belonged to these ten. In only three of the 20 couples were more than 40 % of the proposed attributions ignored or neglected. All three belonged to the five Group S couples.

In nine couples fewer than 35 % of the attributions were classified as constructive. None of these nine were amongst the solvers. Correspondingly, none of the nine couples with the highest proportion of destructive attributions were solvers. With respect to the quality of the attributions proposed, all the solvers - irrespective of which group they belonged to - were characterized by the very same pattern, i.e., a relatively high proportion of constructive, and a relatively low proportion of destructive, attributions. With respect to reactions upon the attributions, however, distinctively different patterns were revealed between Group B and Group N solvers. The four solving Group N couples and the one solving Group S couple did take a stand (accepted or rejected) in 80 %, 72 %, 67 % (the S couple), 67 % and 64 % of the cases respectively, as opposed to only 12 %, 32 %, 46 % and 46 % respectively for the four Group B solvers. Hence the solution of the induced communication conflict is evidently reached via highly differential strategies.

Table 9: The distribution (in percentage) of acts of attribution in terms of interaction between type of attribution and type of reaction. (For explanation, see text.)

Type of attribution		Constructive			Irrelevant			Destructive			Total
Type of reaction	N	Taking a stand	Ambiguous response	Neglect	Taking a stand	Ambiguous response	Neglect	Taking a stand	Ambiguous response	Neglect	
Group N	5	45	9	6	13	8	4	12	4	0	101%
Group S	5	24	8	8	5	11	8	13	7	16	100%
Group B	10	8	14	4	6	10	5	14	29	10	100%
Group BI	4	20	34	5	9	5	8	5	8	6	100%
Group BII	3	7	10	3	5	11	6	15	31	12	100%
Group BIII	3	3	7	2	4	13	2	16	43	9	99%
Solvers	9	37	22	6	11	5	6	5	5	3	100%
Non-solvers	10	11	6	6	5	13	6	13	25	14	99%

In order to grasp the interaction at these critical moments of the communication process, we have in Table 9 presented the combined scoring, where every act of attribution is scored in terms of both quality of attribution and type of reaction. In total, nine different categories result (3 qualities of attribution x 3 types of reactions). To visualize how different the patterns of interaction at these critical moments of communication really were, we have in Figure 5 presented the theoretically most interesting categories. We have left out the 'irrelevant attributions', because it is not easy to say how such irrelevant attributions will actually influence the communication process. Furthermore, it is argued that the essential question regarding the reaction is whether or not a clear stand is taken; hence only four critical categories result: constructive/destructive attributions on which a clear stand is/is not taken by the other. It can easily be imagined how the communication process will develop differently, depending upon whether it is characterized by 'constructive attributions on which a clear stand is taken' or by 'destructive attributions on which no clear stand is taken'. The different patterns of interaction at these critical moments of the communication process of the Groups S, N and B couples are clearly revealed in Figure 5. When the potential monitoring and corrective function of the attribution process (cf. above) is realized, it becomes evident that highly different cooperation climates and communication processes will result in the three experimental groups.

Furthermore, the different patterns revealed in Table 9 and Figure 5 seem to bear directly upon the three experimental groups. The pattern of the solving Group B couples (sub-group BI) deviates from the Group N pattern, and the non-solving Group B and the S couples demonstrate distinctively different patterns.

Particularly with respect to the spouses' reactions to the other spouse's attributions, different styles of communication are revealed in the three experimental groups. In the Group N couples the predominant reaction is to take a stand irrespective of whether the other spouse's attribution is constructive, irrelevant, or destructive. In the Group B couples - and this holds for all the three sub-groups - the predominant reaction pattern is an ambiguous response irrespective of whether the spouse's attribution is constructive, irrelevant, or destructive. In the Group S couples the reaction pattern covaries with the quality of the other spouse's attribution: if the attribution is constructive a stand is taken, if the attribution is destructive it is neglected or ignored.

By taking a stand to the other's attributions, the Group N couples render critical evaluation and appropriate change of their communication pattern possible. By the highly frequent ambiguous responses to each other's attributions in the Group B couples, the potential clarifying aspect of the attribution is spoiled or destroyed, and the uncertainty reflected at these critical moments of communication is enhanced instead of reduced. Finally, the tendency to pretend as if we communi-

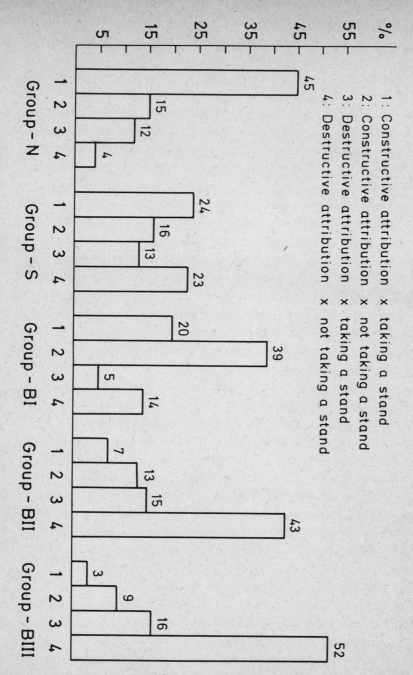

Figure 5: The interaction at the moments of attribution described in terms of 'type of attribution' x 'type of reaction'. (For explanation, see text.)

cate adequately is again reflected in the pattern of the Group S couples: they take a stand when the attribution is constructive, but do not seem to manage the challenge of destructive attributions and consequently ignore or neglect these attributions made by the spouse.

On the average, the 20 couples in the total sample continued 3.1 (0-18) times past the error on the maps. However, the Group S couples continued past the error almost three times (on an average 7.2 times) as often as the Groups N and B couples (respectively 2.0 and 2.6 times on an average). The Group S couples' ignorance of the discrepancy underlying their communication is typical of the as if attitude reported in the communication of families containing schizophrenic members (cf. Sølvberg & Blakar, 1975, Mossige, Pettersen & Blakar, 1976). The Group S couples seem to behave as if they understand each other even in situations when it is clear to an out-side observer that they obviously cannot understand each other.

Again, a development over time was found in the Group N couples, but not in the two psychopathology groups. None of the Group N couples continued past the error in the last third of the time spent in the situation, whereas they had all continued past the error at least once in the first or the second third of the time spent. The Group S couples demonstrated a high and stable frequency of the number of times they continued past the error: 2.2 times in the first, 2.8 times in the second, and 2.2 times in the last third of the time spent in the situation.

A closer examination of the Group B couples reveals a complex picture. First and foremost, of the 20 couples in the total sample only 4 never continued past the error. All these 4 belonged to Group B. On the other hand, 3 of the Group B couples revealed a pattern typical of the Group S couples in that they many times (4, 5, and 9 times respectively) continued past the error. However, these sub-groups do not in any simple manner fit into the three sub-groups into which we have above divided the Group B couples on the basis of their communication efficiency. Of the 4 solvers (sub-group BI) two never continued past the error, whereas the other two fitted the Group N pattern. And the two Group B couples continuing most frequently past the error did not belong to sub-group BII, adhering to the general Group S pattern, but to sub-group BIII.

On the average, the 20 couples returned 12.1 (3-23) times to the starting point. In terms of mere number of returns, there were no systematic differences between the groups. The Group S couples returned 15.6 (8-23) times, on an average, as compared to 10.8 (3-22) and 11.0 (6-21) times in Groups B and N respectively. This apparent difference is mostly due to the fact that Group S (4 non-solvers) has the longest mean time spent in the situation, and does not necessarily reflect systematic group differences regarding, e.g., rigidity in the pattern of communi-cation.

By returning to the starting point, commonality is re-established. But if intersubjectivity is to be maintained in the new trial(s) following the return(s), something ought to be done at these critical points in order to improve the basis for their intersubjectivity in the communication. Hence, it may come as a surprise that as frequently as at every fourth (26 %) return to the starting point, the couples do not make any explicit attributions of their communication difficulties. The Group B couples make relatively few (20 %) returns without explicit attributions as compared to Groups S (31 %) and N (33 %). It may come as a great surprise that the Group N couples have a higher proportion of returns without explicit attributions than the two psychopathology groups. However, when development over time is taken into account, Group N reveals a pattern distinctively different from both Groups S and B. In Groups S and B no development over time is found. Their proportion of returns without explicit attributions is the same in the first as in the last third of the total number of returns made, i.e., a relatively high proportion in Group S and a relatively low proportion in Group B. On the contrary, a development over time is found in the Group N couples, starting with a very high proportion (47%) in the first third of the returns and decreasing to a very low proportion (16%) in the last third.

The flexibility in or change of communication strategy found in the Group N couples, as opposed to the rigidity or lack of change in both of the two psychopathology groups, may reflect the N couples' ability to cope adequately with the demands of the communication situation. The first time(s) communication difficulties are encountered in the present experimental situation it seems reasonable, in mutual understanding, tacitly to ascribe the difficulties to the obvious complexity of the (experimental) route. However, when they repeatedly run into trouble, an 'explanation' is needed. Only the Group N couples manage to cope with these over time changing demands of the interaction situation.

Furthermore, the lack of flexibility and change over time reflects different communication patterns and styles in Groups S and B. The constantly low proportion of returns without explicit attribution in Group B may reflect these couples' preoccupation with communication difficulties, whereas the constantly high proportion in Group S may reflect these couples' ignorance of or withdrawal from communication difficulties encountered.

This latter point may be corroborated by examining the ratio of the total number of explicit attributions made to the number of returns. On the average, the Group N couples returned 11.0 times to the starting point, and made 15.6 attributions, thus yielding a ratio of 1.4 attributions per return. If we à priori do take - as we argued above - the ratio of Group N to be 'optimal' in the present situation, Group B is found to have a too high ratio (22 attributions to 10.8 returns, giving a ratio of 2.0 attributions per return) and Group S a too low ratio (20 attributions to 15.6 returns, giving a ratio of 1.2 attributions per return) respectively.

Most interestingly, this ratio of the total number of attributions to the number of returns proves not to be correlated to communication efficiency. The 9 solvers (4 N, 1 S, and 4 B couples) have a ratio of 1.7 attributions per return, whereas the 10 non--solvers (6 B and 4 S couples) have a ratio of 1.6. On the other hand, the ratio - reflecting the degree of preoccupation with communication difficulties - seems to bear upon the different experimental groups. This is clearly reflected in the fact that the three Group B sub-groups demonstrated the same high ratio: 2.0, 2.0, and 2.1 attributions per return in sub-groups BI, BII and BIII respectively. Finally, this ratio corroborates the different communication patterns of the Group B as compared to the Group N solvers (cf. above), in that the Group B solvers demonstrate a high ratio (2.0), as compared to the Group N solvers (1.3).

Finally, a very simple registration of every utterance explicitly expressing resignation, or that the couple wants to give up, gave additional information about the cooperation climate of the communication in the present situation. On the average, the couples made 2.9 such utterances of resignation. However, the range (from 0 to 13 times) was large. The Group N couples made only 0.4 (0-2) such utterances, as compared to 3.0 (0-10) and 5.0 (0-8) for Groups B and S respectively. However, none of the 9 solvers made any such utterance of resignation, whereas 9 of the 10 non-solvers made one or more (5.4 such utterances on an average for the non-solvers).

In the discussion the theoretical-methodological and the substantial aims of the present study (cf. the introduction) cannot - and should not - be kept entirely apart. For example, in discussing the methodological issues bearing upon the problem of different demand characteristics in resarch of this kind (see Part I p. 48-51, and Haley, 1972, Blakar, 1975a, 1978a), one has to analyze the communication patterns of the different couples, which actually reflects the substantial issue of the present study. In other words, in answering the question whether or not the differences found between Groups S and N couples (Sølvberg & Blakar, 1975) are due to methodological errors only (i.e., different demand characteristics), one is thereby forced to answer the substantial question bearing upon whether or not the Group B couples demonstrate a communication pattern different from the Group S couples. Hence the essential question of the present study is whether the findings done 'carry any implications for the subordinate classes' Groups S versus B couples, or whether they merely 'relate to the superordinate distinction between people (here their parents) under psychiatric care and people outside it' (cf. Bannister's arguments quoted above).

However exploratory it may be, we feel that the present study has really revealed <u>different</u> communication styles and patterns <u>typical of each of the three experimental Groups N, S, and B couples</u>. If, on the basis of having listened to the tapes over and over again, in addition to having conducted the above presented systematic analyses, we were to say <u>what</u> is typical of the communication pattern of each of the three different groups of parental couples, we would start by under-lining <u>the lack of development over time</u> that characterizes the communication of the Group S and B couples, as compared to the Group N couples. It should immediately be added that this is almost the only characteristic common to the two psycho-pathology groups as opposed to the Group N couples. On most other aspects the two groups deviate in <u>different</u> ways from the pattern typical of the Group N couples.

Underlying the different patterns of communication revealed in the above analyses, there seems to be a fundamental difference with respect to what may be called 'the basic dynamics' of communication. In order to establish intersubjectivity and make communication possible at all, one has <u>to believe</u> in the possibility of communication. It may be argued that successful communication is rendered possible by a 'self-ful-filling prophesy' (cf. Rommetveit, 1979b, 1979d, in press). <u>In believing</u> in the possibility of making something known to each other (i.e., of communicating), the participants in the act of communicating render communication possible. In a way, but in distinctively different ways, <u>both</u> the Group B <u>and</u> the Group S couples seem to fail at this basic dynamic aspect of communication.

The Group S couples ignore and neglect the communication difficulties, pretending <u>as if</u> they understand each other. Their own communicative behavior thus hinders all potential unravelling of the underlying communication difficulties and consequent re-establishing of intersubjectivity. However, their monotonous 'yes', 'uhm', etc., following the spouses' vague and egocentric (cf. Sølvberg & Blakar, 1975, Mossige, Pettersen & Blakar, 1976, Kristiansen, 1976, Kristiansen, Faleide & Blakar, 1977) explanations, do <u>not</u> give the impression that they <u>themselves</u> really believe in this perfect mutual understanding. On the contrary, we as observers and listeners have a strong feeling that they fear the confrontation in such critical moments of communi-cation difficulties, <u>because</u> - for reasons unknown to us - the confrontation will merely once again remind them about <u>the impossibility of the two of them communi-cating together</u>. Their interaction is characterized by <u>resignation</u>. If we should try to make explicit the intention possibly underlying their communication, it might be something like: 'The best we can do is to pretend/behave <u>as if</u> we understand each other.' In simple, straightforward situations, as in the practice route, this stra-tegy may prove successful. However, in interaction situations requiring critical evaluation of and change in the pattern of communication, their resignation or lack of confidence in the possibility of the two of them communicating together naturally makes them ignore or neglect (most of) the communication difficulties encountered, thereby hindering maintenance of intersubjectivity and further fruitful communication.

Whereas the behavior of the Group S couples appears to be monitored by an intention to communicate, otherwise their pretending as if could not possibly be understandable, the Group B couples to a large extent seem to be undertaking quite another project. For reasons unknown to us, the Group B couples seem most of all to be preoccupied in fighting each other. Sometimes they join forces, but then in order to fight the surrounding world (here represented by the experimenter). As was mentioned above and corroborated by different findings, the Group B solvers as opposed to the Group N solvers were characterized more by their fighting the experimenter than by themselves working their way through the induced communication conflict.

In direct contrast to the Group S couples, who ignored or withdrew from the communication difficulties, the Group B couples almost seemed to focus on and be preoccupied with communication difficulties. Typical enough, when no difficulties are induced by the interaction situation, as was the case on the simple practice route, they themselves may create their own communication conflicts. And unlike the Group N couples, the Group B couples did not seem to focus on the communication difficulties in order to resolve and unravel them. On the contrary, the communication conflicts seemed to be welcomed as 'tests' in an ever ongoing fight in order to prove the incapability or disqualification of the spouse. Attributions of communication difficulties were used more as weapons against the spouse (or the surrounding world/the experimenter) than in constructive attempts to unravel the communication difficulties encountered.

Underlying the communication of the Groups S and B couples as opposed to the Group N couples, there seems thus to be a lack of mutual confidence in each other. In the Group B couples the communication process even seems to be flavored by an overt, mutual distrust. This is in contrast to the Group S couples, in which the communication process seems to be characterized more by a lack of confidence (lack of confidence in oneself as well as in one's spouse).

Now that the success or failure in the present communication conflict situation of altogether more than 100 couples or families has been analyzed (for reviews, see Part III, and Blakar, 1978a, b), the critical influence exerted upon the communication process by cognitive and motivational, as well as emotional, factors has been demonstrated (cf. Moberget & Reer, 1975, Fætten & Østvold, 1975, Rotbæk, 1976, Haarstad, 1976, Øisjøfoss, 1976, Teigre, 1976, Kristiansen, 1976, Endresen, 1977). For example, Kristiansen (1976), in his analysis of the degree of egocentrism (versus decentration) in the communication of parental couples, found that he had to distinguish between egocentrism resulting from cognitive factors (they seemed not to be <u>capable</u> of decentering and taking each other's perspective) and from emotional/motivational factors (they seemed to be capable, but they <u>would not</u> or they <u>dared not</u> decenter and take each other's perspective). Naturally, these distinctions are analytical only; in practice the communication process is a product of an interaction among these factors. (Cf. how anxiety produced cognitive rigidity in the communication in the present conflict situation; Stokstad, Lagerløv & Blakar, 1976, see also p. 136 - 145.)

The relative failure of the Group B couples as compared to the Group N couples in the present communication conflict situation seems obviously to be due to moti- vational/emotional factors, whereas the helplessness of the Group S couples may make one question their (cognitive) capabilities to communicate. The almost im- pressive verbal fluency and the relatively higher educational and socio-economic level of the Group B couples do not suggest any lack of cognitive capabilities. On the other hand, the high proportion of communication difficulties among themselves in the simple situation (the practice route) points directly toward motivational/ emotional factors in the couples' <u>relation</u> underlying the communication situation.

An outside observer may get the impression that they, even for briefer periods - will not or dare not 'give up' their own premisses and perspectives to the extent necessary to establish <u>shared</u> premisses on which further communication may be based. On the contrary, they continually explicitly question the premisses held and the proposals made by the spouse. To accept their spouses's premisses and per- spectives seems to be felt almost like 'giving up oneself and totally surrendering'. In contrast, the Group N couples are characterized by a mutual give-and-take attitude in their attempts at establishing shared premisses on which the communi- cation may prove to work. They seemed not to feel threatened by accepting the premisses and proposals of the other spouse. They seemed not even to experience it as threatening - either to oneself or to the relationship - to accept that 'it is my fault that we missed again'. This naturally does not imply that the Group N couples did not get angry with each other, and that they did not wrangle. They did! But unlike the wrangling of the Group B couples, in which the conflict and the wrangling almost seemed to be their main 'common' project, the wrangling of the Group N couples represented steps or stages on their way toward an unravelling of the induced communication conflict.

On the surface, the communication pattern of the Group S couples seemed more 'normal', i.e., more similar to the communication pattern typical of the Group N couples. Unlike the Group B couples they did not express any overt suspicion toward the experimenter's integrity; they did not 'attack' the experimenter; they did not openly wrangle all the time question whatever the spouse proposed; and first and foremost, in the simple situation they revealed a communication efficiency, with respect to mean time as well as range - almost identical to that of the Group N couples.

The Group S couples' mastering of the communication task as such testified to on the simple practice route stands out in striking contrast to their helplessness and almost complete failure with respect to the induced communication conflict. However, their mastering of the task as such makes us hesitate to attribute their helplessness in the conflict communication situation (the experimental route) to a lack of (cognitive) capatilities to communicate. On the contrary, their predominant tendency to pretend 'as if we understand each other' - even in situations when it is evident to an outside observer that they do not - points toward motivational/ emotional factors in the couples' relation underlying the communication situation.

However preliminary, the findings of the present study suggest that the different types of communication difficulties of the parental couples with a schizophrenic or a borderline offspring respectively may reflect differential patterns of motivational/emotional factors defining their relationship.

EGOCENTRISM AND INEFFICIENCY IN THE COMMUNICATION OF FAMILIES CONTAINING SCHIZOPHRENIC MEMBERS

Svein Mossige, Rita Bast Pettersen and Rolv Mikkel Blakar [12]

Part I (p.13-53) gives the general historical, theoretical, and methodological backgrounds of the present study. In brief, the point of departure and the final aims of the present study may be summarized as follows: (0) We believe that the communication perspective is a fruitful one in the study of psychopathology in general and of schizophrenia in particular, but that this branch of research has suffered from the use of an implicit and vague concept of communication. (1) Starting from a general communication theory, Blakar (1973a) developed a method directed toward an identification of some prerequisites for communication, and (2) Sølvberg & Blakar (1975) showed that this method was sensitive to differences in the communication of parental couples with and without a schizophrenic child. The present study, therefore, aims (3) at a replication of the Sølvberg & Blakar study, while at the same time we (4) will widen the scope and investigate the communication pattern of parental couples together with their schizophrenic/normal child. Sølvberg & Blakar (1975) not only testified to differences in efficiency of communication, but the analysis also suggested intriguing qualitative differences. Hence the most important aim of the present study is (5) to carry out a more systematic analysis of the qualitative differences in the communication patterns of the different families.

The method, its theoretical background and our modifications

In the present study Blakar's standardized communication conflict situation was employed. A presentation of the method, its theoretical background, and the rationale of this clinical application is given in Part I (p. 26-32). The results from the exploratory Sølvberg & Blakar study (see Part I, p. 32-47) were so promising that they inspired various further studies. (For an overview, see Part III and Blakar, 1975a, 1978a.) Even though nothing definite can be said with respect to causality on the basis of this type of study (cf. Blakar, 1974a, Blakar & Nafstad, 1980b) a most natural extension is to examine the communication of the parents together with the referent person him(her)self. Also historically the parent-child triad has become the 'natural' (but alas, not very frequently researched) unit within communication-oriented research on psychopathology. This is clearly reflected in the following quotation from Haley's (1959, p. 358) account of the development in the field:

A transition would seem to have taken place in the study of schizophrenia; from the early idea that the difficulty in these families was caused by the schizophrenic member, to the idea that they contained a pathogenic mother, to the discovery that the father was inadequate, to the current emphasis upon all three family members involved in a pathological system of interaction. (Our italics.)

Since the number of participants was to be expanded from two (only the parents) to three (the referent person and the parents), the roles in the communication situation had to be reconsidered. We chose to place the parents in the role of the explainer (i.e., with the map with the routes marked in), and the patient in the role of the receiver (i.e., with the map with no routes marked in). We felt that this would most resemble the structure in ordinary parent-child situations. Further, we chose to give the parents one copy of their map only. This to ensure that they could not 'retreat' each behind his or her own map, but had to cooperate in making the two routes known to their child.

Compared to the exploratory Sølvberg & Blakar study (see p.32-47), we tightened up on the termination criteria in the communication conflict situation, and we used the criteria as described by Hultberg, Alve & Blakar in the preceding chapter (see p. 75-76).

On the basis of pretests indicating that the communication task seemed to be more complicated with three than with only two participants, the length of time was expanded from 40 to 50 min. It has to be underlined that the experimenter was instructed not to stop immediately at the 50 min limit if any solution was in sight or any constructive changes in the pattern of communication were taking place; he could then continue ' to see what happened'. Hence, the time limit (50 min) is primarily an analytical criterion that is applied in the analysis afterwards.

Analyses and hypotheses

We define communication as to make common (communicare) (cf. Part I, p. 18-19). Hence, the general purpose of the present study is to examine the process by which the members of differential families (families with and without a schizophrenic member) make something known to each other. More specifically, we intended to test the efficiency of this particular process, as well as to identify and investigate qualitative aspects of the communication process in the different types of families.

Consequently, three different types of analysis were planned and conducted on the tape-recorded familial interactions:

I: Quantitative measures (time used, number of returns to the starting point, etc.) reflecting efficiency and style in communication.

II: Blind-scoring of the tapes.

III: A detailed analysis of some theoretically relevant qualitative aspects of communication.

All the three types of scoring represented natural continuations of Sølvberg & Blakar's study, and particularly the third analysis (III) represented a substantial extension.

I: As a measure of efficiency in communication we simply registered the time each family triad used on each of the two communication tasks, and on the complicated route, whether they resolved the induced communication conflict according to the predetermined criteria. On the basis of previous studies (Haley, 1967 a, b, 1968, 1972, Murell & Stachowiack, 1967, Sølvberg & Blakar, 1975) we expected the Group S families to show a more inefficient communication than the control families. The present experimental method, involving two apparently similar, but in reality highly different, communication settings, in that the one is simple and straightforward, whereas the other one induces a communication conflict, put us in a favorable position with respect to specifying our hypothesis regarding efficiency of communication under various conditions (cf. Part I, and Blakar, 1978a, Stokstad, Lagerløv & Blakar, 1976, 1979). The inefficiency of the Group S families compared to the Group N families will be particularly revealing in cooperation situations that are vague and complicated, requiring critical evaluation of and change in the communication pattern, i.e., the difference will be most pronounced on the complicated route, where the communication conflict is induced. With respect to the simple route, we were in severe doubt. First, in Sølvberg & Blakar's study the two groups of parental couples did equally well. On the other hand, the participation of the patient member made us expect the Group S families to be more inefficient even on the simple route.

II: Since the present study is highly exploratory, and we are just as interested in generating as in testing hypotheses, the following more open analysis was included: Three communication-oriented students trained in clinical psychology were given the tape-recordings, and asked (a) to describe the interaction, and (b) on the basis of their descriptions to predict which of the families contained a schizophrenic member. Because the families' degree of success in the conflict situation on the experimental route could possibly betray some of the Group S families, the scorers were given the recordings of the simple practice route only.

III: We have elsewhere (Blakar, 1975e, 1978a, Blakar & Nafstad, 1980a) argued that methods and concepts to be employed in communication-oriented studies of psycho-pathology should be anchored (a) in a general theory of communication as well as (b) in characteristics of the specific category of psychopathology on which attention is being focused. And we have claimed (Blakar, 1975e, 1978f) that the lack of progress in the field is primarily caused by lack of a general theory of communication. (For critical reviews, see Haley, 1972, Riskin & Faunce, 1972, Jacobsen & Pettersen, 1974, Blakar, 1976a).

However, if one turns to social-developmental psychology, a whole set of relevant and theoretically grounded concepts offer themselves. In Part I (p. 46-47) various examples on such concepts were given.

In the present study we chose to analyze and describe the communication in terms of the family members' degree of egocentrism versus decentration throughout the communication process. This choice reflects the above-mentioned preferred two-fold anchoring. First, the ability and/or willingness to decenter (at least to some extent) and take the perspective of the other person(s) is a basic prerequisite for successful communication, and extreme egocentrism may strongly hinder communication. In particular, when problems are encountered in the communication process, a minimum of decentration is required in order to re-establish shared premises for further communication. Secondly, an earlier study within our project (Sølvberg & Blakar, 1975) indicated that egocentrism may be a particularly significant characteristic of communication in the schizophrenic's family. Apart from this study, however, we have come across no studies on communication and schizophrenia explicitly applying the concept of egocentrism versus decentration, although for example Lidz (1973) has applied the concept of egocentrism in theoretical accounts of the interaction in the schizophrenic's family. However, many phenomena said to be typical of the schizophrenic's family may easily be covered by the concept of egocentrism. Only a few examples will be offered as illustrations. Thus Morris & Wynne (1965, p. 35) described the attention in parental couples with a schizophrenic offspring as being characterized by 'an unwarranted assumption of shared meaning'. This was expressed by their 'assuming mutual understanding which has not grown out of the preceding interaction'. Lennard et al. (1965, p. 176) point out that the parents of schizophrenics are rather insensitive to 'the child's effort to join their interaction, however limited it might be'. Thus Fleck et al. write about the 'narcissistic communication' barriers characteristic in schizophrenic families by which: 'certain mothers - or fathers - are quite incapable of responding spontaneously to their children's behavior unless the parent has evoked such behavior. Thus, a parent may respond to a young child's behavior only if it is elicited by the parent'.

Decentration in communication is characterized by the fact that the sender antecipates the receiver's decoding, takes the receiver's perspective into account, and encodes on the receiver's premises. The following statement where the sender tries to describe a point on the map, is an example: '... then you come to a crossing, there you are in the upper left-hand corner of a rectangle which is to your right under the crossing...'.

Egocentrism, on the contrary, is characterized by the fact that the participants do not take each other's perspective, and do not speak and listen, respectively, on each other's premises. In a situation resembling the one just mentioned in the above example, an egocentric statement would be: ' ... and then you go down here and across there, and then you come to a crossing ... '.

Our use of the concept of egocentrism is inspired by Piaget's (1926) analysis of children's language, but the concept's more social flavour is influenced by Mead's (1934) 'the generalized other'. Only by the communicants taking the perspective of the other(s) into account, so that they (sender and receiver) may establish commonality, is conversation or communication rendered possible.

In addition to the actual lack of sharing of perspectives, there is another important aspect of egocentric communication, i.e. that this lack is constantly covered up in that the communicants act as if their communication were not egocentric. 'Egocentrism ... is characterized by an underlying postulate that the other always sees and keeps the same thing in mind as oneself, i.e., by an unreflected presupposed convergence of memory and attention between speaker and listener' (Rommetveit, 1972a, p. 48-49. Our translation.)

The concept of egocentrism/decentration may thus be applied to characterize both the persons involved (he/she is egocentric) and the communication process itself (the communication is egocentric, cf. Blakar, 1974c, 1977). That these two levels do not necessarily coincide, may be seen from the following example. If a person (sender) is egocentric in his way of speaking, this can be compensated for by a particularly decentered receiver, so that the communication may nevertheless flow tolerably well. This is for example often the case in child-adult interactions.

So far in theory. Our problem was how to operationalize and score degree and development over time of egocentrism and decentration in the communication pattern of our sample of interacting family triads. Two extremely different approaches might be considered. One might listen to the tape-recordings and assess the total communication of each family on a scale expressing degree of egocentrism/decentration. Concretely, this could for example be done by a rank-ordering procedure whereby the families were rank-ordered with respect to degree of egocentrism/decentration. On the other hand, each single utterance might be scored with respect to decentration/egocentrism (e.g., on a scale varying from +3 to -3), and mean scores and development over time could be calculated for each family triad as well as for each family member. However, whereas the first procedure would tend to camouflage the very problem and not contribute substantially to an understanding of the type and degree of egocentrism in the two types of families, the latter procedure would be almost meaningless, in that a major part of the individual utterances could not reasonably be scored as being either egocentric or decentered. The latter procedure would hence lead to entirely artificial scoring.

Consequently, the following scoring procedure was developed. We chose the utterance as our unit of analysis. Instead of assessing every single utterance as being egocentric/decentered, however, the first step of the analysis was to identify from the tapes every single utterance which, on the basis of the ongoing communication process, could be assessed as markedly egocentric or decentered respectively. In order to develop a 'standard' for 'markedly egocentric/decentered' in the actual communication situation, the scorer listened over and over again to earlier tapes from the very same experimental situation. For each such egocentric/decentered utterance, furthermore, the interaction sequence in which it appeared, the point of time at which it appeared, as well as the family member who uttered it, were registered.

By means of this procedure, the number of respectively egocentric and decentered utterances found will naturally vary from family to family. In order to compare the style of communication over families or groups of families, the ratio between the number of egocentric to decentered utterances has to be used. And this ratio of egocentric to decentered utterances in the first versus the last part of the time spent, finally, gives us a picture of development over time.

The most obvious objection against this procedure is that some (markedly) egocentric/decentered utterances may be overlooked. However, the absolute number of such utterances in this particular experimental situation is of negligible theoretical interest. More important is the general problem of applying such a scale consistently over all the families.

Two methodological problems have to be mentioned in particular, because they reflect profound theoretical implications bearing directly upon the very nature of egocentrism in communication.

First, in assessing an utterance as being egocentric/decentered, the wider context and the communication process as such has to be taken into account. Only on the basis of what the participants at a certain point of time have established as a shared social reality (Rommetveit, 1974, Blakar & Rommetveit, 1975), can anything said be assessed as egocentric/decentered. Hence, the scorer has to follow the communication process carefully over time in order to 'know' at each point of time what the participants may tacitly take for granted. And this leads us to the second problem, i.e., that the scorer is an outside observer to the communication process, with no immediate access to the participant's experience. A particularly salient fallacy for such an outside observer is to judge as egocentric a sequence of communication that actually is characterized by ellipsis (Rommetveit, 1974, Strøno, 1978) and thus in a way reflects almost perfect commonality on behalf of the participants.

Concerning hypotheses, it follows from what was said above, that we expect the communication of the Group S families to be more egocentric and less decentered, i.e., that the ratio of egocentric to decentered utterances will be higher than in the Group N families. Furthermore, we expect that the Group N families, when encountering the induced communication conflict, will become more decentered in order to resolve it. Hence, in the Group N families a development over time toward a more decentered communication will be expected. However, we do not expect the Group S families to possess this capacity and/or willingness to respond to the induced communication conflict by a more decentered attitude. On the contrary, it may even be that as the communication conflict is encountered, the family members will stick even more firmly to their own individual perspectives, and thus the communication may become even more egocentric (cf. Stokstad, Lagerløv & Blakar, 1976, 1979, Kristiansen, Faleide & Blakar, 1977).

The sample and the matching

An important issue in this exploratory study was to establish two comparable groups, one consisting of families with a schizophrenic member (Group S), and one matched control group without (Group N). During this exploratory research we chose to limit ourselves to small, but heavily controlled and strictly matched, groups.

First, we concentrated on establishing Group S. Since Lidz's (1957, 1958) research indicates that the interaction pattern in families containing schizophrenic members varies with the sex of the patient member, we chose to restrict ourselves to schizophrenics of one sex only. For practical reasons this happened to be families with a schizophrenic daughter. For our choice of S-families we used mainly the same criteria as Sølvberg & Blakar (1975, p. 523). The definition of schizophrenia is that generally held within Norwegian psychiatry, i.e., according to Kraepelin. Our point of departure was that the reference person (the daughter) in Group S had been diagnosed as being a schizophrenic at the psychiatric institution, and that there should be no doubt with regard to the diagnosis. [13] The latter is one of the reasons why we at the present stage of our research have chosen to restrict ourselves to small, but heavily controlled, samples (cf. Blakar & Nafstad, 1980a).

The use of the diagnostic category entailed that all reference persons would be over 15 years old. We put the upper age-limit at 30 - and within this range we sought the youngest possible reference persons to ensure that they had not been separated from their families for too long. Since we were to study the interaction in the parent-child triad, it was important that they really lived together.

The parental home should represent the reference person's primary group, and she must have been living at home until her 16th birthday. The reference person had to be unmarried and childless, and absence from home should only be in connection with school, work, etc. To avoid as far as possible the potential influence of the socialization effect from longer periods in psychiatric institutions (Goffman, 1961), we preferred reference persons with the shortest possible period of psychiatric hospitalization. In order not to exclude too many families with a schizophrenic daughter, we decided that a maximum of four years could have passed since her first hospitalization. Finally, neither of the reference person's parents were to have been given any psychiatric diagnosis, and they had to be the reference person's biological parents.

Having scanned our pool of potential subjects in the hospital's archive of schizophrenic patients, we identified six female patients as satisfying the above criteria. All these patients and their parents agreed to participate in the study.

Having established Group S, much effort was put into establishing a matching Group N. Ideally, each of the matching N families were to be 'identical' with the respective S family, apart from the fact that the daughter in the S family should be schizophrenic. Variables such as age, number of years of marriage, education, employment, social group, annual income, domicile, living conditions, number of children and their sex and age, were all satisfactorily matched. (For further details on the matching, see Jacobsen & Pettersen, 1974, p. 92-96.) Group N therefore represented a 'normal group' in the sense that they constituted comparable ordinary families without problems that had led any of the family members into contact with treatment or penal institutions. Nothing else is implied by 'normality' in this case.

Presentation and discussion of results

As was the case in the earlier studies with student subjects and married couples, all the families became absorbed and involved in the communication task.

All the 12 families managed the simple practice route, i.e., the daughter reached the predetermined end-point via the correct route by means of the parents' explanations. However, variation in time spent (ranging from 1 min 45 sec to 15 min 15 sec) indicates that the task was by no means equally simple for all of them. Regarding the two different groups, Group S used 9 min 19 sec on an average (ranging from 1 min 45 sec to 15 min 15 sec) as compared to 3 min 46 sec (ranging from 2 min 40 sec to 5 min 23 sec) for Group N. There was thus a tendency, although not significant, toward less efficient communication by the Group S families even in the simple and straightforward situation. Furthermore, the number of returns to the starting-point reflects different styles of co-operation. Whereas the Group N families made on an average 0.8 returns (range 1-0), the Group S families returned 4.3 (range 9-0) times on an average. This last finding may indicate a more stereotyped and repetitive communication pattern in the Group S families.

Regarding the experimental route with the induced error, only 4 of the 12 families managed to resolve the induced communication conflict according to the predetermined criteria (cf. p.106) within the 50 min limit. Eight of the 12 families

Table 10: Time used (mean and range) on the practice route for the parental
couples with and without a schizophrenic offspring and the family
triads with and without a schizophrenic member

	Group S	Group N
Parental couple (Sølvberg & Blakar's study)	4 min 50 sec (2 min 9 sec - 9 min 56 sec) (N = 5)	4 min 57 sec (2 min 2 sec- 8 min 52 sec) (N = 5)
Family triad (The present study)	9 min 19 sec (1 min 45 sec - 15 min 15 sec) (N = 6)	3 min 46 sec (2 min 40 sec - 5 min 23 sec) (N = 6)

went on for more than 50 min, and consequently were stopped and shown the discrepancy between the maps. None of the families was stopped according to criterion
(4) above. Regarding the two different groups of families, not one of the 6 Group S
families managed to resolve the communication conflict. All the 4 families who did
manage, thus belonged to the 6 Group N families. The 4 solvers used on an average,
30 min 52 sec (ranging from 24 min 0 sec to 39 min 30 sec).

Before more general theoretical implications are discussed, the outcome of the
present study will be directly compared to the Sølvberg & Blakar study of parental
couples with and without a schizophrenic offspring.

Table 11: Distribution of solvers/non-solvers on the experimental route over
parental couples with and without a schizophrenic offspring and family
triads with and without a schizophrenic member

	Group S	Group N	Total
Parental couple (Sølvberg & Blakar's study)	1 solver 4 non-solvers (N = 5)	5 solvers 0 non-solvers (N = 5)	6 solvers 4 non-solvers (N = 10)
Family triad (The present study)	0 solvers 6 non-solvers (N = 6)	4 solvers 2 non-solvers (N = 6)	4 solvers 8 non-solvers (N = 12)
Total	1 solver 10 non-solvers (N = 11)	9 solvers 2 non-solvers (N = 11)	10 solvers 12 non-solvers (N = 22)

As can be seen from Tables 10 and 11, the present study essentially replicates
and extends their findings, the only exception being that the Group S families tend
(not significantly) to communicate less efficiently than the Group N families even in
the simple situation (on the practice route), when the patient member herself participates.

Even though these quantitative measures are intended primarily to serve as a
point of departure for more qualitative analyses (cf. Part I, p. 41), some more
general conclusions regarding communication in the two types of families seem
justified at the present stage.

First and foremost, general conclusions regarding differences in efficiency of
communication between families containing and not containing a schizophrenic
member cannot be formulated without explicit reference to the type(s) of interaction
or cooperation situation (cf. Stokstad, Lagerløv & Blakar, 1976, 1979). At present,
the most appropriate conclusions would be:

If the cooperation situation is vague and complicated, requiring a critical evaluation and change in patterns of communication, families containing a schizophrenic
member do communicate significantly less efficiently than matched control families.
This holds whether the parental couples are alone or together with their schizophrenic offspring.

If the cooperation situation is plain and simple, in the sense that no re-adjustment
from the family's usual pattern of communication is required, then the picture is
more complex. If only the parental couple participate, then no difference is revealed
regarding efficiency of communication. When on the other hand the patient member
herself participates, then there is a tendency for families containing a schizophrenic
member to communicate less efficiently, even in a plain and simple communication
situation.

In trying to explain this latter finding, at least the following three different conditions may be of relevance:

(1) The schizophrenics may really be more inefficient (e.g., regarding cognitive
capacities) than the matched controls.

(2) The parent's expectations and attitudes toward the patient member may hinder
efficient communication.

(3) The three-person constellation (the parent-child triad) is more complex than the
the dyad (the parental couple), and hence even the simple practice route is changed
into a more vague and complicated cooperation situation (cf. our hypotheses above).
This latter hypothesis seems hard to hold in view of the fact that the Group N
family triads are, if anything, even quicker than the Group N parental couples.

The blind-prediction procedure

However rough, the blind-scoring procedure and the scorers' descriptions of each family's communication pattern may yield a first idea about possible qualitative differences in the communication of the two groups. First and foremost, all three scorers correctly identified 5 of the 6 Group S families on the basis of the tape-recorded interaction on the practice route. Furthermore, it was one and the same Group S family which all three scorers failed to identify. This suggests that potential pathological characteristics of communication are highlighted in this experimental situation to such an extent that they can fairly easily be 'seen' by clinical psychologists.

A closer examination of the scorers' descriptions of the communication patterns showed that the Group S families (as compared to the Group N families) were characterized by (a) less ability and/or willingness to listen to and take into account what the others say; (b) less ability and/or willingness to take the perspective of the other(s) (both (a) and (b) are closely connected to degree of egocentrism/ decentration); (c) less adequate confirmations of each other; (d) more pseudo-agreement. These findings are much in line with what has been reported from other studies under varying conditions (e.g., Goldstein & Rodnick, 1975, Herman & Jones, 1976, McPherson et al., 1973, Wynne et al., 1976).

Egocentrism and decentration

On the simple practice route, an average number of 2.8 (range 0-9) egocentric, and an average of 1.7 (range 1-3) decentered, utterances were identified. In Table 12 the ratio of egocentric to decentered utterances for each of the 6 families in the two different groups, is presented. The ratio of egocentric to decentered utterances is much higher (in fact 12 times as high) in the Group S families than in the Group N families. And this is not an artificial product of group means, because in 5 of the 6 Group S families there are more egocentric than decentered utterances (the only exception being S-1, with 0 egocentric and 1 decentered utterance), whereas this pattern is reversed in 5 of the 6 Group N families (the only exception being N-4 with an equal number).

On the experimental route, an average number of 6.5 (range 1-15) egocentric, and an average of 4.3 (range 2-8) decentered, utterances were registered. These relatively low numbers in relation to time spent in the experimental situation confirm that only utterances that in an extreme manner revealed egocentrism or decentration respectively were scored. In Table 13 the ratio of egocentric to decentered utterances for each of the 6 families in the two different groups is presented. Again, the ratio of egocentric to decentered utterances is much higher (in fact four times

Table 12: Ratio of number of egocentric to number of decentered utterances
in each family on the practice route

Family No.	S-1,N-9	S-2,N-8	S-5,N-4	S-7,N-11	S-10,N-3	S-12,N-6	Total
Group S families	0/1	4/1	8/2	2/1	9/1	7/3	30/9 *
Group N families	0/1	1/2	1/1	0/3	1/2	0/2	3/11 *

* $\frac{30}{9} = \frac{330}{99}$; $\frac{3}{11} = \frac{27}{99}$

as high) in the Group S than in the Group N families. In all the 6 Group S families
there are a higher number of egocentric than decentered utterances, in 4 of the
6 Group N families the pattern is reversed. Interesting enough, the 2 Group N
families that conform to the Group S pattern were the very two families that did
not manage to resolve the induced communication conflict.

Table 13: Ratio of number of egocentric to decentered utterances in each
family on the experimental route

Family No.	S-1,N-9	S-2,N-8	S-5,N-4	S-7,N-11	S-10,N-3	S-12,N-6	Total
Group S families	6/5	7/3	13/4	6/2	15/2	7/3	54/19 *
Group N families	4/8	6/5	7/3	1/5	4/6	2/5	24/32 *

* $\frac{54}{19} = \frac{1728}{608}$; $\frac{24}{32} = \frac{454}{608}$

A relevant question then is whether the families demonstrate a stable pattern of
egocentrism/decentration over the two communication situations: the simple practice
route and the experimental route with the induced communication conflict. The 12
families were rank-ordered with respect to ratio of egocentric to decentered
utterances on the two routes. A correlation (rho) of .92 [14] indicates that the degree
of egocentrism/decentration is rather stable.

In order to test for the possible development toward a more egocentric or decentered communication over time, the number of egocentric and decentered utterances
elicited in the first and second half of the time spent on the experimental route were

compared. No development was found in the Group S families, nor in the two non-solving Group N families (N-4 and N-8). However, in the 4 Group N families that resolved the induced communication conflict, a marked tendency toward a higher proportion of decentered utterances was found.

In order to pursue the question concerning the potential influence of egocentrism/ decentration on communication efficiency, the 12 families were rank-ordered with respect to ratio of egocentric to decentered utterances and time used. On the simple practice route a correlation (rho) of .86 was found between ratio of egocentric to decentered utterances and time spent. On the experimental route no such correlation coefficient could be calculated, since 8 of the 12 families did not solve the communication conflict, and thus did not get any real solution time. But the influence of the degree of egocentrism/decentration upon communication efficiency is unequivocally revealed in this more complicated situation too, in that whereas the 4 solvers had more decentered than egocentric utterances, the pattern was reversed for the 8 non-solvers. Regarding the latter analysis, this is not presented as a substantially interesting empirical finding, but more as a test of the adequateness of our operationalizations of the concepts 'communication efficiency' and 'egocentrism/decentration'. According to our theoretical framework (cf. above) a high degree of egocentrism should - by logic - result in inefficient communication.

The above analysis reveals unequivocal differences between families with and without schizophrenic members with respect to egocentrism/decentration in their pattern of communication. However, the above strictly numerical presentation of the findings has covered up the different types of egocentrism that were actually revealed through our detailed analysis. Furthermore, via the above presentation the reader has been given little or no information about how, concretely, egocentrism manifested itself in the communication process. Hence, some more qualitative material will be presented and commented upon.

First and foremost, two qualitatively different types of egocentrism in communication were found. Whereas cases of the first type were found in every single one of the 12 families, the latter type, reflecting a more severe kind of egocentrism, was found in 3 of the 6 Group S families only. Characteristic of the first type is that the speaker in making an utterance tacitly assumes as already known by the receiver and thus assumes as being shared by them something that actually cannot be known by the receiver (at that point of time). In particular, this type of egocentrism is revealed in use of deictic linguistic elements. Words and phrases such as 'here', 'there', 'that corner', 'this street', are used without any intersubjectivity having been established as to what the phrase is actually referring to. This kind of utterance seems to be uttered under the assumptions that 'you are present at the same place as I, and you are seeing and keeping in mind the same things as I'. An

illustrative example is the following utterance made by the father in one of the Group
S families: 'Have you come out on the corner of that street, there ... that line,
there?' In the interaction preceding this utterance, no adequate contract concerning
orientation (cf. Rommetveit, 1972a, 1974, Blakar, 1972a, Blakar & Pedersen, 1978,
Moberget & Reer, 1975) had been endorsed between the father and the daughter
(toward whom the utterance is directed). Therefore, the daughter has no possibility
(apart from mere guessing and intuition) of understanding what is meant by 'that
street, there' and 'that line, there'.

However egocentric, this type of utterance is nevertheless definitely directed or
addressed toward a particular receiver. From the point of view of making something
known to that potential receiver (i.e., to communicate) the inadequacy is that the
sender fails to take the receiver's perspective and anticipate the receiver's decoding
(Mead, 1934, Rommetveit, 1974, Strøno, 1978).

The other type of egocentrism is more pronounced in that the speaker does not
seem to direct or address himself to any particular receiver at all. In its most
pronounced form it resembles a monologue in vacuo, or actually, a set of parallell
monologues (cf. Piaget, 1926). An illustrative example is the following 'interaction'
sequence where mother and daughter alternatively speak politely, but where
neither does the utterance seem to be directed toward any receiver nor does the
'receiver' seem to take into account what is being said:

D: Wait a moment ... one, two, three, four, ... what did you mean now ... what
did you first say?

M: Four - crossroads.

D: Let's see ... there we have a crossing.

M: Yes, there we have one, and there is one, and there is one ...

D: And there is one ...

M: And then you come right out on the corner.

An observer to this 'pseudo-dialogue' or parallel monologues may note that neither
the mother nor the daughter at any point of time seems to test or control whether the
other really understands the message (Blakar, 1973c, Rommetveit & Blakar, 1979).

To us as outside observers, these sequences of interaction gave a strong impression
that the members of these families had in fact given up all attempt at communication,
and had abandoned the possibility of making anything known to each other. (This resignation found in families containing a schizophrenic member stands out in contrast
to the 'combative' attitude revealed in the equally disturbed communication of parents
of borderline patients interacting in the present experimental cooperation situation.
Cf. Hultberg, Alve & Blakar, 1978.) In Mishler & Waxler's (1968) study of interaction
in schizophrenics' families a similar phenomenon was reported. In some of the
families they found that the members talked to each other in a set of successive

monologues - politely, orderly, and rigidly, thus hampering any form of direct confrontation between family members. Rigidity and lack of direct confrontations are outstanding characteristics of the latter type of egocentrism observed in the present study too. The rigid pattern is reflected in the manner in which each member repeats (not necessarily verbatim) his utterances without getting/taking a response from the other(s). And the false and unwarranted assumptions of convergence and commonality hamper any direct and clarifying confrontations.

Rather than marking clearly distinguished categories, the difference between the two types of egocentrism is one of degree. A theoretically interesting and frequently observed intermediate case was observed in connection with endorsement of contracts monitoring the communication process (contracts concerning categorization, perspective, orientation etc., cf. Rommetveit, 1972a, 1974, Blakar, 1972a, 1978a, Moberget & Reer, 1975). Just to illustrate, a critical contract concerning perspective in the present cooperation situation is the one with respect to the use of 'left' and 'right'. 'Left' and 'right' may adequately be exploited from the perspective of the car-driver as well as from the perspective of the speaker (and the listener) as seated at the table. In order to avoid misunderstandings, however, the participants have to endorse - explicitly or implicitly - a contract concerning the use of these terms. The following reply uttered by a university student in the present situation demonstrates how bewildering this issue may really be to all of us, and how essential a contractual monitoring is with respect to (re-)establishing the required intersubjectivity: 'When you say to the right, do you mean to the left to me?' Egocentrism with respect to this particular contract was revealed, for example, in that the parents were encoding from their own perspective as seated at the table, whereas the daughter was decoding from the perspective of the car-driver, or vice versa, or even in that the one and the same family member might without any explicit explanation inconsistently vary with respect to perspective over time.

Whereas the more pronounced type of egocentrism was found in 3 of the 6 Group S families only, examples of the first type were found in all the 12 families. Furthermore, even the egocentrism of the first type was often more pronounced in the Group S families. Typical is the following explanatory utterance elicited by a father in one of the Group S families: 'Drive down ... to the edge there ... and so to that ... that out, uh ... drive down there ... as far as to the house furthest in the middle there ... then you stop there ....'

No intersubjective convergence as to what 'there' and 'that' should mean had grown out of the interaction preceding this utterance. And it is worth noticing that even though such an utterance must have been extremely confusing to the daughter (the one toward whom the utterance is being directed), she did not say that she did not understand the father's explanation. Nor did the mother. In the Group S families there was actually a strong tendency to behave as if one had really understood such egocentric utterances. Thus the communication at these critical points was often characterized by pseudo-agreement (Wynne et al., 1958). In the Group N families, however, the receiver much more frequently responded by pointing out that the actual explanation was unclear, insufficient, not understandable, etc. Sequences of the following type, reflecting both egocentrism on behalf of one family member, and another family member's attempt to diagnose the communicative difficulties and reestablish commonality, were thus characteristic to the Group N families:

M: And then you go up there.

D: Up there ... what do you mean by up there?

There is every reason to believe that egocentric utterances of this type are elicited time and again by every 'normal' speaker. The different reactions to them, however, may partly explain why no development was found toward a more decentered communication over time in the Group S families. Without the corrective feedback that an explanation is really inadequate, it is not unlikely that the explanation will be repeated over and over again. And the tendency by the receiver in the Group N families to point out in various ways that such egocentric utterances imply inadequate explanations may represent a continuous pressure on the speaker to decenter. This may thus explain the change toward the gradually more decentered communication found on the experimental route in the 4 solving Group N families. And the lack of adequate feedback from the receiver in the Group S families may actually reflect that in the Group S families they have more severe difficulties in distinguishing between communicative difficulties resulting from their own behavior (e.g., their egocentrism) and communicative difficulties resulting from external, situational factors (e.g., the erroneous maps). For studies on attribution of communicative difficulties in the present experimental cooperation situation, see Hultberg, Alve & Blakar, 1978, Haarstad, 1976.

The above quantitative results indicated a linkage between degree of egocentrism/decentration and efficiency of communication. This more refined qualitative analysis gave clues as to how, more concretely, egocentrism may severely hamper communication. In two of the six Group S families the daughter was at some phases during the communication process more or less convinced about the inbuilt error on the maps, and explicitly demonstrated (some) insight into the missing prerequisite for successful communication. (In none of the other four Group S families did any of the family members explicitly state or utter any doubt as to the credibility of the maps.) However, neither of the two families managed to reach a joint conclusion on this issue. And in both cases the parents' egocentrism and lack of ability and/or will to take the daughter's perspective seemed to represent the main hindrance. The following two excerpts from the communication in these two families will illustrate:

Example No. 1:

D: No, the maps are quite different.

F: Are they ... ehm ... OK ... then it is a question if the point of departure is ...
ehm ... if we have started from the same point.

Example No. II:

F: But they should be equal.

D: But they are not ... they could have been if it had not been for that line.

F: Yea, but it started ... ehm ... it seemed so straight, ehm ... you come to the
first corner.

D: Yea, but if we accept that the routes on the two maps are different ...

F: Yea, but it then becomes so difficult for us to follow.

In the latter example the father even explicitly states or admits that it is difficult
or impossible for them (the parents) to take her (the daughter's) perspective. Thus
in at least two of the Group S families, at least one of the family members (in both
cases the daughter) seems to be convinced about the deceptive communication situation, but it seems to be almost impossible for these families to carry through the
critical re-evaluation of the ongoing communication required in order to re-establish
the basic preconditions for successful communication. This observation may be
described and understood in terms of the daughter's inability to get her insights
across, as well as in terms of the parent's insensitivity toward their daughter's
messages. However, if system theory ever is appropriate in describing family
interaction, we feel it is in the above critical sequences of communication.

During these two short excerpts of communication, the Group S families
demonstrate that they are closed systems really (cf. e.g., Speer, 1970). In these
sequences where a fundamentally new perspective involving change in and restructur-
ing of their communication is being set forth (the maps are different), the family's
resistance to change, is revealed.

> These family organisms (the family of the schizophrenic, author's comment) grow
> their component parts so that they will fit with predetermined names, roles and
> abstractions - with no responsiveness to individual or environmental growth that
> does not fit with expectations. This kind of family has limited evolutionary power
> ... I have called it a closed system family. (Brodey, 1967, p. 77).

But the family systems - open or closed - are constituted of individual members
with personal characteristics and abilities. And we have found that the family members
constituting the Group S families seem to be significantly more egocentric than the
members consituting the Group N families. And the closed system often reported in
families containing schizophrenic members may thus partly be a product of the egocentrism of the individual members.

That the Group S families represent a closed as opposed to an open system, may

be seen clearly from how the family members in the following excerpt from a Group
N family really are open to each other's perspectives, and thus may mutually profit
on feedback:

F: And you should be in the top corner of a square ... aren't you there?

D: No!

F: Because then you don't have a line upwards towards A, but you have a line down
   towards D.

D: Yes, but there's no square.

F: Yes, go one line more then, so you're perhaps on a square now.

D: No!

At this point we have briefly to comment upon a question that became more and
more urgent to us during the analysis. Are the members of the Group S families
unable to or are they not willing to decenter and take each other's perspective (cf.
Blakar, 1975e, 1978a, Kristiansen, 1976)? At first, this question may seem to be
merely speculative. However, it may prove to be of great practical importance,
e.g., in communication-oriented family therapy. At present, we have no answer
to offer, but we feel that the issue has to be researched. In the present analysis
the concept of egocentrism has been applied in a strictly descriptive fashion. What
we have been describing as egocentrism in communication may thus prove to
represent different conditions. To mention but a few possibilities: in one family the
egocentrism found may reflect a lack of proper cognitive ability to decenter (Piaget,
1926) on behalf of one or more of the family members. In another family the egocentrism may reflect the family members' high level of anxiety, in that each member
is scared of giving up his own perspective (cf. Stokstad, Lagerløv & Blakar, 1976).
Thus our analysis of egocentrism in the family's communication is open to be pursued
in different directions (cf. Part III, and Kristiansen, Faleide & Blakar, 1977, Strøno,
1978, Blakar, Paulsen & Sølvberg, 1978).

Concluding remarks

The present paper cannot be brought to an end without some brief comments on the
most serious methodological shortcomings of the present study. First and foremost,
our samples (6 Group S and 6 Group N families) are small. However, at present the
samples are being enlarged.

More critical than the issue of mere number of families is the fact that all the
reference persons are of one sex (female) only (cf. the theory of Lidz et al. 1957,
1958). In a recent follow-up of the present study, Glennsjø (1977) has compared the
patterns of communication in this situation of families containing male and female
schizophrenics respectively. Her study thus offers an experimental test on Lidz's
theory. As far as her analysis goes, no systematic differences between the two
categories of families was found.

However, most critical is the fact that one diagnostic category (schizophrenia) only was included in the present study. Since the demand characteristics of the experimental situation obviously may be different for the two groups (Group S versus Group N), our findings may represent mere tautologies (cf. Haley, 1972, Blakar, 1975a, 1978a, 1978f). [15] However, the results from a series of recently completed studies applying the same experimental method make this explanation very unlikely, or at least insufficient. For example, Haarstad (1976) found that families containing a daughter given the diagnosis anorexia-nervosa revealed a communication pattern different from both Group N and Group S. If the group differences found could be accounted for by different demand characteristics of the experimental situation, all the various 'pathological' families and parental couples should have behaved more or less similarly - at least such systematic group differences should not have been expected.

Keeping the above-mentioned methodological limitations in mind, we will now return to our original point of departure to see whether any more general conclusions may be drawn on the basis of the present study (see p. 105):

(0). With respect to the study of psychopathology in general and schizophrenia in particular, we feel that the present study has testified to the fruitfulness of the communication approach, provided the concept of communication is defined in terms of general theory. And with respect to qualitative analysis of the communication process, it seems that we have managed to develop a scoring procedure that enables us to assess the degree of egocentrism (decentration) and the development of egocentrism (decentration) over time.

With respect to substantial results, the present study (1) replicates the previously reported finding that families containing schizophrenics communicate less efficiently in cooperation situations than matched controls. However, it now has to be under-lined that nothing may reasonably be concluded concerning a family's or category of families' communication efficiency without explicit reference to the actual communi-cation situation. The communication efficiency of families containing schizophrenics is particularly revealing in vague and complicated communication situations requiring critical evaluation and modification of the habitual communication patterns.

(2) With respect to qualitative differences in the communication patterns, it was found that the communication of the families containing schizophrenics was charac-terized by more egocentrism. Not only was a relatively higher frequency of ego-centric utterances found, but the observed egocentrism proved to be of a more severe and pronounced type than the egocentrism observed in the control families. Even though the induced communication conflict required decentration on behalf of the interacting family members, no development toward a more decentered communi-cation over time was found in the families containing schizophrenics. Furthermore,

the analysis suggested a direct linkage between (degree of) egocentrism and inefficiency of communication.

(3) Finally, the family members' different reactions to the emerging insight into the induced communication conflict indicated varying degrees of openness or closedness in the family systems.

COMMUNICATION IN THE FAMILY OF THE ASTHMATIC CHILD: AN EXPERIMENTAL APPROACH

Rolf Wikran, Asbjørn Faleide and Rolv Mikkel Blakar. [16]

Introduction

Childhood asthma is now predominantly classified as a psychosomatic suffering (cf. Pinkerton & Weaver, 1970). The reason why it has been so difficult to gain insight into illnesses such as childhood asthma is the multifactorial causes (Aas, 1969a; Pinkerton & Weaver, 1970). Aas lists the following types of factors: biochemical, infectious, circulatory, ventilatory, psychogenic, allergic, and 'unknown' factors.

Asthma in childhood may be precipitated, aggravated and prolonged by various factors, and the influence of the same factor seems to vary from patient to patient, and over time within the same patient. However, there seems to be somatic predisposition in all cases of childhood asthma (Freeman et al., 1964; Feingold et al., 1966; Aas, 1969b). But there is no one-to-one relation between the physical basis and the severeness of the asthma (Jennings et al., 1966). Somatic as well as psychic factors may maintain the asthmatic condition (Block et al., 1964).

Since the early 1950's there has been a fundamental change in attitudes toward psychopathology in general. There has been an increasing tendency to conceive of psychopathology as a product of the communication/interaction in the family and close environment, and not only as predominantly genetically determined individual states (Ruesch & Bateson, 1951; Bateson et al., 1956, 1963). This redefinition in terms of communication initiated a lot of research, and various theories were developed (for reviews, see Mishler & Waxler, 1965; Handel, 1967; Framo, 1972; Riskin & Faunce, 1972; Jacobsen & Pettersen, 1974; Blakar, 1976a). It has to be mentioned, however, that the explanatory value of the substantial part of these communication-oriented studies on psychopathology is questionable (cf. Schuham, 1967; Riskin & Faunce, 1972; Blakar, 1975c, 1978a).

In therapy as well as in research there has been an increasing tendency to adopt a communication perspective and conceive of the family as a system, and not work exclusively with the identified patient. Even in connection with different somatic illnesses some writers have argued in favour of such a strategy. In the summary of the survey 'A family perspective of psychosomatic factors in illness: A review of the literature', Grolnick (1972) concludes:

But the above viewpoint goes beyond the simple psychosomatic-organic dichotomy. One must consider whether a given family needs a member's illness, whether that illness be schizophrenia, alcoholism (Albees 'A Delicate Balance'), endocrine pathology, or whatever (p. 479).

The purpose of the present paper is two-fold. First, the literature on childhood asthma will be reviewed in order to see whether any support, direct or indirect, may be found for adopting a communication perspective in gaining insight into childhood asthma. Secondly, an exploratory experimental study of the communication pattern and efficiency of the asthmatic child's family will be presented.

It has to be emphasized that we conceive of the communication perspective as a supplementary perspective. The communication perspective exclusively will never be sufficient to understand bronchial asthma in childhood. (Cf. Part I, p. 47, and Blakar & Nafstad, 1980a.)

Review of the literature

When reviewing the literature, one has to be aware of all the methodological pitfalls in psychosomatic asthma research (cf. Purcell, 1965; Feingold et al., 1966). Having reviewed more than 200 studies from 1950 on, Freeman et al. (1964) conclude: 'In general the yield from all the effort expended to date is small indeed' (p. 565). On the other hand, no other alternative to a critical use of the available literature seems reasonable in the present case.

The most relevant literature fell naturally under the following three headings: 1) personality traits of the asthmatic child, 2) the mother-child relationship, 3) the milieu of the asthmatic child. The present review is not intended to give a general overview of the literature on childhood asthma. However, the literature is reviewed to see what support there may be for adopting a communication perspective on childhood asthma.

1) Personality traits

There has been postulated a dependency conflict in the asthmatic child's relation to his mother (French & Alexander, 1941). A sensation of being avoided by, or separated from, the mother may provoke an asthmatic attack. This attack would thus represent a symbolic cry-out for the mother (French, 1939). Such an explanation may sound like a slogan. On the other hand, Sperling spells this out as a 'psychosomatic relation' where the child is avoided only when in good health and in proper function, claiming to be independent, but, in contrast, is rewarded and cared for when ill and helpless (Sperling, 1955). Several researchers support this hypothesis (Miller & Baruch, 1957; Block, 1969). Alcock (1960) studied four groups of children, using the Rorschach projective technique. She found the asthmatic child to manifest a conflict typically centred around the object-relation and strong emotional loading that did not find an adequate outlet.

In discussing this psychoanalytic interpretation, Pinkerton & Weaver (1970) claim that this 'approach/avoidance-conflict' is only one particular way of conceiving of what they more broadly suggest as an implicit 'aura of ambivalence' present in the family situation. We assume that this ambivalence will affect the familial interaction, and result in confused and indirect communication.

In a heavily controlled study conducted by Garner & Wenar (1959) the psychosomatic children in general showed less capacity for social behavior than the controls, and they demonstrated less ability to give vent to intensive reactions and direct expressions of feelings. Furthermore, they were more suspicious than the children in the control groups.

Moreover, both Alcock (1960) and Garner & Wenar (1959) call attention to the cumulation of emotional loading. It is not unlikely that one may find corresponding latent tensions within the family communication system.

2) The mother-child relationship

As is the case in developmental psychology in general, research on childhood asthma has focused almost exclusively on the mother-child relation, and has tended to ignore the influence of the father, of the parental interaction, etc.

Garner & Wenar (1959) hypothesized that children with psychosomatic disorders lack 'mothering'. Roughly this means that mother and child are not operating in harmony with each other, and the mother is not able to meet the child's needs in an adequate manner. Through observations of the mother-child relationship in connection to differential diseases, they found in psychosomatic illnesses an almost negative interaction, i.e. the mother-child relationship was both close and frustrating. Their interaction was flavored by competition. This was most typical for the mother. In interpreting the results, Garner & Wenar maintain that the child is still a part of the mother's 'self'. The child has not learned to differentiate himself from the mother. Block et al. (1964) reached an analogous conclusion. Abramson (1954) describes the parents and child as 'engulfing' each other. Thus this close and undifferentiated relationship seems to be typical for the whole family.

But the mother-child relation is not established in a social vacuum. As Titchener et al. (1960) comment in connection with ulcerative colitis:

> We are of the opinion that colitigenic mothers are not born nor even made in their own childhood. Their ways of relating to their children come into being in the family situation and their special relationship with future ulcerative patients are largely determined by the dynamics of the family environment (p. 129).

In this connection one of our own studies (Faleide, 1969) is of particular interest. We found that traumatic events in the grandparents' generation seemed to have severely hindered the emotional development of one or both of the parents. One may thus tend to say that the asthmatic symptom of the child is the third generation's reaction to the first (grandparents') generation's conflict.

In clinical work with asthmatic children, we have noticed three characteristics typical of their familial situation. They live under constant emotional repression, in an atmosphere of unclear communication, in which their symptoms are being rewarded (Faleide, 1973). Furthermore, Ackerman (1958) discusses a correlation between inconsistent role expectations and unclear communication in the surroundings, on the one hand, and psychosomatic symptom formation of the child, on the other. Mitchell et al. (1953) claim that the parents of the asthmatic child are inhibited in their emotional expressions. They also found that the parental interaction is charac- terized by the mother's domination and the father's withdrawal. Block et al. (1966) found deprivation to be a dominant trait in the mothers. In our clinical practice we have often noticed the father's 'blindness' regarding the mother's needs (Faleide & Vandvik, 1976).

3) Altered environment

It has been known for a long time that some children lose their asthmatic symptoms immediately upon hospitalization (Coolidge, 1956; Tuft, 1957; Peshkin & Abramson, 1959). Thus Tuft (1957) concluded with regard to the asthmatic child that 'the con- clusion seems inescapable that this relationship to his parents or his environment represented by his parent played the dominant role in the continuation of the former state of asthma' (p. 252).

A study by Long et al. (1958) lends support to Tuft's conclusion. A group of chronically ill asthmatic children hospitalized during an attack were tested for sensitivity to house dust. When symptom-free, the children with sensitivity to house dust were exposed to dust collected from their own homes. None of them reacted with asthmatic attacks.

In Purcell et al.'s (1969) study, parents and siblings of asthmatic children were removed from home, and lived in a hotel for two weeks. The patients were cared for in their own homes by substitute parents, thus keeping the physical surroundings almost perfectly constant. On the basis of interviews with the parents, it was pre- dicted beforehand which children would become symptom-free. The predictions were based on whether the attacks were related to emotional factors. All the children predicted to be positive responders improved significantly during this experimental family separation. Taken together, the studies of Long et al. (1958) and Purcell et al. (1969) strongly indicate that social factors in the family are active in initiating and maintaining asthmatic attacks.

It has been claimed that the children who become symptom-free through hospi- talization (rapidly remitting, RR) have a more psychogenic asthma than the steroid- dependent ones (SD). Indeed, many of the RR-children reported emotional factors as precursors of an attack (Purcell, 1963, 1965), although on the whole, both RR-

and SD-children often considered complicated interpersonal conflict situations in the family to be the precipitator of asthmatic attacks.

Kluger (1969) found it characteristic of the social system of the chronically ill patients that they exploited their physical illness as a medium for communication and interaction. Meissner (1966) describes somatic expressions of disharmony in the familial system of psychosomatic patients. Thus somatizing often seems to be the expression of conflicts in the family of the asthmatic child.

In his communication theory of psychosomatic diseases, Ruesch (1951) holds that the psychosomatic patient has learned to put greater value on his physical than on his psychic processes. Hence the body has acquired great communicational value.

Finally, Kluger (1969) noticed that all the members of the family show less social activity than would normally be expected, taking the age of the child and the socio-economic status of the family into consideration.

In conclusion then, on the basis of the literature it seems reasonable to assume that the communication typical of the family of the child with severe asthma is unclear and characterized by ambivalence, and in particular that overt and open discussions in conflicts are avoided.

Experimental Approach

The above exposition of the literature has clearly demonstrated that a systematic examination of communication patterns in the family of the asthmatic child might represent a substantial contribution. As was demonstrated in the above review, on the basis of the literature rather specific hypotheses about the communication in such families could even be proposed. However, at the present stage of research it would seem more reasonable to conduct exploratory, though systematic, studies for the purpose of identifying and describing qualitative characteristics of the communication typical of such families, rather than to test specific hypotheses. For our more general program on communication-oriented studies on psychopathology, see Part I, p. 32 - 53, and Blakar, 1978a, 1978c.

Every communication-oriented study on psychopathology - irrespective of which diagnostic categories one chooses to study - is immediately confronted with two substantial problems. First, there is the vague or even entire lack of relevant communication theory (cf. Part I and Riskin & Faunce, 1972; Blakar, 1975c, 1976a). Secondly, there is the serious lack of adequate methods (cf. part I and Grinker et al., 1968; Haley, 1972; Blakar, 1974a, 1978a).

The choice or development of methods in this field should ideally be based on an explicit theory of communication and knowledge about families with psychopathological members. Regarding the latter, Haley, (1972, p. 35) concludes in his review of the field: 'The most sound findings would seem to be in the outcome area: When faced

with a task on which they must cooperate, abnormal family members seem to communicate their preferences less successfully, require more activity and take longer
to get the task done.' (Our italics.)

Our own expectations concerning the communication in the family of the asthmatic
child (cf. the above review) would also point to the suitability of a cooperation task.
And we felt that an experimental situation of the type envisaged by Haley would be a
good point of departure.

In the present study Blakar's standardized communication conflict situation
(Blakar, 1973a) was employed. A presentation of the method, its theoretical background, and the rationale for the clinical application is given in Part I (p. 26-32).
The termination criteria in the communication conflict situation were used according
to the modified version described by Hultberg, Alve & Blakar (p. 75).

In the present study we chose to focus upon the parental communication patterns.
This for two reasons. First, we did not want to have the patient himself present, as
possible differences could then be 'explained' as a function of special considerations
being made for the patient member. Secondly, the parents create the basic dyad of
the family, the child being born into a milieu created by the parents.

It is essential to emphasize that a study of this type cannot say anything definite
with respect to causality (cf. Blakar, 1974a, Blakar & Nafstad, 1980a). On the other
hand, there can scarcely exist any longer good reasons (i.e., in communication-
oriented family research) for thinking in terms of simple chains of causality; one has
to regard the family as a complex system (Jackson, 1959, 1965, 1966, 1967;
Watzlawick et al., 1967; Jacobsen & Pettersen, 1974; Blakar & Nafstad, 1980a,
see also Part I, p. 51). Even though the parents do play a conclusive role in
the constitution of the family system, there is no doubt that childhood asthma, with
its severe and often dramatic attacks, strongly influences the personality and the
familial situation and interaction (cf. Holthe, 1972). For example, Neuhaus (1958)
and Alcock (1960) hold different positions as to whether the typical personality traits
are one of the consequences or one of the causes of chronic asthma.

Samples and matching

Of basic theoretical importance is the selection of controls. There has been much
diffuse theorizing due to random selection of controls, in particular the so-called
'normal' family has been uncritically used as control (Haley, 1972; Blakar, 1975a;
Hultberg et al., 1978). To make sure that the couples would be as comparable as
possible, we had to select controls that were parents to a severely ill child, but
where there should be no theoretical reason to expect any connection between the
disease and the pattern of communication within the family. Parents of children with
severe, chronic heart disease satisfy these criteria, and have frequently been used

as controls in studies on asthma (Neuhaus, 1958; Glaser et al., 1964; Purcell, 1965; Grolnick, 1972).

For this study, then, we decided to use the two following groups of disorders. In group A (asthma) the patient member had the diagnosis bronchial asthma, strictly used, and the patients were aged from 7-11 years, because this is a relatively stable period. We had to select severe asthmatics so that the reactive factor was to be comparable with the corresponding factor in the heart disease group.

Congenital heart disease represents a stable condition, so for the two groups to be comparable, we aimed at as much stability in the A-group as possible. In establishing the heart disease (HD) group several diagnoses were included, but all had a congenital physical heart defect. The two groups were satisfactorily matched with respect to relevant background variables, such as age, number of years of marriage, education, employment, social group, annual income, domicile, living conditions, number of children and their sex and age (for further details on the matching, see Wikran, 1974, pp. 55-61).

Hypotheses

Even though the present study is highly exploratory, hypotheses concerning the degree of efficiency as well as qualitative differences were set forth. Regarding the possibility of testing specific hypotheses, the very nature of the experimental method is essential (cf. Blakar, 1974a, 1978a). The method consists of two apparently similar, but in reality highly different, communication tasks. Whereas the first one is simple and straightforward, the second induces a communication conflict.

The following rather general hypotheses may in fact be considered tentative conclusions based on the above review of the asthma literature:

(1) Couples from Group A will communicate less efficiently than those from Group HD. And this difference in efficiency will be most pronounced on the experimental route, where - due to the induced communication conflict - a critical re-evaluation of and change in patterns of communication is required. In other words, the Group A couples will have more problems and use a longer time in solving the experimental route where the communication conflict is induced.

(2) Qualitative differences between the communication in Group A and Group HD will be revealed, and such differences are expected whether the communication situation is simple or complicated. On the basis of the literature, the communication of the Group A couples is expected to be more rigid, unclear, and replete with ambivalence. Furthermore, the Group A couples will tend to avoid open - and potentially clarifying - confrontation in conflict situations (also with respect to the experimentally induced communication conflict).

(3) Finally, it is supposed that the qualitative differences (2) will throw light on and partly explain the differences in efficiency of communication (1).

Results and Discussion

As was the case in the earlier studies with student subjects (Blakar, 1973a, Stokstad et al., 1976, 1979) and married couples (Sølvberg & Blakar, 1975), all the couples became absorbed and involved in the communication task.

Let us start by examining the communication on the simple practice route, where they are not being influenced by the experimental manipulation. The most striking observation in Table 12 is the wide within-group variation found in the A-group. Group A is actually divided into two separate sub-groups: A-2, A-4, and A-5 with a mean time of 3 min 27 sec, which is almost identical to that of the Group HD, which used a mean time of 3 min 29 sec, and the two couples A-1 and A-3, demonstrating an extremely inefficient communication.

Table 12. Time spent and number of returns to the starting point on the training route

Couple No.	A-1/HD-6	A-2/HD-7	A-3/HD-8	A-4/HD-9	A-5/HD-10
Asthma group	-* 27 times	54 sec 1 time	37 min 31 sec 14 times	3 min 49 sec 2 times	5 min 37 sec 2 times
Heart disease group	2 min 46 sec 1 time	2 min 27 sec 1 time	2 min 17 sec 1 time	3 min 0 sec 1 time	6 min 48 sec 1 time

* A-1 did not master the training route within 40 min.

A direct comparison with the previous study on parents with and without schizophrenic children (Sølvberg & Blakar, 1975) shows how inefficient the communication in this sub-group (A-1 and A-3) really was. The parents of the schizophrenic patients (S-group) used a mean time of 4 min 50 sec (ranging from 2 min 5 sec to 9 min 56 sec), whereas the parents of the controls (N-group) used 4 min 57 sec (2 min 2 sec - 8 min 52 sec). That the HD-group and the other A sub-groups (A-2, A-4, and A-5) were a little more efficient than the S- and N-groups is likely to be due to their younger age and higher socio-economic level.

Of the nine couples who started on the experimental route (A-1 did not manage the training route within 40 min, and consequently was not started on the experimental route), eight couples managed to solve the experimental route according to the predetermined criteria. All five HD-couples managed, whereas only three of the A-group couples succeeded. As would be expected from the practice route, it was A-3 that did not succeed within the 40-min limit. If the time the solvers used is

examined, no difference is found between the two groups. The three A-group
solvers used a mean time of about 30 min, and the five HD-couples a mean time
of about 32 min.

Such a dichotomy in the A-group did not come as a surprise. First, on the
basis of the multifactorial causality (see above), a rather heterogeneous group had
to be expected. Secondly, as part of the training of the experimenter (cf. Wikran,
1974, pp. 53-55), amongst others three A-couples were tested. Two of them resolved the induced communication conflict, whereas the third one did not.

However, the division into sub-groups made our A-group sample of five too
small, even for this exploratory study. Before qualitative analysis of the communication could reasonably be carried out, we had to enlarge the material in order to
see how real such a dichotomy of the A-parents was. An enlargement of the sample
was also required in order to get an idea of the relative distribution over the two
sub-groups. Hence, as an additional study, as many A-couples as possible within
our time limits were run. When we were obliged to stop experimenting, nine
additional A-couples had been run. All of them managed the practice route; mean
time was 4 min 27 sec, ranging from 42 sec to 8 min 38 sec. On the experimental
route six couples managed, whereas three did not resolve the induced communication conflict. In Table 13 the distribution of solvers and non-solvers in our
total A-sample of 17 couples is given. With respect to efficiency of communication,
about one-third of the A-couples demonstrate an inefficient communication, whereas
the rest of the group communicate as efficiently as the controls (HD- and N-groups).
This distribution holds whether we look at the total sample or at each of the different
part studies (pre-training, main experiment, additional sample). Amongst the six
non-solvers are two couples who in addition demonstrated real problems in mastering
the simple communication task (i.e. the practice route).

From a general methodological point of view the controls (HD-group) are very
interesting indeed. The argument then goes as follows: Blakar (1972a, 1973a).
developed a method for studying some prerequisites for communication. Sølvberg &
Blakar (1975) proved the method to be sensitive with respect to differences in communication of parents with and without schizophrenic offspring. Against this it may
be argued that no communication patterns specific to parents of schizophrenic
offspring had been revealed, but that it had merely been demonstrated that parents
of severely ill children experience this experimental situation differently from
control groups, i.e. that the demand characteristics of the situation are different
for the two groups (cf. Haley, 1972; Blakar, 1975a).

In contrast to the N-group, but on a par with the S-group parents, the HD-
parents knew that they were participating in the experiment because they were parents
of severely ill children. As far as we can tell, the HD-parents did not deviate from

Table 13. Distribution of solvers/non-solvers in the three sub-samples of
A-group couples

Sample	Solvers	Non-solvers	Total
Pretraining sample	2	1	3
Experimental sample	3	2	5
Additional sample	6	3	9
Total	11	6	17

the N-group in the previous study. The communication pattern found by Sølvberg
& Blakar in couples with a schizophrenic offspring can therefore not be said to be
typical of the communication of parents to children with all types of severe illnesses.

It has to be mentioned that Hultberg et al. (1978), in a study applying this same
method, found that the pattern of communication in couples who were parents of
borderline patients deviated both from the pattern found in couples having a schizophrenic offspring and from that found in the parents of the normal controls. (For
a general analysis of demand characteristics in this kind of research, see Part I,
p. 48-51.)

Further qualitative analysis

In order to corroborate the above findings and to make an attempt at identifying
qualitative characteristics specific to the communication of the group A parents,
the following analyses were conducted:

1) A communication-oriented student trained in clinical psychology was given the
10 tape-recordings (five A and five HD) from the main experiment, and asked to
describe the interaction and, on the basis of her descriptions, to predict which of
the couples had an asthmatic child and which had a child with heart disease.

2) Detailed casuistic descriptions of the communication process applying the
conceptual framework of social-developmental theory were worked out
for each of the 10 couples. Some of the more central concepts in this analysis are:
egocentrism versus decentration and taking the perspective of the other (Piaget,
1926; Mead, 1934; Mossige et al., 1976, 1979; Blakar et al., 1978); the type and
quality of the contracts monitoring the communication process (Rommetveit, 1972a,
1974; Blakar, 1972a, Moberget & Reer, 1975; Glennsjø, 1977); attribution of communicative difficulties (Heider, 1958; Ichheiser, 1970; Hultberg et al., 1978;
Haarstad, 1976). For more coherent presentations of the conceptual framework
applied in this analysis, see Part I and Blakar (1975e, 1978a).

In the blind-scoring procedure, the scorer correctly identified four of the five
group A couples. To a certain extent it was thus possible to identify the A-couples
on the basis of their mere interaction in the present experimental situation. A
closer examination of the scorer's descriptions showed that the core cues on which
she relied when identifying a couple as being a group A couple were unclear communication, and the husband's withdrawal.

On the basis of the casuistic descriptions worked out of the couples' communication, we were able to identify some qualitative aspects that seemed typical of the
sub-group (the one-third) of the A group couples demonstrating inefficient communication. These qualitative aspects of their communication pattern, furthermore, seem
to shed some light on why their communication failed so totally. In summary, the
most significant characteristics of the communication of this sub-group were: the
spouses of these couples proved to be highly egocentric, and demonstrated very
limited abilities to take each other's perspective. Their egocentrism was in
particular revealed by their not seeming to 'listen' to and take into account what the
other said. Moreover, their tolerance for vague and unclear communication seemed
very high, and the tendency to pretend that they understood each other was predominant. Although this represents more of an interpretation than an observation,
the high anxiety there seemed to be for (open) conflicts and confrontations has to be
mentioned in this connection. Everything is done to avoid potential conflicts, and
arising conflicts are covered up. Interaction sequences characterized by pseudo-
agreement were thus frequently observed in these couples. The active avoidance
of potential conflicts resulted in an almost total ignorance of testing with respect
to the information being exchanged. And their communication was characterized by
'inactivity', e.g. an almost total lack of questions and fewer proposals than in the
other couples. And little or nothing is done in order to find the causes of (attribute)
the communicative difficulties encountered in the present situation. Another outstanding aspect of these couples was the rigidity of the complementary relationships.
For a presentation of more casuistic material illustrating their pattern of communication, see Wikran et al. (1979).

ANXIETY, RIGIDITY AND COMMUNICATION
AN EXPERIMENTAL APPROACH

S.J. Stokstad, T. Lagerløv and R.M. Blakar [17]

Introduction

Recourse to a communication perspective and application of communication theory
has recently become more and more popular within a wide range of disciplines.
Almost everything - from the sale success of a particular product to a psychotic
breakdown - has been explained in terms of communication. The explanatory value
of the main part of this communication-oriented research, however, is for at least
two reasons questionable. The concept of communication itself has, first of all,
frequently remained underlined and been used in vague and implicit ways. As a
consequence, one is left with a somewhat paradoxical situation where a researcher
who knows a lot about a phenomenon (e.g. schizophrenia) is 'explaining' this
phenomenon by means of another phenomenon (communication, or more adequately,
deviant communication) about which he seems to know far less (cf. Blakar, 1974a;
Sølvberg and Blakar, 1975).

Secondly, there has been a tendency within this type of research to think only
in terms of systems and functions and almost totally ignore individual characteristics
or dispositions of the people constituting the interactional system. But it is questionable to talk about 'senders' and 'receivers' within a 'system' without taking into
account, e.g. each individual sender's/receiver's ability to decenter and take the
perspective of the other, personal characteristics such as rigidity versus flexibility,
level of anxiety, etc. We are of course fully aware of the fact that a person's rigidity,
anxiety and egocentrism, etc. vary over different social situations (e.g. Mischel,
1968, 1973). But to take this to mean that, since 'the person is influenced by the
social situation', personality and personal dispositions should be disregarded, would
be as dangerous as the blindness regarding social variables that has characterized
the dominant traditions within individually oriented psychology. (For an illustrative
example, see Ichheiser's (1970) comments on Freud.)

A pragmatic solution would be in this dilemma, rather than arguing for a social
or an individual psychology, to make clear at each stage of research from which
perspective, the social or the individual, one is exploring the variable in focus. Thus
the individually oriented psychologist would have to make explicit what is presupposed
of social character in his concepts and theory, and correspondingly, the social

psychologist should make clear what he presupposes as regards personality (cf. Blakar, 1974c). The interaction between individual characteristics and social settings (e.g. actual communication situations) should hence be brought into the focus of research.

A field in which the communication perspective has been particularly influential and generated promising research is in the study of psychopathology. Since Ruesch and Bateson in 1951 programmatically redefined psychopathology 'in terms of deficiencies of communication', there has been an ever-increasing tendency to adopt a basic communication/interaction perspective on psychopathology. (For reviews, see e.g. Mishler and Waxler, 1965, Riskin and Faunce, 1972.) In hardly any other field would one expect ignorance of the above-mentioned problems to be so vital, however. (How is it possible to analyze, say, a schizophrenic breakdown without having explicit rules for how to disentangle social and individual variables within the family system?) As one might expect, the optimism that characterized this field in the 1960s (cf. Handel, 1967, Mishler and Waxler, 1965) has therefore been replaced by a more pessimistic and critical attitude (Haley, 1972, Riskin and Faunce, 1972, Jacobsen and Pettersen, 1974). The lack of progress has been ascribed to lack of adequate methods (Haley, 1972) or of 'intermediate concepts', connecting observable data to superordinate concepts, such as 'double bind', 'marital skism & marital skew', 'pseudomutuality', to mention a few of the most well known, used in theorizing about families with deviant members (Riskin and Faunce, 1972). Riskin and Faunce as well as Haley point out essential weaknesses. These issues, however, are in our opinion both merely reflections of another even more basic deficiency, namely that the concept of communication has remained vague and undefined (Blakar, 1975e). A particular problem in studies of interaction in families with psychopathological members is to decide what should be ascribed to the familial communication and what to the individual members' abilities and personal dispositions. This problem is clearly reflected in the following quotation from Haley's recent attempt to assess what has been found out about pathological families: [18]

If we accept the findings of the research reported here and assuming it is sound, evidence is accumulating to support the idea that a family with a patient member is different from an 'average' family. As individuals, the family members do not appear different according to the usual character and personality criteria. Similarly, evidence is slight that family structure, when conceived in terms of role assignment or dominance, is different in normal and abnormal families. On process measurements there is some indication of difference: Abnormal families appear to have more conflict, to have different coalition patterns, and to show more inflexibility in repeating patterns of behavior. (Haley, 1972, p. 35.)

An empirical approach to these issues may take place along the following lines: Given a communication situation (e.g. a cooperation task) in which differences (e.g. efficiency/inefficiency in getting the task done) between 'normal' and 'pathological' families are demonstrated, then interaction between 'normal' subjects with varying personal dispositions (for example high versus low anxiety) ought to be studied in the very same cooperation task. Such parallel research, even though revealing very little concerning causality, may be useful in disentangling social (e.g. familial communication) and personal (e.g. anxiety) aspects (cf. Blakar, 1975a, and Part I).

Having created an experimental communication situation (Blakar, 1973a) in which clear-cut differences between the pattern of communication in families with and without psychopathological members have been demonstrated (Sølvberg and Blakar, 1975), we chose in the present study to examine the influence of anxiety upon communication in the very same situation.

Anxiety and Communication

We follow Rommetveit (1972a, 1974) in defining communication as to make common (communicare). Thus the purpose of the present study is to examine how different levels of anxiety affect the process by which two (or more) people make something known to each other.

It may be hypothesized that level of anxiety will affect some basic preconditions for successful communication, of which only a few will be exemplified here. A certain capacity for decentration and ability and willingness to take the perspective of the other is one such precondition. It is not unlikely, however, that a high anxiety person will stick more to his own perspective and be less open to take the perspective of the other. And when communication runs into trouble (quarrels, misunderstandings, etc.) a certain degree of flexibility is particularly needed. It may be hypothesized (see below) that high anxiety then will result in rigidity.

Even though we have found no studies relating level of anxiety directly to communication (e.g. efficiency of communication), a number of studies seem to show that level of anxiety affects various aspects of communication such as speech. For example, 'speech disturbance ratio' (frequency of unfinished sentences, repetitions, stuttering, slips of the tongue, omissions, etc.) was thus by Mahl (1956) found to be highest in anxiety-filled phases of therapeutic sessions. Similar findings are reported by Boomer and Goodrich (1961), and Kasl and Mahl (1965). Gynter (1957), moreover, demonstrated that anxiety (measured on a Welch A-scale) and an ego-involving stress-instruction influenced what she called 'the communication efficiency' in that it caused the subjects to omit a higher number of irrelevant as compared to relevant utterances in an interview situation.

Studies of this kind are problematic for two reasons: First, they do not bear upon communication or interaction as such, but merely on various aspects of the individual's speech. Secondly, it is difficult to ensure independent operationalization of speech/communication variables and anxiety measures. Hence, in the present study effort was taken to ensure that <u>level of anxiety</u> and <u>communication</u> would be conceptualized and operationalized within different frameworks (<u>intra</u>personal versus <u>inter</u>personal). Anxiety was accordingly measured by the widely used and standardized personality inventory M.M.P.I., via Taylor's Manifest Anxiety Scale (MAS) (Taylor, 1953).

As suggested above, one may imagine various ways in which anxiety influences communication, and high/low anxiety will also affect the very emotional climate of the communication process. The main hypothesis of the present study will be ela- borated by means of the intermediate concept of 'rigidity'. Before we proceed to the hypothesis, however, the communication task and the theoretical rationale behind the operationalization of communication efficiency has to be presented.

The communication situation

In the present study Blakar's standardized communication conflict situation (Blakar, 1972a, 1973a) was employed. A presentation of the method and its theoretical background is given in Part I (p. 26-32). The termination criteria were used according to the modified version described by Hultberg, Alve & Blakar (p. 75).

Rigidity as the link between anxiety and inefficiency of communication

It has been suggested (p.138) that (level of) anxiety may influence communication in various ways. The specific hypothesis to be tested in the present study is that <u>high anxiety persons will show more rigidity, which in turn will result in less efficient communication.</u>

Several studies indicate a relation between anxiety and certain features of the individual's cognitive functioning, thus anxiety seems to lead to rigidity (Ainsworth, 1968, Pilisuk, 1963, Beier, 1965). As to rigidity, two issues of direct relevance to the present study have been discussed. First, it has been asked whether the various manifestations of rigidity might be explained by <u>one underlying rigidity factor</u>. But already in the discussion of the authoritarian personality in the early 1950s, it was demonstrated that rigidity is a multidimensional concept, and hence has to be speci- fied in each concrete study (Brown, 1953). In the present study a discrepancy between the two participants with respect to premises is induced, and it is hypothesized that rigidity will be reflected in resistance against giving up and revising the premises on which the individual is communicating. Rigid persons (or persons who develop rigidity in the communication situation) will hence need <u>longer time</u> in resolving the induced communication conflict.

Secondly, there is still the unsettled issue as to whether rigidity is a <u>situationally induced state</u> or a more stable <u>personality trait.</u> Different positions are taken by Luchins (1951), who on the basis of a series of problem-solving experiments concludes that rigidity is a situationally induced state, and Rokeach (1960) and Rubenowitz (1963,

1970), who claim that rigidity is a more or less stable personality characteristic.

In accordance with our general introductory comments, rigidity was therefore induced in two different manners in the present study. The 'personality aspect' of it was assessed by selection of subjects, in that the person's level of anxiety was varied. In addition, different instructions were used to induce different levels of stress on the subjects in the experimentel situation. [19]

The final experimental design therefore included the following four different experimental conditions (see Table 14) where an equal number of male and female dyads were run in each of the four conditions.

Table 14. Experimental design.

| | | Instruction: | |
		Standard instruction	Stress instruction
Level of anxiety:	High anxiety		
	Low anxiety		

Subjects

A total of 155 undergraduate students, aged 19-21 years, 87 females and 68 males were tested on MAS. Average score on MAS was 18.43 (18.37 for the men, 18.48 for the women). The standard error was 7.68 (8.31 for the men, 7.15 for the women).

A split half reliability correlation of 0.88 was found (Spearman-Brown's method, Guildford, 1965). The highest and lowest scores on MAS were selected for the communication experiment. In order to get two extreme groups from our pool of 155 subjects, the number of dyads was restricted to 24 (six in each experimental condition). The final high anxiety group scored from 25-43, whereas the low anxiety group scored from 2-12. [20] The 24 dyads, [21] each consisting of either two high scorers or two low scorers, were run in randomized order and the experimenter did not know their scores on MAS.

Hypotheses

The following hypotheses were put forward:
(I) On the training route, where no conflict is induced between the premisses the subjects have already been given about the maps and what later will prove to be the

case, the anxiety level will not produce differences in solution time (i.e. in development of rigidity). On the experimental route, however, where such a conflict will arise, the anxiety level will produce differences, so that the high anxiety dyads will develop more rigidity and need longer time.

(II) On the training route, the standard versus stress instruction conditions will not produce differences in solution time (i.e. in development of rigidity). On the experimental route, however, these conditions will cause differences such that those given the stress instruction will develop more rigidity and need longer time.

(III) On the training route, there will be no interaction effect between anxiety and instruction conditions as regards solution time (i.e. development of rigidity). On the experimental route there will be such an interaction effect.

Results

A first crucial observation was that all subjects became involved and seemed highly motivated to solve the two tasks (cf. footnote to Table 16), and the experimenter had no particular problems in making them grasp the instructions and start on the practice route.

All the 24 dyads managed the practice route without too much trouble (4 min 45 sec in mean), but the variation in time used (from 1 min 9 sec to 17 min 10 sec) indicates that the task was not equally simple for all of them. These results are almost identical with those obtained in earlier experiments with student subjects in the same communication situation (Blakar, 1973a).

To test for the possible effect of (level of) anxiety and (type of) instruction on communication in the simple situation, an analysis of variance was conducted. Neither main effects nor interaction effects proved significant.

On the experimental route, 17 dyads managed to resolve the induced communication conflict according to the criteria (see p. 75), whereas seven dyads did not, and hence were shown the induced error by the experimenter when more than 40 min had elapsed. In Table 15a and b is given the distribution of solvers/non-solvers over the four experimental conditions.

Table 15a and b. Distribution of solvers/non-solvers over the various experimental conditions

	Solvers	Non-solvers	Total		Solvers	Non-solvers	Total
Low anxiety	12	0	12	Standard instruction	8	4	12
High anxiety	5	7	12	Stress instruction	9	3	12
Total	17	7	24	Total	17	7	24

The effect of (level of) anxiety on communication in this conflict situation is testified to in that all the seven non-solvers were among the high anxiety dyads. However, no effect of the stress instruction is revealed by this rough measure (solvers versus non-solvers). Analysis of variance on time used on the experimental route [22] showed that the effect of anxiety upon communication in the conflict situation was significant: $F(1.23) = 13.68$, $p < 0.01$. No effect of type of stress instruction was found, however. Nor was there any significant interaction between (level of) anxiety and (type of) instruction.

We were thus correct in our expectations that neither (level of) anxiety nor (type of) instruction would influence the efficiency of communication in a simple situation where no critical evaluation and re-adjustment of communication is required. Furthermore, we were correct in our hypothesis that high anxiety would lead to rigidity and inefficient communication when the situation became complex in such a way that critical evaluation and re-adjustment of the communicative strategy was required. Our expectation that the stress instruction would also lead to rigidity and inefficient communication in the conflict communication situation, was not confirmed. It is possible though that our 'stress instruction' was not a successful manipulation. Logically, there are two different alternative explanations: either the stress instruction was not really experienced as stressing, or the situation itself (with the standard instruction) may have been so stressing, that the 'stress instruction' did not make any difference at all. The hypothesis about the impact of situationally induced stress should therefore not be rejected on the basis of the present study only. [23]

In order to explore the effect of anxiety upon communication somewhat further, two different qualitative analyses were conducted:
(1) An analysis of the (level of) precision in the dyads' verbal explanations.
(2) An analysis of the emotional climate of the interaction.

The rationale for analysis of level of precision resides in previous studies (cf. above) indicating a relationship between anxiety and various verbal skills. We wanted to explore, therefore, whether the observed differences could be explained by different degree of precision in the verbal explanations, or if (level of) anxiety affected more basic aspects of communication.

Degree of precision may be defined differently. In the present communication situation precision of explanations was operationalized along the following dimensions: To what extent was an explanatory utterance precise with respect to the critical categories (1) distance, (2) direction and (3) localization on the map. A certain degree of precision with respect to all these three aspects is required if the task is to be successfully accomplished. The dyads' verbal interaction on the experimental route from when they started until they reached the point of the induced error the first time, was scored. Every dyad was scored independently by two trained scorers, and each utterance was given a score (from 1 to 4) according to its degree of precision in relation to the three critical dimensions mentioned above. On the basis of these scores, the 24 dyads were rank-ordered from 1 to 24 according to degree of precision. Interscorer reliability on this final rank order was 0.85.

To test the possible effect of (degree of) precision upon efficiency of communication, the rank-order correlation between time used on the two routes and precision was calculated. No significant correlation was found between time used and degree of precision, either on the practice route (rho = -0.18) or on the experimental route (rho = 0.17). The differences in communication efficiency can therefore hardly be explained as being due to differences in verbal precision in the explanations.

In order to assess the emotional interaction climate of the various dyads, two

Table 16. The twelve scales used to assess the emotional interaction climate, as well as the interscorer reliability co-efficients

Scales		Interscorer reliability	
		Practice route	Experimental route
samarbeidende (cooperative)	konkurrerende (competitive)	0.33	0.88
sikker (sure)	usikker (unsure)	0.71	0.86
formell (formal)	uformell (informal)	0.40	0.46
fredelig (peaceful)	aggressiv (aggressive)	0.51	0.77
strukturert (structured)	ustrukturert (instructured)	0.87	0.80
anspent (tense)	avslappet (relaxed)	0.57	0.62
tolerant (tolerant)	intolerant (intolerant)	0.24	0.81
engasjert (involved)	uengasjert (uninvolved)	0.15	0.00 a
tillit (confident)	mistillit (inconfident)	0.38	0.85
alvorlig (serious)	humoristisk (humourous)	0.55	0.83
rigid (rigid)	fleksibel (flexible)	0.31	0.81
varm (warm)	kjølig (cool)	0.08	0.71

a From the point of view of the method, it is worth reporting that all the dyads scored relatively high on involvement.

scorers were given tape-recordings of the 24 practice routes and the 24 experimental routes in random order and asked to rate the interaction on 12 seven-point scales of the type 'cooperative-competitive' (see Table 16). All scales with interscorer reliability lower than 0.70, were rejected. We were thus left with nine reliable scales on the experimental route, and only two on the shorter practice route.

A factor analysis of the ratings of the experimental route on the nine reliable scales revealed two factors, explaining 67% and 16% of the total variance respectively. Factor I correlated highest with the scales tolerant/intolerant, confident/inconfident and flexible/rigid. Factor I thus seems to reveal something about openness/closedness regarding what is to be made known or exchanged in the dyads. We therefore labelled factor I a 'rigidity factor'. The two scales correlating highest with factor II were humorous/serious and warm/cool. Factor II was therefore labelled an 'emotional tone factor'.

An analysis of variance conducted on the reliable scales and the two factors (see Table 17) revealed no influence of any of the experimental manipulations on the practice route. On the experimental route, however, the communication of the high anxiety dyads was significantly different from that of the low anxiety dyads on eight of the nine scales and factor I. The high anxiety dyads were significantly more rigid (factor I) than the low anxiety dyads, but no such difference was found with respect to factor II. The different instruction conditions did not influence communication significantly in either of the two tasks, as rated on any of the scales or factors.

Table 17. Summary of analyses of variance on scales and factors on the communication on the practice route and the experimental route respectively

Situation	Scale/Factor	Source (level of anxiety)		(type of) instruction		Interaction	
		F	p	F	p	F	p
Practice route	(2) sure-unsure	0.00	–	0.52	–	0.52	–
	(4) structured-unstructured	0.08	–	0.60	–	0.46	–
Experimental route	(1) cooperative-competitive	10.99	0.01	4.33	–	2.62	–
	(2) sure-unsure	163.21	0.01	0.02	–	0.62	–
	(3) peaceful-aggressive	4.60	0.05	3.25	–	0.59	–
	(4) structured-unstructured	16.76	0.01	0.42	–	0.42	–
	(5) tolerant-intolerant	14.73	0.01	1.76	–	0.35	–
	(6) confident-inconfident	13.62	0.01	2.64	–	0.78	–
	(7) serious-humorous	0.06	–	0.72	–	1.19	–
	(8) rigid-flexible	29.73	0.01	3.50	–	1.12	–
	(9) warm-cool	3.64	–	0.83	–	5.01	0.05
	Factor I	42.75	0.01	1.59	–	0.23	–
	Factor II	0.06	–	1.44	–	2.05	–

Concluding Remarks

Two more general theoretical comments may be made on the basis of the present study. First, it demonstrated the possible substantial contributions of studies conducted on the general formula: How does the personal disposition X influence communication?

Secondly, the present study did so by revealing a significant effect of anxiety upon communication. The influence was reflected in efficiency as well as in ratings of emotional climate of the communication process. However, this particular effect was dependent upon situational factors, so that the influence was merely exposed in a complex conflict situation, and not in a simple and straightforward situation. A person's behavior in a social situation can, therefore neither be explained exclusively by a trait or disposition theory nor by situational factors (situationism). We have instead to specify under which social situation conditions a particular personal disposition will be influent.

PART III

A summary presentation and discussion of what has been done (1972–79) within this
research program

In Part I (p.47-53) we discussed our projects on the basis of ideal type theoretical-methodological considerations. But a thorough and systematic investigation of each single one of these issues would have demanded more resources than we have at our disposal. Because of the trivial fact that every project represents a compromise between theoretical-methodological ideals and the resources at one's disposition, we will briefly mention the most important factors that have made it possible to realize at least parts of the ambitious research program hammered out in Part I. First and foremost, inspired by the Sølvberg & Blakar study, a number of students became interested in writing their dissertations in connection with the project. This represented an enormous potential of interest and work, and the strong involvement of the students resulted in solid and thorough efforts. The main disadvantage, however, was that each study has to represent a complete and autonomous piece of work. This implies that it was impossible to direct the proceedings only in accordance with strict theoretical-methodological criteria, and instead each study had to be adapted to each student's special interests. Hence the very enterprise of integrating the parts afterwards becomes more difficult and comprehensive than it otherwise would have been. Parts I and III can be read as examples of such integrative enterprises (cf. also Blakar, in press c, in press b, Blakar & Pedersen, 1980a, 1980b).

Below follows a brief presentation of what has until now (October 1979) been done within the research program outlined above. In the presentation we will adhere strictly to the disposition given by means of the list of theoretical-methodological issues in Part I. Each study will hence be presented and commented upon from the perspective of settling the above issues only. The numbers from 1 to 6 correspond to the list of issues in Part I (p. 47-53).

(1) Replications and expansions of the samples: Paulsen (1977) carried out a replication of Sølvberg & Blakar's study. In this connection the widely acknowledged lack of replicative studies in this field should be underlined (cf. Riskin & Faunce, 1972). This study is, however, not just a replication of the original study, but by moving the study from Oslo (typically urban) to a typical rural district, social/cultural/ecological variables are systematically varied (cf. pt. 4). By combining the original study and the replication, we obtain a subtle 2x2x2 design, which enables us to describe under what conditions the communication patterns of families containing schizophrenic members deviate, and in what manner they deviate (Blakar, Paulsen & Sølvberg, 1978, see ch. 1 in Part II). The crucial point is that not only do we have two types of couples (parents with and without a schizophrenic offspring) with varying sociocultural background (town versus country), but they communicate in two different cooperation situations (one simple and straightforward versus one in which a conflict is induced). With regard to efficiency of communication, the significant differences

between parents with and without a schizophrenic offspring were reproduced. In addition considerable differences in communication efficiency between rural and urban couples in this particular situation were found. This latter finding underlines how cautious one has to be in generalizing in this field of research, and that methods and models have to be adapted in accordance with local social and cultural variations with regard to style and pattern of communication (Blakar, Sølvberg & Paulsen, 1978). (Cf. Dahle's study under pt. 4 below.) Presently, Valdimarsdottir (in preparation) is conducting a replication of the Sølvberg & Blakar study in Iceland. Her results too are in perfect accordance with the findings in the Sølvberg & Blakar study.

Rund (1976, 1978) went a step further and tried to specify more clearly the connection between the parent's pattern of communication and the specific deviance in thought processes displayed by the schizophrenic patient. This was achieved by (a) testing thought deviances of the schizophrenics by means of traditional tests, and by (b) mapping the communication pattern of the parents in the present standardized communication conflict situation. Finally, (c) through a blind scoring procedure it was predicted which patient 'belonged' to which parental couple. The in-part negative results (failure to predict) in this study illustrate the obvious weaknesses of the theories that have been developed on this subject (for example the theories of Theodore Lidz and Lyman Wynne. For more thorough criticism of their theories and research, see Rønbeck, 1977, Glennsjø, 1977).

(2) Different demand characteristics: With regard to the extremely important methodological issue concerning the situational demand characteristics, several independent and substantially interesting studies have been conducted. Alve & Hultberg (1974) studied the communication of parents of 'borderline' patients. Wikran (1974) studied the pattern of communication of parents with children who suffer from asthma as compared to parents whose children had congenital heart diseases. Rotbæk (1976) studied the communication of parents of children who suffered from enuresis. Finally, Fætten & Østvold (1975) studied the communication pattern in couples in which not an offspring, but one of the spouses, was the diagnosed patient member.

However, the substantial findings of all these studies would be of little interest in this context. To examine the methodological problems in focus, the one study of parental couples with a borderline offspring (Group B) will be chosen. The outcome of this study is particularly critical to the Sølvberg & Blakar study. First and foremost, borderline represent a 'non-schizophrenic control' to use Bannister's terminology. Second, the distinction between the diagnostic categories schizophrenia and borderline is very subtle, and it is not likely to be known by the parents. Hence the two categories of parents are likely to enter the situation on the same or comparable expectations, namely that we are participating because we are the parents of a psychiatric patient/a mad person.

Moreover, parental couples having a child with a serious heart disease (Group H) represents a particularly interesting control. Similar to parents having a schizophrenic offspring, they are the parents of a seriously ill person. The illness of their child will also strongly influence family life, although very differently from a schizophrenic member. And like the Group S parents, they will know that they participate because they are parents of a seriously ill child. But contrary to schizophrenia (and borderline), there is absolutely no reason to assume that the illness can be understood in terms of the familial communication pattern.

Given these four categories of parental couples, Group N, Group S, Group B, and Group H, a variety of possible combinations with regard to differences and similarities in patterns of communication can be imagined. Only a few of the theoretically most interesting ones with specific reference to the Sølvberg and Blakar study will be examined.

A possible outcome is: $S = B = H \neq N$, i.e., that Group S, Group B and Group H demonstrate similar patterns, and a pattern different from that of Group N. The implication of this outcome would be that the Sølvberg & Blakar study carried absolutely no specific information concerning families containing schizophrenic members. We would be forced to conclude that the inefficient communication of the Group S couples could not be related specifically to the fact that they had a schizophrenic offspring. The inefficiency would most likely be due to a general effect of being selected to participate because one had a seriously ill child.

Whereas the first outcome would be conclusive with regard to the Sølvberg & Blakar study, the following would not: $S = B \neq H = N$. This would imply that the inefficiency of the Group S parents in the conflict situation could not be ascribed to a general effect of having a seriously ill child. Moreover, this outcome would distinguish between couples with and without children 'under psychiatric care', to use Bannister's terminology again. However, this outcome would not allow any conclusions with reference to the sub-category of schizophrenia specifically.

Another possible outcome is: $S \neq B = H = N$. This outcome would have represented strong indications that the findings done in the Sølvberg & Blakar study were specific to the category of schizophrenia. But let us now turn to the outcomes that were revealed within this integrated project, namely: $S \neq B \neq H = N$. In our contention, no other combination of outcomes could have been more supportive with respect to further elaborations of the conceptual and methodological issues of the field, while at the same time providing intriguing substantive evidence. First, parents of seriously ill children (heart disease) do not deviate in their pattern of communication from so-called normal parental couples. Furthermore, both Group S and Group B demonstrated patterns of communication different from Group N, and moreover, they demonstrated patterns distinctively different from each other. And most intriguing of all, on various measures the patterns of communication of Group S and Group B couples deviated in opposite directions from the Group N pattern. (For detailed descriptions of the patterns of communication of Group S, Group B and Group N, see ch. 2 in Part II, Hultberg, Alve & Blakar, 1978, Knutsen, 1979.)

(3) Parent-child interaction: As regards the issue of parent-child communication, four autonomous, but interrelated, studies have been conducted until now. In these studies the mother and father together are asked to explain the two routes to their daughter or son. Jacobsen & Pettersen (1974) analyzed the patterns of communication between the parents and their schizophrenic or 'normal' daughter. Differences in communication between Group S and Group N families were revealed just as clearly in this three-person setting as in the Sølvberg & Blakar study involving the parents alone (see ch. 3 in Part II, Mossige, Pettersen & Blakar, 1976, 1979).

As mentioned above, in connection with this latter study it could also be argued that differences in communication could be attributed to different situational demand characteristics for the two groups of families. Haarstad's (1976) investigation of the parent-daughter communication in families in which the daughter was given the diagnosis of anorexia nervosa (Group A families) settled this issue, however, in that families of this category revealed a communication pattern definitely different from both Group S and Group N families. Hence we can conclude as we did above, that the differences exposed in the communication patterns cannot be explained by different expectations held toward the experimental situation only. In this respect Haarstad's study serves exactly the same purpose as Alve & Hultberg's (1974) study presented above. At present the qualitative differences in the patterns of communication in these three categories of families are being further corroborated in terms of degree of open versus closed family systems and degree of egocentrism on behalf of the family members (Antonsen, in preparation); in terms of patterns of confirmation (Aspen, in preparation); and in terms of how they react upon and manage episodes of conflict during the process of communication (Olsen, in preparation).

Moreover, Glennsjø (1977) compared the patterns of communication in families containing a schizophrenic son with those containing a schizophrenic daughter. This particular study thus represents a critical test of the theory developed by Lidz and associates. Glennsjø's study testified to great differences as to how families containing a schizophrenic member structured the communication process, but there were no systematic differences between families containing a male (son) and families containing a female (daughter) diagnosed as schizophrenic. (Cf. Pedersen's study under pt. 4 below.) These findings are contrary to predictions derived from Lidz' theory.

Finally, Vassend (1979) and Valstad (in preparation) has pursued Wikran, Faleide
& Blakar's (1978) study (see ch. 4 in Part II) in connection with children with asthma,
in that he has investigated parent-child interactions in families with and without an
asthmatic child. In addition to a control Group N, two different sub-groups of A
families, depending on how severe the astma was and whether or not psychogenic
factors had been reported in connection to asthmatic attacks, were included in this
study. His study replicates and corroborates the findings reported by Wikran, Faleide
& Blakar (1978). However, the patterns of communication of the 21 families in Vassend's study cannot be directly compared with the families in the above studies, in
that the participating children were much younger.

(4) General variables in communication: As we have demonstrated elsewhere
(Blakar, 1978a, in press a), clinically oriented research in this field has not been
properly integrated with more generally oriented research on communication (cf.
also Riskin & Faunce, 1972). It follows from the research program we have outlined
(Blakar, 1978a, and Part I, p.47-53) that it is absolutely necessary to conduct more
clinically oriented studies of familial communication and psychopathology as an integral part of a more general study of the process of communication. Only within the
frame of general communication theory it is possible to contribute to the understanding of psychopathology from a communication perspective. Concentrating exclusively
upon investigating patterns of communication in families with and without psychopathological members obviously involves the risk of labeling as 'deviant' or 'pathological'
patterns of communication which would prove to be within the 'normal range' if one
took care to systematically explore the variation of 'normal' patterns of communication depending on background variables.

The studies conducted so far (Lagerløv & Stokstad, 1974, Dahle, 1977, Pedersen,
1979, and Strøno, 1978) have demonstrated the impact of general variables (such as
sex, social background, age, anxiety) on the process of communication in this communication conflict situation.

As an illustration of how (a) personality variables are reflected in the process of
communication, Lagerløv & Stokstad (1974) analyzed the communication of persons
with varying levels of anxiety. They compared the patterns of communication among
students with high versus low level of anxiety (as measured by Taylor's Manifest
Anxiety Scale).

It should be emphasized that here we are not referring to extreme or 'pathological'
anxiety, but to levels of anxiety found amongst normally functioning university students. In the simple and straightforward situation (the practice route) there was no
difference in efficiency of communication between the two groups. In the communication conflict situation, however, there was a marked difference in that, whereas all

the low level anxiety dyads solved the induced conflict, more than half of the high level anxiety dyads failed. This study thus testified to subtle person-situation inter-actions in communication (see ch. 5 in Part II, Stokstad, Lagerløv & Blakar, 1976, 1979).

With respect to (b) social (anthropological) variables, Dahle (1977) has analyzed the patterns of communication of couples with differing social backgrounds (urban versus rural, and working class versus middle class couples). And Pedersen (1979a, 1979b) studied how the pattern of communication is structured and defined by sex roles. Dahle has demonstrated that variations in style and efficiency in communica-tion within the range of so-called normal couples, i.e., in those parental couples who do not have an offspring who is given some sort of psychiatric diagnosis, are really considerable, and co-vary systematically with social background. Again the inter-action with type of communication situation should be noted, in that whereas no dif-ferences in communication efficiency were found in the simple and straightforward situation (the practice route), clearcut differences emerged in the conflict situation. Moreover, Pedersen (1979a) has revealed highly different patterns of communication depending on how the sexes of explainer and follower were combined. The four com-binations: (1) man → man, (2) woman → woman, (3) man → woman, (4) woman → man yielded very different patterns of communication. Of the findings it may be briefly mentioned that - according to common sense 'knowledge' about sex-roles - male → female dyads revealed the most efficient communication, and female → male the most inefficient. However, this was true of the simple situation only. The pattern was totally reversed in the conflict situation in that male → female dyads were the most inefficient in solving the induced communication conflict (cf. Blakar & Pedersen, 1980a, 1980b). Dahle's and Pedersen's studies yield interesting contributions to an understanding of social control and communication in general (Blakar, 1978a, 1979b).

Finally (c) Strøno (1978) has analyzed the process of communication in this conflict situation within the framework of general developmental psychology. She investigated the communication of children of various ages (6-16 years) and found, as could be expected, an increasing capacity to decenter and take the perspective of the other (Piaget, 1926, Mead, 1934). The communication became more adequate and efficient with increasing age. The categorization system developed by Strøno, in order to identify and describe the various manifestations of egocentrism in the process of communication, has yielded a general framework within which the patterns of com-munication of different categories of families (e.g., families containing a schizo-phrenic member) can be assessed (cf. Blakar & Nafstad, 1980a).

Of course, the presentation of these studies is not intended as an exhaustive analysis of how general social, developmental, and personality variables are reflected in the process of communication (cf. Blakar, 1979b). On the contrary, they were presented here for theoretical-methodological reasons only to demonstrate that systematic studies along these lines are necessary in order to warrant any conclusions from studies conducted on the relation between patterns of familial communication and (development of) psychopathology.

First, only through this type of systematic study (especially of the kind that Dahle has conducted) can we learn the normal variations. Without thorough knowledge of normal variations in patterns of communication according to social class, cultural, and ecological background variables, one will be unable to assess and describe properly deviant or pathological communication. Studies of the kind that Dahle (1977) has conducted are particularly important because the underlying (often implicit) model of 'normal communication' from which pathological communication deviates, is seriously questioned and investigated. We have elsewhere (see ch. 1 in Part II, Blakar, Paulsen & Sølvberg, 1978) argued that a particular experimenter ethno-centrism has been displayed by students of psychopathology and familial communication, in that the 'norm' for 'adequate communication' has been implicitly defined as the communication of the normal middle class family living in cities.

Secondly, knowledge about how general variables (such as level or anxiety, or age) affect the process of communication may contribute to the identification of what (if anything) is failing in the communication of families containing members who have been ascribed psychiatric diagnoses (for example schizophrenia). Conclusions concerning causality cannot be drawn from such covariation studies, but systematic comparisons of the communication of people with, for instance, a high level of anxiety with the pattern of communication of families containing, for instance, a schizophrenic member could give valuable clues for future research.

(5) Methods of analysis: The fact that by simple means we have succeeded in developing a standardized communication situation, which proved sensitive with respect to revealing the patterns of communication of different categories of families, is important. However, with regard to the research program outlined in Part I (cf. Blakar, 1974a, 1978a), this constitutes only a first, albeit critical, step. One next step was the development of methods that will enable systematic analyses to be made of qualitative characteristics pertaining to the communication of the different categories of families or parental couples.

As with the development of the standardized communication situation itself (cf. Blakar, 1973a, 1978a, and Part I), we want methods of analysis which are explicitly grounded in and derived from general communication theory. It should be underlined that in this field of research this seems to be far from an obvious qualification. The enormous number of studies applying linguistically inspired, but from the perspective of communication theory highly questionable, units or categories, such as 'number of words per sentence' and 'ratio of nouns to verbs', are illustrative.

We have elsewhere (Blakar, 1978a, Blakar & Nafstad, 1980a) argued that methods and concepts to be employed in communication-oriented studies of psychopathology should be anchored (a) in a general theory of communication as well as (b) in characteristics of the specific category of psychopathology in focus. We have also claimed (Blakar, 1976a) that the lack of progress in the field (for critical reviews, see Haley, 1972, Riskin & Faunce, 1972, Jacobsen & Pettersen, 1974, Jacob, 1975) is primarily caused by lack of a general theory of communication.

In particular, when it comes to qualitative analysis of communication in families with and without psychopathological members, most researchers seem to have given up or forgotten all about a general communication theory. Overwhelmed by the richness of and variation in the material, they have resorted to mere clinical-casuistic descriptions, freely employing everyday language and ad-hoc terms. (For critical reviews of this conceptual and terminological chaos, see Riskin & Faunce, 1972, Blakar, 1976a.)

Riskin & Faunce (1972) point out that 'interdisciplinary isolation' is striking in the field. But if one turns, for example, to social-developmental psychology, a whole set of relevant and theoretically grounded concepts are available. To illustrate, a few examples will be given. A basic precondition for successful communication is the participants' ability to take the perspective of the other (Mead, 1934), and egocentrism (lack of decentration) (Piaget,1926) may strongly hinder communication. Related to this is Rommetveit's (1968) notion that 'encoding involves antecipatory decoding'. Another essential prerequisite for successful communication is that the participants have to endorse contracts (contracts concerning categorization, topic, perspective, etc.) by which the act of communication is being monitored (Rommetveit, 1972a,1974, Blakar, 1972a, 1978a). And when communication runs into more or less serious trouble, it is essential in order to re-establish successful communication that the difficulties are adequately attributed (Heider,1958) by the participants. Only the slightest knowledge about communication in relation to psychopathology should enable one to see that these concepts from social-developmental psychology may be of direct relevance in analysis of patterns of familial communication.

To investigate the above-mentioned concepts we have developed a set of methods of analysis and scoring procedures which help to assess the theoretically relevant qualitative aspects of the process of communication. These methods of analysis will be briefly presented below.

Alve & Hultberg (1974) took as their point of departure the concept of attribution, and developed a procedure to describe the process of communication in terms of the couples' patterns of attribution of communication difficulties (who attributes how to what, and how does the other spouse react to the attribution). Haarstad (1976) adapted the method for application in the more complex (three-person) parent–child interaction. Systematic differences in the various categories of families' or couples' patterns of attribution in the communication conflict situation were revealed (see ch. 2 in Part II, Hultberg, Alve & Blakar, 1978). And Pedersen (1979) has revealed distinctively different patterns of attribution of communication difficulties depending on the constellation of sexes in the roles of explainer and follower respectively. Finally, Guttelvik (1979) conducted an analysis of patterns of attribution of communication difficulties of troubled married couples who have/have not participated in a therapeutic program.

Already in the first exploratory study (Sølvberg, 1973, Sølvberg & Blakar, 1975, see Part I, p. 32-47), the concept of egocentrism (versus decentration) proved useful in capturing qualitative differences in the patterns of communication of parental couples with and without a schizophrenic offspring. Since then a lot of work has been invested in developing systematic scoring procedures for assessing the degree of and the development over time of egocentrism/decentration as displayed by the various categories of participants in the communication conflict situation (Jacobsen & Pettersen, 1974, Kristiansen, 1976, Mossige, Pettersen & Blakar, 1976, 1979, Kristiansen, Faleide & Blakar, 1977, Strøno, 1978, see ch. 3 in part II). In his analysis on utterance level, Kristiansen (1976) managed to assess degree of and development over time during the process of communication of egocentrism as well as types of reaction to the egocentric utterances. By this method of analysis qualitative differences in the patterns of communication of various categories of parental couples (parents of children with psychosomatic illnesses compared with three control groups, i.e., parents of children with congenital heart disease and parents of schizophrenic and borderline patients) were revealed (Kristiansen, Faleide & Blakar, 1977). At present Antonsen (in preparation) is pursuing this analysis in order to assess the potential interplay between degree of egocentrism on behalf of the individual family members and to what degree the family exposes a closed or open family system (cf. Mossige, Pettersen & Blakar, 1979, see ch. 2 in Part II).

Inspired by the analysis of egocentrism, Paulsen (1977) in his study of parental couples (urban versus rural) with and without a schizophrenic offspring, developed a scoring procedure for assessing the couples' ability to cope adequately with free and bound information (cf. Rommetveit, 1974, Blakar & Rommetveit, 1975, Blakar, 1978a). He found that across the social background variation, the Group S couples more frequently and to a larger extent tacitly took for granted (as free information) critical information that could not yet possibly be known to the other spouse. At present Blisten (in preparation) is refining this analysis of the participants' mastering of free and bound information during the process of communication.

The contractual aspect is characteristic of the process of communication (cf. Rommetveit, 1972a, 1972b, 1974, 1978, Blakar, 1972a, 1975b). Having identified the various types of contracts (contracts concerning topic, perspective, roles, categorization, etc,) monitoring the process of communication in this communication conflict situation, and the process by which contracts are endorsed (Blakar, 1972a), Moberget & Reer (1975) developed a systematic procedure for classifying and describing the endorsement of contracts. From a theoretical point of view, the concept of contract was proposed to handle the dynamic aspects of communication. And in the concrete studies of familial communication, the analysis of contracts have enabled us to describe in detail the control relations as reflected in the monitoring of the process of communication. By means of this contractual analysis Øisjøfoss (1976) revealed distinctly different patterns of control in married couples depending on social background variables (urban versus rural, middle class versus labour class). Furthermore, he found a high correlation between flexibility in patterns of control and efficiency in communication (whether they solved the induced communication conflict or not). Pedersen (1979) revealed different patterns of control depending on the constellation of sexes in the roles of explainer and follower. Glennsjø (1977) adapted the scoring procedure for application in the more complex (three-person) parent-child interaction.

From a methodological point of view the greatest advantage of the present design is that we get excerpts of the communication process in two apparently similar, but actually highly different, situations. The one is simple and straightforward (the so-called practice route), whereas in the other a conflict is experimentally induced. In a sense we thus have a 'before-after' design. The difference between the two situations, moreover, is conceptualized within the framework of a general theory of communication (cf. Blakar, 1973a, 1978a, Blakar & Pedersen, 1980b). The fact that in a study where 24 student dyads participated, a rank-order correlation of -0,19 was found between efficiency (time used) of communication in the two situations (Blakar & Pedersen, 1980a) indicates that we really have managed to establish two apparently similar, but in reality highly different, communication situations.

In principle, this methodological advantage may be exploited in many ways to gain insight into and obtain knowledge about the process of communication (Blakar, 1978a). So far we have mainly used various prediction or blind-scoring procedures. The general procedure may be described as follows. The scorer is only allowed to listen to the recording from the simple and straightforward situation (the practice route). On the basis of his analysis of the pattern of communication in the simple situation, he is asked to predict - and give the reasons for his predictions - how these particular participants (family/couple/dyad) will manage to cope with the induced communication conflict. In this manner we can to a certain extent put our insights and the different methods of analysis to a test.

A brief discussion of a study by Teigre (1976) will serve as an illustrative example. He assessed the degree of confidence (in oneself and the other) in the simple situation for 30 married couples, and on the basis of the type and degree of mutual conficence, he predicted the outcome in the communication conflict situation. Similar prediction procedures can in principle be exploited in connection with all the qualitative methods of analysis discussed above. So far, however, predictions from the simple to the conflict situation have only been conducted for the contractual analysis (Moberget & Reer, 1975).

It has to be emphasized that the above prediction procedure should not be confused with the prediction procedure used in the Sølvberg & Blakar study (see Part I). In the latter case the blind scorer listened to the recordings and on the basis of clinical insight predicted which of the recordings belonged to the Group S and which to the Group N couples. This latter procedure too has been further refined (Jacobsen & Pettersen, 1974, Wikran, 1974, Mossige, Pettersen & Blakar, 1976, 1979, Wikran, Faleide & Blakar, 1978, 1979, see ch. 3 and ch. 4 in Part II).

Our primary concern at the present stage is in the reasons the scorers give for their predictions. We obtain information regardless of whether the predictions are correct or not. It is only where one and the same argument sometimes results in correct and sometimes in incorrect predictions that we are left inconclusive regarding the potentiality of the actual analysis.

A third type of prediction procedure that has also been exploited, is (a) to have the parents' pattern of communication assessed in Blakar's standardized communication conflict situation, and (b) to have the identified reference (diagnosed) person assessed either by test procedures or by more clinical descriptions, and then (c) have blind scorers predict which of the patients belong to which of the parental couples (cf. Rund, 1976, 1978). At present this procedure is being used in more large scale studies in our attempt (see p.40) to break away from categorizing families in terms of individual nosology, e.g., 'schizophrenic' families or 'borderline' families, and to develop a family-based nosology or classification system.

In the different types of analysis mentioned above, we have restricted ourselves to one single concept in each analysis (for example contract, attribution of communication difficulties, confidence, egocentrism/decentration, free and bound information). Obviously, these concepts are interconnected. They are all derived from the same theoretical framework (cf. Part I). The interrelations between the various aspects captured in the analyses presented above may perhaps be illustrated thus. The egocentrism of one of the family members may result in his tacitly taking for granted or given (i.e. , as free information) something that could not possibly be known by the others. This may easily result in communication difficulties either directly or indirectly. And in order to re-establish commonality, the (experienced) communication difficulty has to be identified (i.e. , attribution of communication difficulties). As a consequence of the (adequate or inadequate) attribution of the communication difficulties, the underlying contracts are frequently modified or new contracts are endorsed to prevent further tangles of the same kind (cf. Blakar, 1978a).

In order not to lose track of these integrative aspects, the more systematic and detailed, but very laborious and time-consuming, analyses on, for example, egocentrism/decentration have continually been supplemented with more free case studies in which all these concepts have been exploited in describing the patterns of communication in the various categories of families or couples. Within the project this type of analysis has been refined in a series of studies (Wikran, 1974, Fætten & Østvold, 1975, Rotbæk, 1976, Dahle, 1977, Blakar, 1976, Blakar, Lavik & Østvold, 1980). The integrative aspect has also been taken care of, in that two or more of the above qualitative analyses have been conducted on the same set of families. For example, Guttelvik (1979), Knutsen (1979) and Pedersen (1979a) in their respective studies conducted both an analysis of patterns of attribution of communication difficulties and an analysis of control relations. Combined, these two analyses yielded very nuanced pictures of the patterns of communication. In recent and ongoing studies much effort has been invested in simplifying and standardizing the various scoring procedures (cf. Pedersen, 1979a, Knutsen, 1979, Guttelvik, 1979, Blisten, in preparation).

All the above-mentioned methods of analysis are based on concepts derived from a social-developmental theory, i.e. , the theoretical framework within which the standardized communication conflict situation itself was developed. From the perspective of generalization, it is essential that the process of communication in this particular conflict situation has also been analyzed within quite different theoretical frameworks. Within the framework of symbolic interactionism Bråten (1974, 1978) has exploited the conflict communication situation in his study of coding processes. It is worth mentioning that in his studies Bråten used video-tape, so that non-verbal communication in the situation can be analyzed as well. In connection with the identification of coding mechanisms involved, Enge (1978) has developed a computer program to simulate the process of communication in the conflict situation. Havik and his students (Ellingsen et al. , 1976) took as their point of departure Kelly's so-called personal construct theory, and, on the basis of Kelly's Role Construct Repertory Test, predicted the communication pattern of various married couples in the conflict situation. Within the framework of attribution theory, McKillip (1975) studied the participants' evaluations of each other before, during, and after they had been involved in the induced communication conflict. He found marked differences between subjects who knew/did not know each other, in that those who did not know each other were much more prone to change their opinion of the other.

By far the most thorough and systematic analysis of the process of communication in this situation conducted within alternative conceptual frameworks is the one by Andersson & Pilblad (1977). They analyzed the interaction of 30 parental couples in this particular situation by means of Bales' new system for categorizing interaction, SYMLOG (Bales & Cohen, 1974). First and foremost, striking differences in the patterns of communication of the solvers compared with the non-solvers were exposed. Secondly, this method of analysis revealed systematic differences between different categories of parents. As Andersson & Pilblad themselves pointed out, the differences in patterns of communication between Group S, Group B, and Group N couples revealed in their SYMLOG analysis are consistent with the findings reported from the analyses conducted in terms of, for example, contractual monitoring of the process of communication and patterns of attribution of communication difficulties.

A linguistically oriented analysis of the patterns of communication in this particular conflict situation has long been awaited and invited (cf. Blakar, 1979b). Recently, Holmefjord Olsen (in prep.) has undertaken this enterprise.

(6) The conceptual framework: The distinction between pt. 5 (development of methods of analysis) and pt. 6 (further development of the conceptual framework) does not of course reflect a division of labour. Theoretical clarification represents a necessary prerequisite for the development of adequate methods of analysis, whereas the development of methods of analysis promotes theoretical clarification. The various methodological developments described above all contributed to theoretical clarification. As a transition to pt. 6, we will therefore consider an issue which was originally encountered as an irritating methodological problem in the analysis of the process of communication, but which proved to involve intriguing, basic theoretical issues: When is a problem in an act of communication unravelled? When is a communication conflict solved? The trivial problem of analysis which originally compelled us to undertake the very enterprise of analyzing these issues in general was the fact that we soon ran into trouble in applying our simple set of criteria (see p. 75) for distinguishing between those who managed (solvers) and those who did not manage (non-solvers) to unravel the induced communication conflict (cf. Blakar, 1978a, Mossige, Pettersen & Blakar, 1976, 1979, Wikran, Faleide & Blakar, 1978, Hultberg, Alve & Blakar, 1978). This problem will not be discussed in any detail here, only a brief illustration of the nature of the problems will be given. This presentation will be directly related to the set of termination criteria originally developed by Sølvberg & Blakar (see p. 33):

First, in some cases only one of the participants recognized the deception in the

maps, while the other(s) would show great surprise when the error was afterwards uncovered by a direct comparison of the two maps. This type of solution, which we have
classified as an individual solution, is very different from cases in which all of them
(both) are firmly convinced about the existence of the error (a social solution). If the
experimenter too readily accepted an individual solution, we would lose the chance to
study how the member with insight about the deception convinces or fails to convince
the other(s). Actually, this phase could be very revealing as to factors such as power
and control.

Furthermore, various combinations of degrees of cognitive insight into the deception
and social conviction vis-à-vis the experimenter have been observed. On the one extreme, we have the couples or families in which one (or all) members claim with conviction that something is wrong, and consequently there is no reason in continuing, but
without their having identified and localized the error on the maps. On the other extreme,
we have the couples or families who have obviously achieved a certain insight about the
deceptive maps (the degree of insight may vary from vague doubt to full understanding),
but who are unsure of their own judgment and therefore hesitate to reveal their suspi-
cions to the experimenter. The latter involves a distinct contrast to those who on the
basis of vague and diffuse suspicion only put the experimenter under a heavy social
pressure to admit that something is wrong (see ch. 2 in Part II). The phase when the
participants advance and work their way from vague and diffuse suspicion toward full
understanding of the deception and thus unravel the communication conflict in which they
have been involved (or fail to do so) could be very revealing with regard to their pattern
of communication. In order not to lose critical information about the process of communication, we have reconsidered and tightened up the termination criteria (see p. 33
and p. 75) in that we have decided that the experimenter should (a) 'press' the couples
or families as much as possible toward criterion (1), and not accept solutions according to criterion (2). Furthermore, the experimenter should (b) hesitate to accept individual solutions, and see if the couple or family can reach a joint conclusion.

Not only among the solvers (i.e., those who manage to have the experimental session
terminated according to the criteria within the 40-minutes limit) have different patterns
been identified. Also the non-solvers (i.e., those who continue for more than 40 minutes)
reveal distinctly different patterns of behavior. The most important distinction within
this latter category is between those who one or more times explicitly question the credibility of the maps, but without achieving any conclusion or identification of the error,
and those who never explicitly question the credibility of the maps. In this connection
it has to be mentioned that the analysis of attribution of communication difficulties (cf.
above) is particularly revealing with respect to how various participants may oscillate
between attributing the communication difficulties to the situation (the maps), to themselves or to the other participant(s) (Hultberg, Alve & Blakar, 1978, see ch. 2 in Part II).

At present Valstad (in preparation) is pursuing this analysis in that he is developing a procedure to assess the families' patterns of behavior in the various episodes
during the process of communication at which lack of commonality (i.e., conflict with
regard to premisses) can be identified. Owing to the deception, the families will continually encounter such conditions. Moreover, the deception helps the outside observer
to identify instances of conflict. Valstad's preliminary data indicate distinctively different patterns of behavior by different categories of families at these critical moments
of interaction.

The issue to be demonstrated here, however, is how the analysis of these methodological problems entailed an explication of general theory concerning social conflicts
and their solution. In order to develop adequate criteria for terminating the experimental session, and accept the induced communication conflict as being unravelled,
an explicit model or theory of conflict solution had to be outlined (Endresen, 1977,
Blakar, 1978a). [24] The above-mentioned aspects (social versus individual solution,
cognitive insight versus social pressure, etc.) represent essential problems for a
general theory or model of social conflict solution. Only from such a model is it possible to derive a set of theoretically grounded criteria. Here it should be noted that
the set of criteria originally launched in the exploratory Sølvberg & Blakar study (see
p. 33) were based primarily on an intuitive hunch.

Naturally, the above-mentioned clinically oriented studies have all contributed theoretical and conceptual clarification. The development of scoring procedures in
connection with some of the key concepts of social-developmental theory has
in fact been one of the major purposes in several of the above studies - egocentrism/
decentration (Jacobsen & Pettersen, 1974), attribution of communication difficulties
(Alve & Hultberg, 1974, Haarstad, 1976), the contractual aspect of the process of communication (Glennsjø, 1977), free and bound information (Paulsen, 1977), just to mention some illustrative examples. However, as is always the case in clinically oriented
research, these studies were all devoted more or less exclusively to the study of one
particular type of psychopathology (schizophrenia, anorexia nervosa, borderline syndrome, etc.). We have elsewhere (Blakar, 1976a), pointed out various methodological
pitfalls in the predominant strategy of research in the field, according to which the
study of familial communication and psychopathology is conducted exclusively within
'a clinical context' with little or no contact with general theory on communication.
Hence, if our conceptual framework was elaborated in connection with clinically
oriented studies of the above types only, we would be guilty of ignoring our own criticism.

In connection with the present clinical project on familial communication and psychopathology, we have attempted to amend the methodological-theoretical conditions in
four mutually supplementary manners:

First and foremost, by continuing work within the psychology of language and communication theory in general. [25] (Cf. Blakar, 1978a, in press b.)

Secondly, a series of analyses aiming at more general theory construction has been conducted on the basis of studies in the present communication conflict situation. For example, Brisendal (1976) developed a theoretical framework for identifying preconditions for mutual understanding (versus lack of understanding and misunderstanding). Endresen (1977) developed a theoretical framework and a corresponding model for solution or unravelling of social conflicts. Moreover, Svenheim (1979) has shown on the basis of the above studies how the framework of systems theory when applied to the field of family research has to take into account personal characteristics and individual capacities.

Thirdly, the conceptual framework has been elaborated in connection with more systematic re-analyses of the material collected in the clinically oriented studies presented above. Just to give a few examples, aspects of the process of communication have been corroborated in terms of confidence (in self and the other(s)) (Teigre, 1976); decentration and the ability to take the perspective of the other(s) (Kristiansen, 1976); (flexibility in) distribution of control (Øisjøfoss, 1976, Knutsen, 1979); the interplay between open versus closed family systems and egocentrism/decentration on behalf of the individual family members (Antonsen, in preparation); and, patterns of confirmation in familial communication (Aspen, in preparation). In these latter studies the theoretical and conceptual analysis has been subjected to exploratory empirical tests, in that material from the above-presented clinically oriented studies has been re-analyzed.

Finally, the studies of how general variables (such as sex, age, level of anxiety, etc.) are reflected in the process of communication (cf. pt. 4 above) have significantly contributed to the elaboration of the general conceptual framework for the study of familial communication and deviant behavior.

Concluding comments

Although the present volume has reported on the yield of the joint efforts of many people over some years, the findings presented and the conclusions reached should be interpreted as highly explorative. This does not imply a modest downgrading of our work and the potential contributions we have made. It reflects, however, an acknowledgement of the complexities and subtleties of the fundamental human problems that we have addressed.

The most honest conclusion at the present stage is thus that almost every study conducted within the above research program so far has posed as many new questions and issues as it has settled. Communication-oriented research on psychopathology –

the present project included - constitutes therefore but a very intriguing challenge. However, the studies conducted so far have strongly convinced us that systematic investigation of the pattern of familial communication constitutes at least one promising way to gain insight into the complex processes leading to an individual developing deviant or psychopathological behavior. The above projects have fully demonstrated that the hurdles of this field of research are many and difficult, but also that an exhaustive exploitation of the conceptual framework of social-developmental theory will represent an important supplement to the understanding of the various forms of deviant behavior and psychopathology in general and of schizophrenia in particular.

REFERENCES

Aas, K. (1969a).   Allergiske barn. Oslo: J.W. Cappelens forlag.

Aas, K. (1969b).   Allergic asthma in childhood. Arch. Dis. Child., 44, 1-10.

Abramson, H.A. (1954). Evalutaion of maternal rejection theory in allergy. Ann. Allerg., 12, 129-140.

Ackerman, N.W. (1958). Psychodynamics of Family Life. New York: Basic Book.

Ackerman, N.W. , Beatman, F.L. & Sherman, S.N. (eds.) (1961). Exploring the Base for Family Therapy. New York: Family Service Ass. of America.

Ainsworth, L.H. (1958). Rigidity, insecurity and stress. J. Abn. and Soc. Psychol., 56, 67-75.

Alcock, T. (1960). Some personality characteristics of asthmatic children. Brit. J. Med. Psychol., 35, 133-141.

Alve, S. & Hultberg, M. (1974). Kommunikasjonssvikt hos foreldre til borderline pasienter. Unpublished dissertation, University of Oslo.

Andersson, R. & Pilblad, B. (1977). En metodologisk studie av samhandling i föräldradyader. Unpublished dissertation, University of Oslo.

Argyle, M. (1969). Social Interaction. Atherton: Methuen.

Athanassiades, J.C. (1974). An investigation of some communication patterns of female subordinates in hierarchical organizations. Human Relations, 27, 195-209.

Bakan, D. (1967). On Method. San Francisco: Jossey-Bass.

Bales, R.F. & Cohen, S.P. (1974). Systematic multiple level observation of groups (SYMLOG). Mimeographed, Harward University, Cambridge Mass.

Bannister, D. (1968). Logical requirements of research into schizophrenia. Brit. J. Psychiatry, 114, 181-188.

Bateson, G. (1960). Minimal requirements for a theory of schizophrenia. Arch. Gen. Psychiat., 2, 477-491.

Bateson, G., Jackson, D.D., Haley, J. & Weakland, J.H. (1956). Toward a theory of schizophrenia. Behavioral Science, 1, 251-264.

Bateson, G., Jackson, D.D., Haley, J. & Weakland, J.H. (1963). A note on the double bind - 1962. Family Process, 2, 154-161.

Becker, E. (1962). The Birth and Death of Meaning. New York: The Free Press, McMillan.

Becket, S. (1945). Waiting for Godot. New York: Grove Press.

Beier, E.G. (1951). The effect of induced anxiety on flexibility of intellectual functioning. Psychol. Monogr., 65, No. 9.

Bem, D. J. & Allen, A. (1974). On predicting some of the people some of the time. The search for cross-situational consistencies in behavior. Psychological Review, 81, 506-520.

Bernstein, B. (1971). Class, Code and Control. London: Routledge and Kegan Paul.

Blakar, R. M. (1970). Konteksteffektar i språkleg kommunikasjon. Unpublished dissertation, University of Oslo.

Blakar, R. M. (1972a). Ein eksperimentell situasjon til studiet av kommunikasjon: Bakgrunn, utvikling og nokre problemstillingar. Mimeographed. Institute of Psychology, University of Oslo.

Blakar, R. M. (1972b). Om ordassosiasjons-forsøk som metode og innfallsport til språkpsykologisk innsikt. Working Papers in Linguistics from Oslo, 1, No. 3, 65-92.

Blakar, R. M. (1973a). An experimental method for inquiring into communication. European Journal of Social Psychology, 3, 415-425.

Blakar, R. M. (1973b). Språk er makt. Oslo: Pax.

Blakar, R. M. (1973c). Context effects and coding stations in sentence processing. Scand. J. Psychol., 14, 103-105.

Blakar, R. M. (1974a). Schizofreni og kommunikasjon: Foreløpig presentasjon av ei eksperimentell tilnærming. Nordisk Psykiatrisk Tidsskr., 28, 239-248.

Blakar, R. M. (1974b). Kvifor det er nødvendig å ta eit eksplisitt kommunikasjonsperspektiv i studiet av språkprosessar. Tidsskrift for Samfunnsforskning, 15, 169-176.

Blakar, R. M. (1974c). Distinguishing social and individual psychology. Scand. J. Psychol., 15, 241-243.

Blakar, R. M. (1975a). Psykopatologi og kommunikasjon: Vidareføring av vår eksperimentelle tilnærming. Tidsskrift for Norsk Psykologforening, 12, No. 8, 16-25.

Blakar, R. M. (1975b). Human communication - an ever changing contract embedded in social contexts. Mimeographed, Institute of Psychol., University of Oslo.

Blakar, R. M. (1975c). Double-bind teorien: Ei kritisk vurdering. Tidsskrift for Norsk Psykologforening, 12, No. 12, 13-26.

Blakar, R. M. (1975d). How the sex roles are represented, reflected and conserved in the Norwegian Language. Acta Sociologica, 18, 162-173.

Blakar, R. M. (1975e). Psykopatologi og kommunikasjon: Rapport frå ein eksperimentserie. Mimeographed, Institute of Psychology, University of Oslo.

Blakar, R. M. (1976a). Psykopatologi og kommunikasjon: Ei kritisk vurdering av dette forskningsområdet. Tidsskrift for Norsk Psykologforening, 13, No. 6, 3-18.

Blakar, R. M. (1976b). Klinisk-kasuistiske analyser av kommunikasjonen til 30 ektepar med og utan barn med psykopatologi i ein standardisert eksperimentell kommunikasjonssituasjon. Mimeographed, Institute of Psychology, University of Oslo.

Blakar, R. M. (1977). Ruminations about conceptual and methodological problems in disentangling social and individual psychology. Tidsskrift for Norsk Psykologforening, 14, No. 5, 2-11.

168

Blakar, R. M. (1978a). Kontakt og konflikt. Oslo: Pax.

Blakar, R. M. (1978b). Psykopatologi og kommunikasjon I: Ei kritisk vurdering av dette forskningsfeltet. In Hem, L. & Holter, H. (eds.) Sosialpsykologi. Oslo: Universitetsforlaget.

Blakar, R. M. (1978c). Psykopatologi og kommunikasjon II: Ei eksperimentell tilnærming. In Hem, L. & Holter, H. (eds.), Sosialpsykologi. Oslo: Universitetsforlaget.

Blakar, R. M. (1978d). Klinisk psykologisk forskning: Common sense utsagn eller empiriske funn. Impuls, 32, No. 4, 16-34.

Blakar, R. M. (1978e). Statistical significance(s) versus theoretical clarifications: A comment on the Doane-Jacob & Grounds dispute. Informasjonsbulletin frå Psykopatologi- og kommunikasjonsprosjektet, No. 9, 3-9.

Blakar, R. M. (1978f). Psychopathology and communication: Report from a research project. Informasjonsbulletin frå Psykopatologi- og kommunikasjonsprosjektet, No. 8, 4-61.

Blakar, R. M. (1979a). Language as a means of social power: Theoretical-empirical explorations of language and language use as embedded in a social matrix. pp. 131-169 in Mey, J. L. (ed.). Pragmalinguistics: Theory and Practice. The Hague: Mouton.

Blakar, R. M. (1979b). Språk som makt og kvinneundertrykking. Språksosiologi som motefag. pp. 209-270 in Kleiven, J. (ed.)(1979). Språk og samfunn. Oslo: Pax.

Blakar, R. M. (in press a). The social sensitivity of theory and method. In Brenner, M. (ed.). Social Method and Social Life. London: Academic Press.

Blakar, R. M. (in press b). Psychopathology and familial communication. In Brenner, M. (ed.). The Structure of Action. Oxford: Basil Blackwell.

Blakar, R. M. (in press c). Towards a theory of communication in terms of preconditions: A conceptual framework and some empirical explorations. In Giles, H. & StClair, R. (eds.). Language and the Paradigms of Social Psychology. New York: Laurence Erlbaum.

Blakar, R. M. (in press d). Statistical significance(s) versus theoretical clarifications: A comment on the Doane-Jacob & Grounds dispute. Family Process.

Blakar, R. M., Lavik, A. & Østvold, M. (1980). Hysteri og kommunikasjon. Ei kartlegging av kommunikasjonsmønsteret til ektepar der kona er tildelt diagnosen hysteri. In Blakar, R. M. & Nafstad, H. E. (eds.) (1980). Klinisk psykologisk og anvendt samfunnsvitskapeleg forskning: Utfordringar og problem. Monography No. 5, Tidsskrift for Norsk Psykologforening.

Blakar, R. M. & Nafstad, H. E. (1980a). Familien som ramme for studiet av psykiske lidingar og avvikande atferd: Nokre generelle teoretiske og metodologiske problem. In Blakar, R. M. & Nafstad, H. E. (eds.) (1980). Klinisk psykologisk og anvendt samfunnsvitskapeleg forskning: Utfordringar og problem. Monography No. 5, Tidsskrift for Norsk Psykologforening.

Blakar, R. M. & Nafstad, H. E. (eds.) (1980b). Klinisk psykologisk og anvendt samfunnsvitskapeleg forskning: Utfordringar og problem. Monography No. 5, Tidsskrift for Norsk Psykologforening.

169

Blakar, R.M., Paulsen, O.G. & Sølvberg, H.A. (1978). Schizophrenia and communication efficiency: a modified replication taking ecological variation into consideration. Acta Psychiat. Scand., 58, 315-326. (See ch. 1, Part II.

Blakar, R.M. & Pedersen, T.B. (1978). Control and self-confidence as reflected in sex-bound patterns in communication: An experimental approach. Informasjonsbulletin frå psykopatologi- og kommunikasjonsprosjektet, No. 7, 3-35.

Blakar, R.M. & Pedersen, T.B. (1980a). Control and self-confidence as reflected in sex-bound patterns in communication: An experimental approach. Acta Sociologica, 23, 33-53.

Blakar, R.M. & Pedersen, T.B. (1980b). Sex-bound patterns of control in verbal communication. Paper presented at the conference 'Language and Power' at Bellagio, Italy, April 4th.-8th. 1980.

Blakar, R.M. & Rommetveit, R. (1975). Utterances in vacuo and in contexts: An experimental and theoretical exploration of some interrelationships between what is seen or imagined. International J. Psycholinguistics, No. 4, 5-32, and, in Linguistics, (1975), No. 153, 5-32.

Block, J. (1969). Parents of schizophrenic, neurotic, asthmatic, and congenitally ill children. Arch. Gen. Psychiat., 20, 659-674.

Block, J., Jennings, P.H., Harvey, E. & Simpson, E. (1964). Interaction between allergic potential and psychopathology in childhood asthma. Psychosom. Med., 26, 307-320.

Block, J., Harvey, E., Jennings, P.H. & Simpson, E. (1966). Clinicians' conceptions of the asthmatogenic mother. Arch. Gen. Psychiat., 15, 610-618.

Boomer, D.S. & Goodrich, D.W. (1961). Speech disturbance and judged anxiety. J. Cons. Psychol., 25, 160-164.

Bowers, K.S. (1973). Situationism in psychology: An analysis and a critique. Psychological Review, 80, 307-336.

Brisendal, C.G. (1976). Om å misforstå: En kommunikasjonsorientert analyse. Unpublished dissertation, University of Oslo.

Brodey, V.M. (1967). A Cybernetic Approach to Family Therapy. In G.H. Zuk & I. Boszormenyi-Nagy (eds.) Family Therapy and Disturbed Families. Palo Alto: Science and Behavior Books Inc.

Brooke, E.M. (1959). National statistics in the epidemiology of mental illness. J. Ment. Sci., 105, 893-908.

Brown, R. (1953). A determinant of the relationship between rigidity and authoritarianism. The J. Abn. and Soc. Psychol., 48, 469-476.

Bråten, S. (1974). Coding simulation circuits during symbolic interaction. pp. 327-336 in Congress Proceedings from Association Internationale de Cybernetique. Namur, Belgia.

Bråten, S. (1978). Competing modes of cognition and communication in simulated and self-reflective systems. Paper presented at the Third Richmond Conference on Decision Making in Complex Systems.

Chessick, R.D. (1968). The 'Crucial Dilemma' of the Therapist in the Psychotherapy of Borderland Patients. Amer. J. Psychotherapy, 4.

Coolidge, J.C. (1956). Asthma in mother and child as a special type of intercommunication. Amer. J. Orthopsychiat., 26, 165-176.

Crafoord, C. (1972). Borderline personligheten - översikt och synpunkter. Svenska föreningen för psykisk hälsovårds monografiserie, No. 2.

Dahle, M. (1977). Sosial bakgrunn og språklig kommunikasjon. Unpublished disserta-
    tion, University of Oslo.

Deutsch, H. (1942). Some forms of emotional disturbance and their relationship to
    schizophrenia. Psychoan. Quarterly, 11, 301-321.

Doane, J.A. (1978a). Family interaction and communication deviance in disturbed
    and normal families: A review of research. Family Process, 17,
    357-376.

Doane, J.A. (1978b). Questions of strategy: Rejoinder to Jacob and Grounds. Family
    Process, 17, 389-394.

Ellingsen, G.R., Iversen, O. & Ohnstad, K. (1976). Kommunikasjon og impervious-
    ness. Stenciled report, Institute of Psychology, University of
    Bergen.

Endresen, A. (1977). Modell för lösning av kommunikasjonskonflikt. Unpublished
    dissertation, University of Oslo.

Enge, T. (1978). Degree of hierarchy in semantic information processing during
    interaction: An exploration through computer simulation. Un-
    published dissertation, University of Oslo.

Faleide, A. (1969). Haldningar og meiningar hos foreldre til astmabarn. Ei spørje-
    skjema undersøkjing. Mimeographed, Institute of Psychology,
    University of Oslo.

Faleide, A. (1973). Vurdering av psykoterapeutiske metoder ved astma bronchiale
    hos barn. Individualterapi. Mimeographed, Institute of Psycho-
    logy, University of Oslo.

Faleide, A. & Vandvik, J.H. (1976). Samtalegruppe med astmatiske barns foreldre.
    Tidsskrift for Den Norske Lægeforening, 22, 1140-1142.

Feingold, B.F., Singer, M.T., Freeman, E.H. & Deskins, A. (1966). Psychological
    variables in allergic disease: A critical appraisal of methodology.
    J. Allergy, 38, 143-155.

Ferreira, A.J. & Winter, W.D. (1968a). Decision-making in normal and abnormal two-
    child families. Fam. Proc., 7, 17-36.

Ferreira, A.J. & Winter, W.D. (1968b). Information exchange and silence in normal
    and abnormal families. Fam. Proc., 7, 251-276.

Folkard, S. & Mandelbrote, B. (1962). Some ecological aspects of schizophrenia in
    Glouchestershire. The International J. of Social Psychiatry, 8,
    256-271.

Framo, J.L. (ed.) (1972). A Dialogue between Family Researchers and Family Thera-
    pists. New Yorker: Springer Publishing Co.

Freeman, E.H., Feingold, B.F., Schlesinger, K. & Gorman, F.J. (1964). Psycho-
    logical variables in allergic disorders: A review. Psychosom. Med.,
    26, 543-575.

French, T. (1939). Psychogenic factors in asthma. Amer. J. Psychol., 52, 86-101.

French, T. & Alexander, F. (1941). Psychogenica in bronchial astma. Psychosomatic
    Med. Monogr., 4, 1.

Fresch, J. (1964). The psychotic character: Clinical psychiatric considerations.
    Psychiatric Quarterly, 38, 81-96.

Fætten, A. & Østvold, M. (1975). Hysteri og kommunikasjon. Unpublished disserta-
    tion, University of Oslo.

Garfinkel, H. (1972). Studies of the routine grounds of everyday activities. In D. Sudnov (ed.). Studies in Social Interaction. New York: The Free Press.

Garner, A.M. & Wenar, C. (1959). The Mother-Child Interaction in Psychosomatic Disorders. Urbana: University of Illinois Press.

Glaser, H.H., Harrison, G.S. & Lynn, D.B. (1964). Emotional implications of congenital heart disease in children. Pediatrics, 33, 367-379.

Glennsjø, K.B. (1977). Marital schism og marital skew - en kommunikasjonsteoretisk tilnærming. Unpublished dissertation, University of Oslo.

Glucksberg, S., Krauss, R.M. & Weissberg, R. (1966). Referential communication in nursery school. Method and some preliminary findings. Journal of Experimental Child Psychology, 3, 333-342.

Goffman, E. (1961). Asylums. Essays on the Social Situation of Mental Patients and other Inmates. New York: Anchor Books.

Goldstein, M.J., Gould, E., Alkire, A., Rodnick, E.H. & Judd, L.L. (1968). A Method for studying social influence and coping patterns within families of disturbed adolescents. J. Nerv. Ment. Dis., 147, 233-251.

Goldstein, M. & Rodnick, E. (1975). The family's contribution to the etiology of schizophrenia: Current status. Schiz. Bull., 1, 48-63.

Grinker, R.R., Werble, B. & Drye, R.C. (1968). The Borderline Syndrome. A Behavioral Study of Ego-functions. New York: Basic Books.

Grolnick, L. (1972). A family perspective on psychosomatic factors in illness: A review of the literature. Family Process, 11, 457-485.

Guilford, J.P. (1956). Fundamental Statistics in Psychology and Education. New York: McGraw-Hill Book Co.

Guttelvik, P.E. (1979). En kommunikasjonsorientert eksperimentell evaluering av ekteparterapi. Unpublished dissertation, University of Oslo.

Gynther, R.H. (1957). The effects of anxiety and situational stress on communicative efficiency. J. Abn. and Soc. Psychol., 54, 274-276.

Haley, J. (1959). The family of the schizophrenic: A model system. J. Nerv. Ment. Dis., 129, 357-374.

Haley, J. (1963). Strategies of Psychotherapy. New York: Grune & Stratton.

Haley, J. (1967a). Experiments with abnormal families. Archives of General Psychiatry, 17, 53-63.

Haley, J. (1967b). Toward a theory of pathological systems. In G.H. Zuk & I. Boszor-menyi-Nagy (eds.) Family Therapy and disturbed Families. Palo Alto: Science and Behavior Books.

Haley, J. (1968). Testing parental instructions of schiophrenic and normal children: A pilot study. J. Abnorm. Psychol., 73, 559-565.

Haley, J. (1971). Family therapy: A radical change. In Haley, J. (1971). Changing Families. New York: Grune & Stratton.

Haley, J. (1972). Critical overview of present status of family interaction research. In Framo, J.L. (ed.) (1972). A Dialogue between Family Researchers and Family Therapists. New York: Springer Publishing Co.

Hall, E.T. (1959). The Silent Language. Greenwich, Conn.: Fawett Publications.

Handel, G. (ed.). (1967). The Psychosocial Interior of the Family. Chicago: Aldine.

Herman, B. & Jones, J.E. (1976). Lack of acknowledge in the family Rorschachs of families with a child at risk for schizophrenia. Family Process, 15, 289-306.

Heider, F. (1958). The Psychology of Interpersonal Relations. New York: Wiley.

Hoffart, A. (1978). Common-sense og kommunikasjon: Behandling av noen metateoretiske spørsmål knyttet til Blakarprosjektets virksomhet. Impuls, 32, No. 3, 33-43.

Hoffart, A. (1979). Dagligspråk, samhandling og det ubevisste. Unpublished dissertation, University of Oslo.

Holthe, H. (1972). Foreldres beskrivelse av sine astmatiske barn, på noen atferds- og personlighetsvariabler. Unpublished dissertation, University of Oslo.

Hultberg, M., Alve, S. & Blakar, R.M. (1978). Patterns of attribution of communicative difficulties in couples having a 'schizophrenic', a 'borderline' or a 'normal' offspring. Informasjonsbulletin frå Psykopatologi og kommunikasjonsprosjektet, No.6, 4-63. (See ch.2, Part II.)

Hymes, D. (1967). Models of the interaction of language and social settings. J. Soc. Iss., 23, No. 2, 8-28.

Haarstad, B.E. (1976). Anoreksia nervosa. En eksperimentell studie av familiens kommunikasjon. Unpublished dissertation, University of Oslo.

Ichheiser, G. (1970). Appearances and Realities. Misunderstandings in Human Relations. San Francisco: Jossey-Bass.

Jackson, D.D. (1957). The question of family homeostasis. Psychiat. Quart. Supp., 31, 79-90.

Jackson, D.D. (1959). Family interaction, family homeostasis and some implications for conjoint family psychoterapy. In Masserman, J. (ed.). Science and Psychoanalysis Vol. II. Individual and Family Dynamics. New York: Grune & Stratton.

Jackson, D.D. (1965). Family rules. Arch. Gen. Psychiat., 12, 589-594.

Jackson, D.D. (1966). Family practice: A comprehensive medical approach. Comprehensive Psychiatry, 7, 338-344.

Jackson, D.D. (1967). The individual and the larger contexts. Fam. Proc., 6, 139-147.

Jacob, T. (1975). Family interaction in disturbed and normal families: A methodological and substantive review. Psychol. Bull., 82, 33-65.

Jacob, T. & Grounds, L. (1978). Confusions and conclusions: A response to Doane. Family Process, 17, 377- 387.

Jacobsen, S.M. & Pettersen, R.B. (1974). Kommunikasjon og samarbeide i den schizofrenes familie. Unpublished dissertation, University of Oslo.

Jennings, P., Block, J., Harvey, E., Nurock, A., Simpson, E. & Yarris, J. (1966). Two components of the allergic process compared: Allergic potential and severity of asthma. J. Allergy and Clin. Imm., 39, 148-159.

Kasl, S.V. & Mahl, G.F. (1965). The relationship of disturbances and hesitations in spontaneous speech to anxiety. J. Pers. and Soc. Psychol., 1, 425-433.

Kernberg, O. (1967). Borderline personality organization. J. Amer. Psychoanal. Assoc., 15, 641-685.

Kluger, J. M. (1969). Childhood and the social milieu. J. American Academy of Child Psychiatry, 8, 353-366.

Knight, R. P. (1953). Management and psychotherapy of the borderline schizophrenic patient. Bulletin of the Menninger Clinic., 17, 138-150.

Knutsen, A. (1979). Kontroll i kommunikasjonen til foreldre til borderline-pasienter. Unpublished dissertation, University of Oslo.

Kringlen, E. (1972). Psykiatri. Oslo: Universitetsforlaget.

Kristiansen, T. S. (1976). Kommunikasjon hos foreldre til barn med psykosomatiske lidelser. Unpublished dissertation, University of Oslo.

Kristiansen, T. S., Faleide, A. & Blakar, R. M. (1977). Kommunikasjon hos foreldre til barn med psykosomatiske lidelser: Ei eksperimentell tilnærming. Tidsskrift for Norsk Psykologforening, 14, No. 12, 2-24.

Kuhn, T. S. (1970). The Structure of Scientific Revolutions. Chicago: University of Chicago Press.

Labov, W., Cohen, P., Robins, C. & Lewis, J. (1968). A study of the non-standard English of negro and Puertorican speakers in New York City. Final report, U. S. Office of Education cooperative research project No. 3288. New York: Columbia University.

Lagerløv, T. & Stokstad, S. J. (1974). Angst og kommunikasjon. Unpublished dissertation, University of Oslo.

Laing, R. D. (1969). Self and Others. London: Tavistock Publications.

Lennard, H. L., Beaulieu, M. R. & Embrey, N. G. (1965). Interaction in Families with a schizophrenic Child. Arch. Gen. Psychiat., 12, 166-183.

Lidz, T. (1963). The Family and Human Adaptation. New York: International Univ. Press.

Lidz, T. (1973). The Origin and Treatment of Schizophrenic Disorders. New York: Basic Books.

Lidz, T., Cornelison, A., Terry, O. & Fleck, S. (1957). The infrafamilial environment of the schizophrenic patient: Marital schism and marital skew. Amer. J. Psychiat., 114, 241-248.

Lidz, T., Cornelison, A., Carlson, D. T. & Fleck, S. (1958). Intrafamilial environment of the schizophrenic patient: The transmission of irrationality. Archives of Neurology and Psychiatry, 79, 305-316.

Litzowitz, N. S. & Newman, K. N. (1967). Borderline personality and the theatre of the absurd. Arch. Gen. Psychiat., 16, 268-280.

Long, R. T., Lamont, J. H., Whipple, B., Bandler, L., Blom, G. E., Burgin, L. & Jessner, L. (1958). A psychosomatic study of allergic and emotional factors in children with asthma. Amer. J. Psychiat., 114, 890-899.

Luchins, A. S. (1942). Mechanization in problem solving: the effect of Einstellung. Psychol. Monogr., 54.

Mahl, G. F. (1956). Disturbances and silences in the patient's speech in psychotherapy. J. Abn. and Soc. Psychol., 53, 1-15.

Masterton, J. F. (1972). Treatment of the Borderline Adolescent: A Developmental Approach. New York: John Wiley.

McKillip, J. (1975). Letter to the present author.

McNemar, Q. (1962). Psychological Statistics. New York: Wiley & Sons Inc.

174

McPherson, S. (1970). Communication of intents among parents and their disturbed adolescent child. J. Abnormal Psychol., 76, 98-105.

McPherson, S., Goldstein, M. & Rodnick, E. (1973). Who listens? Who communicates? How? Arch. Gen. Psychiat., 28, 393-399.

Mead, G.H. (1934). Mind, Self and Society. Chicago: Univ. of Chicago Press.

Meissner, W.W. (1966). Family dynamics and psychosomatic processes. Fam. Proc., 5, 142-161.

Miller, H. & Baruch, D.W. (1957). The emotional problems of childhood and their relation to asthma. Amer. J. Dis. Child, 93, 242-245.

Mischel, W. (1968). Personality and Assessment. New York: Wiley.

Mischel, W. (1973). On the empiric dilemmas of psychodynamic approaches: Issues and alternatives. Journal of Abnormal Psychology, 82, 335-344.

Mishler, E.G. & Waxler, N.E. (1965). Family interaction processes and schizophrenia: A review of current theories. Merrill-Palmer Quarterly of Behavior and Development, 11, 269-315.

Mishler, E.G. & Waxler, N. (1968). Interaction in Families. An Experimental Study of Family Processes and Schizophrenia. New York: Wiley.

Mitchell, A.J., Frost, L. & Marx, J.R. (1953). Emotional aspects of pediatric allergy - the role of the mother-child relationship. Ann. Allerg., 11, 744-751.

Moberget, O. & Reer, Ø. (1975). Kommunikasjon og psykopatologi: En empirisk-teoretisk analyse med vekt på begrepsmessig og metodologisk avklaring. Unpublished dissertation, University of Oslo.

Morris, G.O. & Wynne, L.C. (1965). Schizophrenic offspring and styles of parental communication: A predictive study using family therapy experts. Psychiatry, 28, 19-44.

Moscovici, S. (1967). Communication processing and the properties of language. In Berkowitz, L. (ed.), Advances in Experimental Social Psychology. Vol. III, New York: Academic Press.

Mossige, S., Pettersen, R.B. & Blakar, R.M. (1976). Egocentrism versus Decentration and Communication Efficiency in Families with and without a Schizophrenic Member. Informasjonsbulletin frå Psykopatologi og Kommunikasjonsprosjektet, No. 4, 4-53.

Mossige, S., Pettersen, R.B. & Blakar, R.M. (1979). Egocentrism and inefficiency in the communication of families containing schizophrenic members. Family Process, 18, 405-425. (See ch. 3, Part II.)

Murrell, S.A. & Stachowiack, J.C. (1967). Consistency, rigidity and power in the interaction patterns of clinical and nonclinical families. J. Abn. Psychol., 72, 265-272.

Nafstad, H.E. & Gaarder, S. (1979). Barn - utvikling og miljø. Oslo: Tiden.

Neuhaus, E.C. (1958). A personality study of asthmatic and cardiac children. Psychosom. Med., 20, 181-186.

Ødegaard, Ø. (1945). The distribution of mental diseases in Norway. Acta Psychiatrica et Neurological, 20, 247-284.

Øisjøfoss, Ø. (1976). Makt og kontroll i ekteskapet. Unpublished dissertation, University of Oslo.

Olson, D.H. (1972). Empirically unbinding the double bind: Research and conceptual reformulations. Family Process, 11, 69-94.

Orne, T.T. (1962). On the social psychology of the psychological experiment: With particular reference to demand characteristics and their implications. American Psychologist, 17, 776-783.

Øvreeide, H. (1970). Verbal kommunikasjon mellom barn. Muligheter og begrensninger. Unpublished dissertation, University of Oslo.

Paulsen, O.G. (1977). Schizofreni og kommunikasjon: En replikasjonsstudie. Unpublished dissertation. University of Oslo.

Pedersen, T.B. (1979a). Kjønn og kommunikasjon: En eksperimentell tilnærming. Unpublished dissertation, University of Oslo.

Pedersen, T.B. (1979b). Sex and communication: A brief presentation of an experimental approach. Paper presented at International conference on social psychology and language, Bristol, England, July 16th-20th, 1979.

Piaget, J. (1926). The Language and Thought of the Child. New York: Harcourt, Brace.

Peshkin, M.M. & Abramson, M.A. (1959). Psychosomatic group therapy with parents of children having intractable asthma. Ann. Allerg., 17, 344-349.

Pilisuk, M. (1963). Anxiety, self-acceptance, and open-mindedness. The J. Clin. Psychol., 19, 388-391.

Pinkerton, P. & Weaver, C.M. (1970). Childhood asthma. In Hill, O.W. (ed.). Modern Trends in Psychosomatic Medicine 2. London: Butterworths.

Purcell, K. (1965). Critical appraisal of psychosomatic studies of asthma. New York State Journal of Medicine, 65, 2103-2109.

Purcell, K., Brady, K., Chai, H., Muser, J., Molk, L., Gordon, N. & Means, J. (1969). The effect of asthma in children of experimental separation from the family. Psychosom. Med., 31, 144-164.

Ringuette, E.L. & Kennedy, T. (1966). An experimental study of the double-bind hypothesis. Journal of Abnormal Psychology, 71, 136-141.

Riskin, J. & Faunce, E.E. (1972). An evaluative review of family interaction research. Family Process, 11, 365-455.

Rokeach, M. (1960). The Open and Closed Mind. New York: Basic Books, Inc.

Rommetveit, R. (1968). Words, Meanings and Messages. New York: Academic Press and Oslo: Universitetsforlaget.

Rommetveit, R. (1972a). Språk, tanke og kommunikasjon. Oslo: Universitetsforlaget.

Rommetveit, R. (1972b). Deep structure of sentences versus message structure: Some critical remarks to current paradigms, and suggestions for an alternative approach. Norwegian J. Linguistics, 26, 3-22.

Rommetveit, R. (1974). On Message Structure. London: Wiley.

Rommetveit, R. (1978). Language and thought. Cornell Review, 2, 91-114.

Rommetveit, R. (1979a). On 'meanings' of situations and social control of such meaning in human communication. Paper presented at Symposium on the situation in Psychological Theory and Research, Stockholm, June, 17-22.

Rommetveit, R. (1979b). On negative rationalism in scholarly studies of human communication and dynamic residuals in the construction of intersubjectivity. In Rommetveit & Blakar (eds.). Studies of Language, Thought, and Verbal Communication. London: Academic Press.

Rommetveit, R. (1979c). The role of language in the creation and transmission of social representations. Paper presented at Colloque sur les Représentationes Sociales, Paris, January, 8-10.

Rommetveit, R. (1979d). On common codes and dynamic residuals in human communication. In Rommetveit & Blakar (eds.) Studies of Language, Thought, and Verbal Communication. London: Academic Press.

Rommetveit, R. (in press). On the meanings of acts and what is meant and made known by what is said in a pluralistic social world. In M. Brenner (ed.) The Structure of Action. Oxford: Basil Blackwell.

Rommetveit, R. & Blakar, R.M. (eds.) (1979). Studies of Language, Thought, and Verbal Communication. London: Academic Press.

Rotbæk, K. L. S. (1976). Enurese. En oversikt over de begreper og teorier som finnes i psykologisk/psykiatrisk litteratur, og en eksplorerende undersøkelse på kommunikasjonsteoretisk grunnlag. Unpublished dissertation. University of Oslo.

Rubenowitz, R. (1963). Emotional flexibility-rigidity as a comprehensive dimension of mind. Stockholm: Acta Psychologica.

Rubenowitz, R. (1970). Personlighetspsykologi. Stockholm: Bokförlaget Aldus/ Bonniers.

Ruesch, J. & Bateson, G. (1951). Communication: The Social Matrix of Psychiatry. New York: Norton.

Rund, B.R. (1976). Tankeforstyrrelser og kommunikasjon. En eksperimentell undersøkelse av forholdet mellom tankeforstyrrelser hos schizofrene og kommunikasjonsmønsteret hos foreldrene. Unpublished dissertation, University of Oslo.

Rund, B.R. (1978). Den schizofrenes tenkning og foreldrenes kommunikasjon - en eksplorerende undersøkelse. Nordisk Psykologi, 30, 238-254.

Rønbeck, K. (1977). Familiekommunikasjon og schizofreni. En eksperimentell undersøkelse og diskusjon av en forskningstradisjons metodiske og teoretiske fundament. Unpublished dissertation, University of Oslo.

Schuham, A. I. (1967). The double-bind hypothesis a decade later. Psychol. Bull., 68, 409-416.

Shafer, R. (1958). Regression in the Service of the Ego: The Relevance of a Psychoanalytic Concept for Personality Assessment. In Lindzey (ed.). Assessment of Human Motives. New York: Holt, Rinehart and Winston.

Smedslund, J. (1964). Concrete reasoning. A study of intellectual development. Monographs of the Society for Research in Child Development, 29, No. 2.

Smedslund, J. (1978). Bandura's theory of self-efficacy: a set of common sense theorems. Scand. J. Psychol., 19, 1-14.

Smedslund, J. (1979). Between the analytic and the arbitrary: A case study of psychological research. Scand. J. Psychol., 20, 129-140.

Smedslund, J. (in press). Analyzing the primary code: from empirism to apriorism. In Olson, D. R. (ed.). The Social Foundations of Language and Thought: Essays in Honour of J.S. Bruner. New York: Norton.

Sorokin, P. A. & Zimmerman, C. C. (1929). Principles of Rural-urban Sociology. New York: Holt.

Speer, D. C. (1970). Family Systems: Morphostasis and Morphogenesis, or 'Is Homeostasis enough?' Family Process, 9, 259-278.

Sperling, M. (1955). Psychosis and Psychosomatic Illness. Int. J. Psycho-Anal., 36, 320-326.

Stokstad, S. J., Lagerløv, T. & Blakar, R. M. (1976). Anxiety, rigidity, and commu- nication: An experimental approach. Informasjonsbulletin frå Psyko- patologi og kommunikasjonsprosjektet, No. 3, 6-36. (See ch. 5, Part II.)

Stokstad, S. J., Lagerløv, T. & Blakar, R. M. (1979). Anxiety, rigidity and commu- nication: An experimental approach. In Rommetveit, R. & Blakar, R. M. (eds.) Studies of Language, Thought and Verbal Communi- cation. London: Academic Press.

Strøno, I. (1978). Egosentrisme og desentrering i verbal kommunikasjon hos barn og ungdom. Unpublished dissertation, University of Oslo.

Svenheim, I. (1979). Double bind og toleranse for flertydighet. Unpublished disserta- tion, University of Oslo.

Sølvberg, H. A. (1973). Kommunikasjon og samarbeide mellom den schizofrenes for- eldre. Unpublished dissertation, University of Oslo.

Sølvberg, H. A. & Blakar, R. M. (1975). Communication efficiency in couples with and without a schizophrenic offspring. Family Process, 14, 515-534.

Taylor, J. A. (1953). A personality scale of manifest anxiety. J. Abn. and Soc. Psychol., 48, 285-290.

Teigre, H. Ø. (1976). Tillit som forutsetning for kommunikasjon. Unpublished dis- sertation, University of Oslo.

Titchener, J. T., Riskin, J. & Emerson, R. (1960). The family in psychosomatic process. Psychosom. Med., 22, 127-142.

Tuft, H. S. (1957). The development and management of intractable asthma of child- hood. Amer. J. Dis. Child, 93, 251-254.

Vassend, O. (1979). Barn med astma: Kommunikasjon og samhandlingsklima i fami- lien i konfliktsituasjonar. Unpublished dissertation, University of Oslo.

Watzlawick, P., Beavin, J. H. & Jackson, D. D. (1967). Pragmatics of Human Com- munication. New York: Norton.

Weakland, J. H. (1974). The double-bind theory by self-reflexive hindsight. Family Process, 13, 269-277.

Weakland, J. H. & Fry, W. (1962). Letters of mothers of schizophrenics. American Journal of Orthopsychiatry, 32, 604-623.

White, R. W. (1963). Ego and Reality in Psychoanalytical Theory. Psychological Issues. Monograph II. Vol. III. No. 3. New York: International Universities Press.

Wikran, R. J. (1974). Kommunikasjon og samarbeide mellom astma-barnets foreldre. Unpublished dissertation, University of Oslo.

Wikran, R.J., Faleide, A. & Blakar, R.M. (1978). Communication in the family of the asthmatic child: An experimental approach. Acta Psychiat. Scand. 57, 11-26. (See ch.4, Part II.)

Wikran, R.J., Faleide A. & Blakar, R.M. (1979). Kommunikasjon og samarbeid mellom astmabarnets foreldre: Ei eksperimentell tilnærming. In Faleide, A. (ed.) Barn - med astma. Ei psykologisk utgreiing. Monography No. 4, Tidsskrift for Norsk Psykologforening.

Wynne, L., Rykoff, I., Day, J. & Hirsch, S. (1958). Pseudo-mutuality in the family relations of schizophrenics. Psychiatry, 21, 205-220.

Wynne, L.C., Singer, M. & Toohey, M. (1975). Communication of the adoptive parents of schizophrenics. In Jørstad, J. & Ugelstad, E. (eds.) Schizophrenia 75. Oslo: Universitetsforlaget.

NOTES

1. Elsewhere (Blakar, in press a) we have analyzed more systematically the pervading tendency to ignore social psychological theory and knowledge in general.

2. Although we do not subscribe to his position in detail, we cannot but join Smedslund (1978, 1979a, 1979b) in his vigorous plea for an aprioristic psychology. The field of family-oriented research constitutes a sad demonstration of how an enormous amount of empirical research is most likely to have represented futile effort-wasting, because the aprioristic, conceptual problems of the field have not been taken seriously. Such an endeavor would have involved, among other things, that the fundamental problems in developing a general theory of communication had been explicitly addressed (cf. Blakar, 1978c, in press d).

3. In earlier writings we have often referred to our approach as 'social-cognitive'. Although essential in describing and analyzing the individual communicant (in the functions of sender and receiver respectively), cognition represents but one aspect. Only from a general developmental perspective can we manage to capture and describe the individual communicant in full complexity (cf. Blakar & Nafstad, 1980a).

4. Throughout the studies covered by the present volume, it has not been necessary to use this criterion. It should be mentioned, however, that in studies involving younger children the time-limit (criterion 3) before the deception is being revealed, has been considerably shortened (cf. Strøno, 1978, Vassend, 1979).

5. As a curiosity only, it may be mentioned that we learned afterwards that the one Group S couple that had managed to solve the communication conflict was the only one of the five that had been given some family therapy in connection with the treatment of their hospitalized daughter.

6. A reasonable counter-argument on the part of the Sølvberg & Blakar study is that the Group S and Group N couples communicated equally efficiently in the simple situation. It was in the communication conflict situation only that the marked differences were revealed. It has then to be explained why the two categories of

couples held different expectations toward one, but not toward the other, of these apparently similar situations.

7. It should be remarked that Sølvberg & Blakar were aware of and explicitly commented upon these restrictions of their study. However, in most studies in this field this fallacy with respect to the subtleties and complexities of social situations seems not to be acknowledged.

8. The authors are indepted to Hilde Eileen Nafstad, Ragnar Rommetveit, and Astri Heen Wold for valuable comments on earlier version of this paper. This research has been supported by the Norwegian Research Council for Social Science and the Humanities. We are grateful to the Presteseter Hospital in Oppland and the Dikemark Hospital in Oslo for their kind cooperation regarding the subjects.. Published in Acta Psychiatrica Scandinavica, 1978, 58, 315-326.

9. We are grateful to Lovisenberg Hospital in Oslo for their kind assistance and cooperation regarding the subjects. The authors are indebted to Hilde Eileen Nafstad, Ragnar Rommetveit, and Astri Heen Wold for valuable comments on an earlier version of this paper. Published in an internal stencilled report series "Informasjonsbulletin frå Kommunikasjons- og Psykopatologiprosjektet" (1978), No. 6.

10. The cooperative hospital was asked to identify patients according to the list of criteria presented and discussed in section I (p. 69-74). In this connection it should be mentioned that at this particular hospital they were at this time carrying out a series of projects concerning the Borderline syndrome. Thus the institution was not only very cooperative, but also particularly competent in the difficult task of applying these criteria.

11. The only exception being married couples in which the wife was diagnosed as being 'hysteric'. In this case the wife/wives put extremely heavy pressure on the experimenter and the husband(s) to make them take responsibility for the communication situation itself (Fætten & Østvold, 1975).

12. We are grateful to the Presteseter Hospital for their kind cooperation regarding the subjects. The authors are also indebted to Ragnar Rommetveit, Hilde Eileen Nafstad, Theodore Lidz and Astri Heen Wold for valuable comments on an earlier version of this paper. This research has been supported by the Norwegian Research Council for Social Science and the Humanities on grants B. 60. 01.-85 and B. 60. 01-100, given to R. M. Blakar. Published in Family Process, (1979) 18, 405-425.

13. In order to ensure a homogeneous sample in this exploratory study, we restricted ourselves to families in which the schizophrenic daughter belonged to the sub-category hebephrenia. In this respect we deviate from the Sølvberg & Blakar study, in which the only criterion was that the patient member was given the diagnosis schizophrenic.

14. If it is presupposed that the degree of egocentrism/decentration represents a relatively stable aspect, this very high correlation (.92) may be interpreted as supporting high reliability in the scoring of egocentrism/decentration.

15. The same criticism is valid with respect to the Sølvberg & Blakar study. However, a series of studies (Hultberg, Alve & Blakar, 1978, Wikran, Faleide & Blakar, 1978, Rotbæk, 1976, Kristiansen, 1976) have revealed that other groups of parental couples (parents of borderline patients, asthmatic children, and children with enuresis respectively) show patterns of communication different from both the Group N and the Group S couples (see Part III).

16. We are grateful to Dr. Sørland, Cardiologic Dept., Assoc. Professor Dr. med. Kjell Aas, and Dr. Dag Nilsson, Dept. of Allergy at the Pediatric Department, Rikshospitalet, Oslo, and The Allergic Institute, Voksentoppen, Oslo, for their kind assistance regarding the subjects. This research has been supported by the Norwegian Research Council for Social Science and the Humanities on grants B.60.01-85 and B.60.01-100 given to Rolv Mikkel Blakar. The authors are indebted to Kjell Aas and Finn Askevold for valuable comments on an earlier version of this paper. Published in Acta Psychiatrica Scandinavica, 1978.

17. The authors are indebted to Hilde Eileen Nafstad, Ragnar Rommetveit, Kjell Raaheim, Per Schioldborg and Astri Heen Wold for valuable comments on an earlier version of this paper. This study was supported by the Norwegian Research Council for Science and the Humanities on grants B.60.01-85 and B.60-01-100 given to R.M. Blakar. Published in an internal stencilled report series "Informasjonsbulletin frå Kommunikasjons- og Psykopatologi-prosjektet" (1976) No.3.

18. This quotation is not chosen because it gives a generally accepted assessment of the field, but because the problems in focus are very well illustrated. For example, Theodore Lidz (personal communication) disagrees with the conclusions drawn by Haley.

19. Whereas the standard instructions merely present the task to the subjects (cf. Blakar, 1973a, for a verbatim presentation of the standard instructions), the stress instruction is intended to put a heavy pressure on the subjects to cooperate efficiently and quickly. In addition to the mere presentation of the task as with the

standard instructions, the impression was given that the task represented a standardized test of the ability to cooperate. And, it was explicitly added that people normally used 2-3 min on the simple route and about 10 min on the more complex route. It was even said that 'students such as you are almost always quicker than that'.

20. Since we started with extreme groups, the regression effect has to be taken into consideration (McNemar, 1962). The 'true' values calculated on the basis of the reliability coefficient are 3·97-12·77 and 24·71-40·05 for the low and high anxiety groups respectively. Both groups are almost exclusively recruited from the highest and lowest quarter respectively of our pool of subjects.

21. A total of 29 dyads were run through the experimental communication situation. One dyad was rejected because one of the participants did not master Norwegian well enough, and another because one of the participants proved to be 26 years old. Three dyads were rejected because they applied particular explanatory strategies that took them through the experimental route without the induced error causing any trouble, and thus these dyads did not face any communication conflict.

22. In the analysis of variance the seven non-solvers were all given a time of 40 min.

23. Reanalysis of the data in connection with a study on sex and communication (Pedersen, 1979, Blakar & Pedersen, 1980a) revealed that in the simple situation, male and female dyads reacted differently upon the stress instruction, in that whereas male dyads were more efficient than when given the standard instruction, female ones were less efficient. Given the standard instruction, male and female dyads did equally well. No such sex-specific influences of the instructions were found in the communication conflict situation.

24. Interesting enough many couples or families containing psychopathological members transform the induced conflict (induced in terms of lacking common premisses) into a conflict involving conflicting personal interests (for example, which of us is right, which of us is stupid).

25. We have in particular been preoccupied by analyzing the organization of the process of communication (Blakar, 1975b, in press c); of the distribution of control in acts of communication (Blakar, 1979b); of language as a means of social power (Blakar, 1975d, 1979a, 1979b); and, of the interplay between individual and social variables in communication (Blakar, 1977). (For a collected presentation, cf. Rommetveit & Blakar, 1979.)